OXFORD WORLD'S CLASSICS

THE CONSOLATION OF PHILOSOPHY

ANICIUS MANLIUS SEVERINUS BOETHIUS (*c*.480–*c*.524/6) was born into a Roman aristocratic family shortly after the fall of the Roman Empire in the West. After the death of his father, who had earlier been praetorian prefect and consul, the boy was adopted into the family of Symmachus, who boasted both aristocratic descent and Christian commitment. Having emerged as a leading senatorial at Rome, Boethius attracted the favourable attention of both Theoderic, king at Ravenna, and Anastasius, eastern emperor at Constantinople. Not only was he advanced to the consulship himself at Rome (510), but his two sons were similarly honoured (522), at a ceremony at which their father was chosen to deliver the encomium to Theoderic. In the same year he was appointed Master of Offices at Ravenna, the highest post in the administration of the court. Earlier he had gained scholarly fame as the author of treatises on Aristotle's logic; he had also demonstrated Christian allegiance by his *Theological Tractates*. But his world came crashing down when in company with the ex-consul Albinus he was charged in 523 with treason against the king. Confined to house-arrest in Pavia, he composed *The Consolation of Philosophy*, in which he described the soul's renunciation of the goods of this world in its journey to the Neoplatonist God, the One and the Good. This work became a seminal document in the cultural history of Europe. It was translated into Old English by Alfred the Great, into Old High German by Notker Labeo, into Middle English by Geoffrey Chaucer; Queen Elizabeth I made her own translation of it. Literary figures as diverse as Jean de Meun, Dante Alighieri, and C. S. Lewis acknowledged its importance to them in shaping the vision of the good life.

P. G. WALSH is Emeritus Professor of Humanity at the University of Glasgow. His translations for Oxford World's Classics include Apuleius, *The Golden Ass*, Petronius, *The Satyricon*, Pliny's *Complete Letters*, and Cicero, *The Nature of the Gods* and *Selected Letters*.

OXFORD WORLD'S CLASSICS

*For over 100 years Oxford World's Classics have brought
readers closer to the world's great literature. Now with over 700
titles—from the 4,000-year-old myths of Mesopotamia to the
twentieth century's greatest novels—the series makes available
lesser-known as well as celebrated writing.*

*The pocket-sized hardbacks of the early years contained
introductions by Virginia Woolf, T. S. Eliot, Graham Greene,
and other literary figures which enriched the experience of reading.
Today the series is recognized for its fine scholarship and
reliability in texts that span world literature, drama and poetry,
religion, philosophy and politics. Each edition includes perceptive
commentary and essential background information to meet the
changing needs of readers.*

OXFORD WORLD'S CLASSICS

BOETHIUS

The Consolation of Philosophy

Translated with an Introduction and Notes by
P. G. WALSH

OXFORD
UNIVERSITY PRESS

OXFORD
UNIVERSITY PRESS

Great Clarendon Street, Oxford OX2 6DP

Oxford University Press is a department of the University of Oxford.
It furthers the University's objective of excellence in research, scholarship,
and education by publishing worldwide in

Oxford New York

Athens Auckland Bangkok Bogotá Buenos Aires Calcutta
Cape Town Chennai Dar es Salaam Delhi Florence Hong Kong Istanbul
Karachi Kuala Lumpur Madrid Melbourne Mexico City Mumbai
Nairobi Paris São Paulo Shanghai Singapore Taipei Tokyo Toronto Warsaw

with associated companies in Berlin Ibadan

Oxford is a registered trade mark of Oxford University Press
in the UK and in certain other countries

Published in the United States
by Oxford University Press Inc., New York

First published as an Oxford World's Classics paperback 2000
Reissued 2008

British Library Cataloguing in Publication Data

Data available

Library of Congress Cataloging in Publication Data

[De consolatione philosophiae. English]
The consolation of philosophy/Boethius; translated with an
introduction and explanatory notes by P. G. Walsh
Includes bibliographical references.
1. Philosophy, Medieval. I. Walsh, P. G. (Patrick Gerard).
II. Title.
B659.D472E5 1999 100—dc21 98-30457

ISBN 978-0-19-954054-9

5

Typeset by Joshua Associates Ltd, Oxford
Printed in Great Britain by
Clays Ltd, St Ives plc

PREFACE AND ACKNOWLEDGEMENTS

This is an appropriate time to launch a new translation of *The Consolation of Philosophy*. In the past few years there has been a significant revival of interest in Boethius; this has been marked by several studies which have partially restored him to the prominence which he enjoyed for over a millennium from the Carolingian age onwards. My rendering, with its accompanying Introduction and annotation, has sought to exploit these important researches.

The translation is based on Ludwig Bieler's admirable edition in the Corpus Christianorum series. The annotations have bene fited conspicuously from the notable commentary of J. Gruber. Henry Chadwick's general study of Boethius, and the volume of essays edited by the late-lamented Margaret Gibson entitled *Boethius, his Life, Thought, and Influence*, have furnished much of the information on which the Introduction is based. My debts to Gerard O'Daly's *The Poetry of Boethius* for interpretation of the verses, and to R. W. Sharples' edition of the taxing philosophical content of Books 4–5, will be obvious from the frequent citations in the notes. Details of these works are presented in the Select Bibliography.

I am grateful to the anonymous readers who offered their widely varying criticisms of the specimen translations submitted before the project was approved, and especially to Hilary O'Shea for her encouragement and the expedition which she showed in guiding this and three previous translations through the Press.

P.G.W.

CONTENTS

ABBREVIATIONS

AJP	*American Journal of Philology*
Am. Hist. Rev.	*American Historical Review*
Bieler	L. Bieler, *Anicii Manlii Severini Boethii Philosophiae Consolatio*[2], CCL 94 (Turnholt, 1984)
CCL	Corpus Christianorum, series Latina
CR	*Classical Review*
CSEL	Corpus scriptorum ecclesiasticorum latinorum
Chadwick	H. Chadwick, *Boethius, The Consolations of Music, Logic, Theology, and Philosophy* (Oxford, 1991)
Courcelle	P. Courcelle, *La Consolation de Philosophie dans la tradition littéraire* (Paris, 1967)
GIF	*Giornale Italiano di Filologia*
Gruber	J. Gruber, *Kommentar zu Boethius, De Consolatione Philosophiae* (Berlin, 1978)
HSCP	*Harvard Studies in Classical Philology*
Jones, *LRE*	A. H. M. Jones, *The Later Roman Empire 284–602* (2 vols.; Oxford, 1964)
Kirk–Raven–Schofield[2]	G. S. Kirk, J. E. Raven, and M. Schofield, *The Presocratic Philosophers*[2] (Cambridge, 1983)
Klingner	F. Klingner, *De Boethii Consolatione Philosophiae* (Berlin, 1921; repr. Zurich, 1966)
Matthews	John Matthews, 'Anicius Manlius Severinus Boethius', in Gibson (see Bibliography), 15–43
MGH	Monumenta Germaniae Historica
OCD	*Oxford Classical Dictionary*
O'Daly	Gerard O'Daly, *The Poetry of Boethius* (London, 1991)
ODCC	*Oxford Dictionary of the Christian Church*
O'Donnell	J. J. O'Donnell, *Boethius, Consolatio Philosophiae* (2 vols.; Bryn Mawr, 1984)
PL	*Patrologia latina*

Relihan	J. C. Relihan, *Ancient Menippean Satire* (Baltimore, 1993)
RhM	*Rheinisches Museum*
Roman. Forsch.	*Romanische Forschungen*
Ross, *Aristotle*[5]	Sir David Ross, *Aristotle*[5] (London, 1949)
Sharples	R. W. Sharples, *Cicero On Fate, and Boethius, The Consolation of Philosophy IV 5–7, V* (Warminster, 1991)
Scheible	H. Scheible, *Die Gedichte in der Consolatio Philosophiae des Boethius* (Heidelberg, 1972)
Vig. Christ.	*Vigiliae Christianae*

INTRODUCTION

The modern reader who embarks on *The Consolation of Philosophy* with no knowledge of the controversies which have surrounded it for more than a millennium is confronted by a series of puzzling questions. Is the dialogue an authentic record of Boethius' response to his recent condemnation and impending execution, or does the mostly dispassionate flavour suggest that the work is an elaborate fiction, unrelated to the author's harrowing experiences? If indeed the work is one of self-consolation composed under the shadow of death, how far if at all does the author's espousal of Christian belief impinge upon the philosophical doctrines? And if the treatise is to be read as a serious and engaged philosophical reflection, why does Boethius choose to address the problems in what had hitherto been a predominantly playful form, the combination of prose and verse largely associated with Menippean satire? These questions demand an investigation of Boethius' earlier political career, and in particular his condemnation, in the complex world of sixth-century Italy; of his philosophical (and theological) studies, which as a latter-day Cicero he pursued throughout his adult life; of his literary as distinct from his philosophical enthusiasms, which reflect intimate acquaintance especially with the Latin poetry of the first centuries BC and AD.

I. THE HISTORICAL BACKGROUND

The Italy[1] into which Anicius Manlius Severinus Boethius was born in the early 480s had witnessed the deposition of 'the last Roman emperor of the West', Romulus Augustulus, by the German Odoacer, who had earlier served under Roman generals before fomenting a successful rebellion in 476. Until the time of

[1] For this and the following section, see the excellent accounts of Chadwick, ch. 1; Matthews, 15 ff.; Gruber, 1 ff.

the emperor Honorius, Milan had been the regular Italian residence of the Western imperial court, but when that city was besieged by Alaric in 401, Ravenna, protected by its marshes and lagoons, had become the choice for the new centre of the court. Odoacer, when proclaimed king, maintained the continuity of Western government there. He recognized the overlordship of the eastern emperor Zeno at Constantinople, gained the support of the Roman senate, and, though an Arian, ruled Catholic Italy harmoniously until 489 when he faced an armed invasion by the Ostrogoth Theoderic.

Theoderic had earlier been a youthful hostage at Constantinople, where he had received a Roman upbringing. In 471 he had become king of the Ostrogoths, who were settled at that time in Pannonia, south and west of the Danube. He remained in close contact with Constantinople, and became consul in 484. In 489 Zeno prompted him to invade Italy, with the aim of supplanting Odoacer. After four years of intermittent campaigning, Odoacer surrendered; having yielded Ravenna to Theoderic, he was promptly executed there.

Meanwhile at Constantinople the elderly Anastasius had succeeded Zeno as eastern emperor in 491. He confirmed Theoderic's position as king of Italy, and gave him discretion to nominate Roman consuls for approval at Constantinople. The Roman senate accepted him as successor to Odoacer and as the equivalent of a western emperor. Theoderic had earlier become thoroughly Romanized, an admirer of the traditional Roman culture and of the stability of Roman law. He promoted cordial co-operation with the Roman senate, and continued to allow the offices of consuls, praetorian prefect, and governors in Italy to remain in the hands of the Roman aristocracy. Though he himself as an Ostrogoth remained an Arian by religious conviction, he made no attempt to proselytize. He sought to maintain religious harmony by leaving Catholic churches unmolested, and indeed on a visitation to St Peter's at Rome in 500, he venerated it 'as if he were a Catholic'.[2]

Though relations between Ravenna and Constantinople vacillated during Anastasius' tenure of power in the east, Theoderic was able to maintain his independence against any attempt to

---

[2] *Anonymus Valesianus*, 65 (cited by Chadwick, 3).

deliver Italy from its barbarian overlords. An important factor which militated against the restoration of political unity between east and west was the ecclesiastical tension between the Roman papacy and the eastern churches. The situation changed dramatically, however, when Anastasius died in 518. He was succeeded by Justin I (518–27), an Illyrian peasant from the Latin-speaking diocese of Dacia. Religious unity was now rapidly restored between the Holy See and all the eastern churches except Egypt's. Justin himself was an illiterate and an indifferent administrator, but he promoted his favourite nephew, Petrus Sabbatius, better known by his adoptive name of Justinian, to be the most influential figure at court as a skilled negotiator in both political and ecclesiastical spheres. Relations between Ravenna and Constantinople became increasingly soured; this spirit of increasing distrust, as we shall see, sparked off the condemnation of Boethius on a charge of treason in 524.

Justinian, a native Latin speaker of considerable culture, who was steeped in Rome's history and had profound respect for Roman law, regarded it as his life's mission to restore the glories of the Roman empire, and to deliver the city of Rome from barbarian servitude. Though his wife Theodora was a monophysite, believing that the incarnate Christ had only one, divine, nature, he himself was an unswerving supporter of the doctrine of the two natures, human and divine, of Christ ratified by the Council of Chalcedon (451). The resultant ecclesiastical reconciliation between east and west paved the way, following the deaths of Boethius and of Theoderic (who died of a stomach complaint in 526), for military conquest. Belisarius, the celebrated general of Justinian, first overthrew the Vandal kingdom of Africa in 533–4, and then between 535 and 540 completed the subjugation of the Ostrogothic kingdom of Italy.

II. THE CAREER OF BOETHIUS

Boethius was born into one of the aristocratic families which dominated Roman life in the final decades of the fifth century. The Anicii were one of the clans of conspicuous wealth who had become Christian following the conversion of Constantine, but who continued to walk proudly in the traditions of imperial Rome. The tag of Ennius, 'moribus antiquis res stat Romana virisque' ('the Roman state stands firm on the manners and men of old'), might have been written as commentary on this supremely conservative society. Though shorn of military power and ultimately dependent on the decrees of the Ravenna court, they contrived to maintain their privileged life in a circumscribed society, and to retain the domestic offices of state. Boethius' own father had been city-prefect, praetorian prefect, and consul.

Soon after holding these posts the father died, and the boy was adopted into the family of the leading Roman of the day, Quintus Aurelius Memmius Symmachus, who had been consul in 485. Two conspicuous features in the life of this aristocrat deserve particular emphasis for their influence on the adopted son. First, though proud of his pagan ancestry (and especially of his descent from the fourth-century orator who, as prefect of the city, had unsuccessfully sought to have the Altar of Victory restored to the Roman senate-house), Symmachus was a highly committed Christian, intimately involved in both the theological controversies of the day and the disputes which bedevilled the occupancy of the papal throne; a further indication of the Christian devotion of the family is shown in the fact that two of Symmachus' daughters took the veil. Secondly, he combined with this Christian commitment an enthusiasm for the traditional literary culture. He wrote a history of Rome in seven books; unfortunately only a single extended fragment has survived (which in discussion of the third-century emperor Maximin lays emphasis on his persecution of Christians, but also on the ways in which Roman manners could civilize barbarian rule). He was also closely involved in an edition of Macrobius' *Commentary on the Dream of Scipio*, as the subscription in an extant manuscript indicates. Boethius exploited this work of Macrobius in his *Consolation*.[3]

The close intimacy between the two men was further enhanced when Symmachus gave his daughter Rusticiana to Boethius in marriage. She bore him two sons. Symmachus and Boethius. As described by Philosophy in the *Consolation*, her modesty and

---

[3] The fragment of the *Roman History* is preserved in the *Getica* of Jordanes (15. 83 ff.); for the echo of Macrobius in the *Consolation*, see 2. 7. 3 n. For Boethius' admiration for Symmachus, 2. 3–4.

chaste life were beyond compare; she was 'the image of her father'. Her loyalty to her husband was demonstrated throughout his imprisonment. After his execution, she devoted herself to charitable works. When Belisarius invaded Italy, she showed contempt for personal danger at the hands of the Goths by having the statues of Theoderic torn down from their pedestals in Rome.[4]

With the advantage of his own aristocratic descent and the support of his adoptive family, Boethius' early career was one of unalloyed prosperity. Like Symmachus, he became a leading figure in the Roman establishment. With the benign support of Theoderic on the one hand and of Constantinople on the other, he became sole consul in 510 while still in his late twenties; though this dignity endowed more prestige than power, his presidency over the games which incumbents of the consulship were expected to mount must have made him a popular figure in Rome. His claim that during a period of Campanian famine he successfully opposed the praetorian prefect Faustus' compulsory purchase of grain is probably to be dated to this period. Twelve years later in 522 an even more signal honour was conferred on him when his two sons, who were barely out of their teens, were jointly invested with the consulship; this was clearly intended as a tribute to Boethius himself, for on the day of their installation he was chosen to pronounce the encomium to King Theoderic, and later he was installed between his sons in the Circus to receive the plaudits of the Roman crowd.[5]

This moment of ceremonial glory was the prelude to further advancement. Theoderic, ever conscious of the desirability of maintaining harmonious relations with the Roman establishment, and eager to recruit this outstanding figure of social and intellectual eminence, offered him the post of Master of Offices in the Ravenna court. This position, which dated back to the era of Diocletian and Constantine, had grown in importance since that

---

[4] For Rusticiana's wifely virtues, see 2. 4; her dedication to charitable works, Procopius, *History of the Wars of Justinian*, 7. 2, 27; destruction of Theoderic's statues, Procopius 7. 2. 29.

[5] Whether Boethius travelled abroad for higher education is a disputed question. It has been suggested that he acquired his philosophical expertise at Athens (cf. C. J. De Vogel, *Vivarium* (1971), 49–66; (1972), 1–40), or at Alexandria (so P. Courcelle, *Late Latin Writers*, tr. H. Wodeck (Cambridge, Mass., 1969), 275 ff.), but neither thesis can be definitely established. For his burgeoning career at Rome, see the refs. in n. 1 above; his opposition to the Praetorian Prefect, 1. 4; his honours in 522, 2. 4.

time. It made Boethius the intermediary between the king and all who sought access to him. Cassiodorus, successor to Boethius in the office, has left a description of it as dictated by Theoderic himself.[6] The duties included maintenance of discipline in the palace, with control of the *scholares* or Imperial Guard, introducing senators into the royal presence, dealing likewise with foreign ambassadors, and superintending public entertainments. A considerable attraction for Theoderic in having such highly literate men as Boethius and Cassiodorus as his chief functionary at court was the facility and authority with which they drew up documents in negotiations with the Roman senate, with his allies and other external powers, and with ecclesiastical dignitaries. As he himself concedes, Boethius made enemies for himself both at court and in the Roman senate; he was clearly zealous in dealing with cases of corruption and injustice that came to his notice, but the history of his fall suggests that he alienated others by the imperious exercise of his position.

In 523–4 the Roman senator Albinus, a senior figure of great distinction who had been consul in 493 and Praetorian Prefect a few years later, and who as a close confidant of Pope Hormisdas had played a prominent role in the ecclesiastical reconciliation between east and west, was accused of having written insultingly of Theoderic to officials in the entourage of Emperor Justin. The informer was Cyprian, the private secretary of the king. Though Albinus denied the charge, Theoderic was persuaded of the truth of the allegation, and Albinus was condemned at Verona on a charge of treason, without formal trial. Theoderic's suspicion of a plot against his regime being hatched at Constantinople may well have had some justification. He himself had attained the throne of Italy in 493 with the complicity of the eastern emperor Zeno, and now that the religious differences between east and west had been settled, the continuing dominance of Arian Ostrogoths over *Roma Aeterna*, the heart of Classical and Christian traditions, was increasingly resented in both Constantinople and Rome. Moreover, the king's age (he was now in his seventies and had ruled for thirty years) and his precarious health, to which he succumbed three years later, may have increased his fears.

---

[6] Cassiodorus, *Variae*, 6. 6.

Boethius had been in office at Ravenna for only a year, and one suspects that his continuing self-identification with Rome rather than with Ravenna was a sore disappointment to Theoderic. His response to the condemnation of Albinus was certainly less than diplomatic. The Ravenna Chronicler, writing a generation after the event, records it like this: 'Then Boethius the patrician, who was Master of Offices, said in the king's presence: "Cyprian's charge is false. But if Albinus so acted, then I and the whole senate acted with one mind. It is false, my lord king".'[7] The boldness of this declaration suggests that he expected the king to dismiss the accusation; instead, Theoderic interpreted Boethius' words as proof that he and the senate were parties to a conspiracy. His suspicions were reinforced by accusations laid by ex-courtiers dubbed by Boethius as men of dubious reputation, to the effect that Boethius was shielding the senate from the accusation of treason. The charges made against him, chiefly that of treason, included one of 'sacrilege', by which it was suggested that he was indulging in the black arts of magic to achieve his ends—a claim hotly denied by Boethius himself and absurd to modern ears, but one to which serious attention was repeatedly paid in the era of late antiquity.[8] Though Boethius makes serious accusations of corruption against his accusers, two of them, the brothers Cyprian and Opilio, subsequently attained positions of influence at court, Cyprian in particular becoming royal treasurer and eventually Master of Offices.

Albinus and Boethius were both arrested and imprisoned. Albinus may have been summarily executed, for he disappears from the scene. Boethius was confined at Ticinum (modern Pavia), and the city-prefect Eusebius was summoned from Rome to receive the instruction of the king. The result was that a senatorial court was convened at Rome and passed the death-sentence on Boethius, who was given no opportunity to leave his confinement to speak in his own defence. The condemnation, which Boethius bitterly criticizes in the *Consolation* as a betrayal by his fellow-senators, had all the appearances of submission to *force majeure*; Eusebius may have carried back from Ravenna the

---

[7] *Anon. Vales.* 85. For the date and status of this work as a source for Theoderic's final years, see S. J. R. Barnish, *Latomus* (1983), 572 ff.

[8] See 1. 4. 37 and n..

command to convict, with the alternative of disbandment of the senate.

The length and nature of Boethius' imprisonment are controverted, and depend on whether Boethius' own version of his conviction and projected punishment are historical. One scholar has suggested that the entire setting of the *Consolation* is fictitious, and that even the names of Boethius' accusers are symbolic—Basilius representing kingly power, Opilio wealth, Gaudentius pleasure. But several of the personalities involved are undoubtedly historical, including the brothers Cyprian and Opilio; and Boethius' repeated censure of Theoderic and his court closely accords with the historical accounts of events in 524 and after.[9] None the less, there is a certain incongruity in this leisured and academic discussion allegedly composed when its author was confronting an imminent and violent death, and consideration should be given to the possibility that a stay of execution was still possible, and that the conditions under which Boethius was confined were reasonably humane.

Boethius may well have believed that Theoderic would hesitate to steel himself to order the execution of a distinguished senatorial who had been his chief official. Such arbitrary savagery was contrary to the king's temperament and earlier practice; according to Procopius, the executions of Boethius and Symmachus were a unique blot on his reign, 'the first and last injustice which he committed against his subjects, because he passed judgement on the two men without making a full enquiry as had been his usual practice'. The historian attributes this departure from his routine to the influence of envious men who had accused the two senators before the king of plotting a *coup d'état*.[10] But a spectacular deterioration in relations between Ravenna and Constantinople may also have harmed Boethius' prospects of a reprieve. Justin, early in 525, was reportedly harassing Arians in the east by forced conversions and by seizure of their churches. Theoderic sent a powerful embassy to remonstrate and to demand a reversal of this policy. It was headed by Pope John I, and it included five other bishops and four senior senators. Though Justin was believed to

---

[9] For the thesis that the dialogue is a fiction, see E. Reiss, *Class. Journ.* (1981), 37 ff., repr. in his *Boethius* (Boston, 1982), 82 ff. For a rebuttal, D. Shanzer, *Hermes* (1984), 352 ff.
[10] See Matthews, 35.

have acceded to the request for restoration of ecclesiastical proper-ties, this concession was overshadowed by the enthusiastic recep-tion of the embassy, whose visit culminated in the ceremonial crowning of Justin as emperor by Pope John. This gesture set the seal on the reconciliation of the western and eastern churches, and intensified Theoderic's suspicions of the emperor. When the embassy returned to Ravenna, the ambassadors were imprisoned and maltreated; Pope John, who was a sick man, died in confinement there in 526. It is conceivable that Theoderic was holding Boethius and Symmachus as hostages to ensure the success of the embassy, and that he gave orders for their execution after disturbing reports from Constantinople in 525 indicated that the rift with Ravenna was widening. Though the conventional dating of Boethius' execution is late 524, it could equally have occurred in 525, or even in 526 as the *Liber Pontificalis* has it.[11]

The nature of Boethius' confinement at Pavia is similarly obscure. If Boethius' own testimony in the *Consolation* is taken as historical, it is clear that the conditions under which he was held were markedly more primitive than those of his ancestral home. When Philosophy rebukes him for his tearful lamentation, he reminds her of her earlier visits to his library, which with its sumptuous furnishings contrasted markedly with his present abode.[12] On the other hand, to envisage him as confined in durance vile would clearly be an exaggeration; he has the books and leisure to compose his crowning work unimpeded. Accord-ingly we may assume that he was kept under house-arrest in the Ager Calventianus, an area near Pavia inhabited by impoverished peasants, which the prisoner laments as a place of exile.[13]

The sources offer differing versions of the manner of execution. The Ravenna Chronicler records that a cord was twisted round his head so tightly that it caused his eyeballs to protrude from their sockets, and that his life was then beaten out of him by a club. Boethius as a Roman senator might have anticipated a less brutal

[11] For this thesis, see Chadwick, 59 ff., and 2. 2. 14 n. It must be conceded that the contemporary accounts give no hint that he died as a victim of the moves towards unification of east and west; see Helen Kirkby in *Boethius*, ed. M. Gibson (Oxford, 1981), 61–2.

[12] See 1. 4. Tester's Loeb trans. misleads here.

[13] See 2. 4. A. Fortescue, in the chapter 'De religione Boethi' in his edn. of *De consolatione philosophiae* (London, 1923), speculates that he was in exile, but not in prison.

mode of execution, since being cudgelled to death was by Roman law restricted to individuals of the lower classes. Such niceties, however, would have been of little concern to Ostrogoth officials superintending an execution for so heinous a crime as treason. The authority of the source makes this version more probable than that recorded in the *Liber Pontificalis*, that Boethius was dispatched by a sword thrust.[14]

III. LITERARY ACTIVITIES

The traditionalism which is so distinctive in the lives of the Roman aristocracy of the fifth century is especially reflected in the literary pursuits which many of them combined with their duties in public life. We have seen that Symmachus, father-in-law of Boethius, wrote a history of Rome and was active in editing Macrobius. Turcius Rufius Apronianus Asterius, consul in 494, edited the text of Virgil's *Eclogues* in the very year of his consulship. Vettius Agorius Basilius Mavortius, consul in 527, revised the texts of Horace and the Christian poet Prudentius.[15] Cassiodorus, successor to Boethius as Master of Offices at Ravenna, in the course of his secular career wrote a summary of Roman history called *Chronica*, and twelve books on the history of the Goths, as well as a treatise *On the Soul*.[16] Boethius himself decided to emulate Cicero the philosopher. In a passage containing perceptible echoes of the prefaces to Cicero's philosophical works, he writes:

Though the duties of my consular office hinder my devoting all my leisure and full attention to these studies, it seems none the less appropriate to any commitment towards the state to instruct the citizens in the learning of a subject over which one has burnt the midnight oil. The virtue of men of old consigned dominion and rule over other cities to this state alone, so I shall not deserve badly of my fellow-citizens if I at any rate perform the remaining task of schooling the manners of our state in the arts of Greek wisdom. So

[14] For the Ravenna Chronicler's version, see *Anon. Vales.* 85 ff.; *Liber Pontificalis* l. 276 records the alternative. Symmachus' outrage at the execution led to his arrest and subsequent execution (*Anon. Vales.* 92).

[15] For these examples, see Matthews, 19 ff.

[16] See J. J. O'Donnell, *Cassiodorus* (Berkeley, 1979), 36 ff., 103 ff.

even this is not superfluous to the duty of a consul, for it was always the way of Romans to lend by imitation more and more honour to all that was fine and praiseworthy throughout the world.[17]

Boethius' astonishingly bold plan of publication rivals that of Cicero, who sought to bring the riches of the whole of Hellenistic philosophy before the minds of Roman readers. For his part, Boethius promised to do the same with Plato and Aristotle:

It is my firm intention . . . to translate into Latin every work of Aristotle that comes into my hands, and to write Latin commentaries on all of them; thus I shall translate in due order all the elements of subtlety of logic, of serious moral insight, of the keen vision of natural truth which Aristotle has penned. In addition I shall provide Latin dress for all Plato's dialogues by translating and also writing commentaries on them. On completing these tasks I shall not disdain to reconcile, so to say, the ideas of Plato and Aristotle, and to demonstrate that the two do not disagree in all matters, as most critics hold, but that they accord with each other on most issues, these being the most important in philosophy.[18]

This ambitious programme of a youthful enthusiast was never fulfilled; as we shall see, his researches on Aristotelian logic dominated his studies until his departure to Ravenna, and two other large-scale projects also preoccupied him. The second of these, his excursion into the controversies of theology following the decrees of the Council of Chalcedon, must demand our attention later. The first was in his view a necessary preliminary to the study of logic; this was a plan to clarify the nature and importance of the four mathematical disciplines in the seven liberal arts (his is the first extant use of the word *quadrivium* to describe the combination). He hints at this project in the exordium to his treatise on the first of the four, the *De arithmetica*, which he dedicated to Symmachus. This work in two books is in large part a translation of the *Introduction to Arithmetic* by the celebrated mathematician of the second century AD, Nicomachus of Gerasa. To this magisterial account of the abstract properties of number Boethius himself was able to add little of importance.

[17] *Commentary on Aristotle's Categories*, II *Praef.* (*PL* 64. 201B; cf. S. Lerer, *Boethius and Dialogue* (Princeton, 1985), 21). The reference to his consulship indicates a date of 510 for these four books of commentary; Boethius was still in his twenties at that time.
[18] *Second Commentary on Aristotle, On Interpretation*, ed. C. Meiser (Leipzig, 1880). Cf. J. Barnes in *Boethius*, ed. Gibson, 74.

Boethius' treatise on the second of the liberal arts, the *De institutione musica* (which has survived in five books, the last incomplete), is based largely on the same Nicomachus' *Introduction to Music* for the first four books, and on Ptolemy's *Harmonics* for the fifth; its importance lay in presenting the Pythagorean theory of cosmic harmony to educated Roman contemporaries increasingly remote from the world of Greek learning.[19] Boethius composed a treatise on the third of the liberal arts, the *De geometria*, for this is twice attested by Cassiodorus, and extracts from it are preserved in medieval manuscripts, which indicate that Euclid was his basic source. But there is doubt whether he composed a work on astronomy, for though Cassiodorus credits Boethius with a translation of Ptolemy on this subject, no traces of this work remain.[20] But the *Consolation* reflects a wide knowledge of the heavenly bodies, so that even if Boethius' researches were not published, he was certainly a keen student of astronomy. This study of the mathematical *quadrivium* was of the greatest importance in forming his vision as a philosopher (and a Christian) of the nature of the world and of God; 'Knowledge of the rational, numerical structure of the universe would lead to knowledge of the divine nature, and to apprehension of God himself.'[21]

In the ancient theory of education, the mathematical disciplines were the first stage,[22] to be followed by study of logic, the essential tool for advancing into the realm of metaphysics. Aristotle and the Peripatetic school which he founded reigned supreme in this branch of philosophy. The standard guide to their doctrines in Boethius' day was the *Isagoge* ('Introduction') of the Neoplatonist Porphyry, which had already been translated into Latin by Marius Victorinus, the Neoplatonist-turned-Christian whom Augustine acknowledges in his *Confessions* as his intellectual model on the

[19] On the *De arithmetica* and the *De institutione musica*, see J. Caldwell in *Boethius*, ed. Gibson, ch. 5; Chadwick, 69 ff. The text of Nicomachus, *On Arithmetic* was edited by R. Hoche (Leipzig, 1866), and translated by M. L. D'Ooge in *Studies in Greek Arithmetic* (New York, 1926). Nicomachus' treatise on music has not survived.

[20] On the fragments of the *De geometria* and the possible existence of a *De astronomia*, see Chadwick, 102 ff.; D. Pingree in *Boethius*, ed. Gibson, ch. 6.

[21] So Alison White in *Boethius*, ed. Gibson, 163. Her chapter offers an informative survey of the widespread diffusion of *De arithmetica* and *De institutione musica* in the medieval schools.

[22] So Plotinus, *Enneads*, 1. 3.

path to conversion. Boethius initially wrote a commentary in dialogue form on the *Isagoge*, based on that earlier Latin version. But his dissatisfaction with its accuracy led him to offer his own translation, together with a second commentary. He was now launched into a threefold mode of instruction on logic.[23] He provided direct translations of the salient works; he wrote commentaries on the various books which comprise Aristotle's *Organon* ('Instrument of Thought')—the *Categories*, *On Interpretation* (he wrote a double commentary on this, which in his own words offers simple elucidation followed by 'a more profound and pointed consideration'), and the *Prior* and *Posterior Analytics*;[24] and monographs on particular subjects arising out of the Aristotelian corpus. The approximate order of the surviving works is as follows:[25]

> *First Commentary on Porphyry's* Isagoge, *c.*AD 504–5
> *On Categorical Syllogisms, c.*505–6
> Translation and *Second Commentary on* Isagoge, *c.*507–9
> *Commentary on Aristotle's* Categories, 510
> *First Commentary on Aristotle's* On Interpretation, *c.*513–14
> *Second Commentary on Aristotle's* On Interpretation, *c.*515–16
> *On Hypothetical Syllogisms, c.*516–22
> (Lost) *Commentary on Aristotle's* Topics, (including *Sophistici Elenchi*), before 523
> *Commentary on Cicero's* Topics, before 523
> *On Topical Differences*, before 523
> Surviving Notes on Aristotle's *Prior Analytics*, before 523.

Since the Greek originals are available to scholars today, the value of Boethius' labours must be measured within the context of his own day and of the succeeding centuries until the rediscovery of Aristotle. For the students of those eras he provided an invaluable service. His translations were deliberately literal rather than literary. Their fidelity to the meaning of the Greek is impressive, especially as Aristotle's teachings in the compressed form in which they were transmitted to posterity were so difficult

[23] For what follows I draw on J. Barnes in *Boethius*, ed. Gibson, ch. 3.

[24] The commentaries on the *Analytics* (if it existed) and on *Topics* have not survived; see Barnes, in *Boethius*, ed. Gibson, 87 n. 8.

[25] See L. M. de Rijk, *Vivarium* (1964), 1–49, 125–62.

to interpret. The commentaries in their line-by-line explications lay no claim to originality, nor do they incorporate wide reading of the many Greek authorities who are quoted, for the citations are taken at second hand, whether from the works of Porphyry or from detailed glosses on a manuscript of the *Organon* of Aristotle, themselves distillations of Porphyry's work.[26] For the monographs, the staple information came from Aristotle, supplemented by the writings of the later Peripatetics and of Cicero. Boethius' contribution to the discipline of logic was thus essentially an exercise in synthesis. He educated his readers and himself in the application of human reason to the wider problems of the nature and existence of God, of the origin and governance of the world, and of man's status and role in that world.

IV. BOETHIUS AND NEOPLATONISM

These broader metaphysical questions, which Boethius addressed in the *Consolation*, had for long been subjected to the rigours of Peripatetic logic in the Neoplatonist schools at Athens and Alexandria.[27] The philosophical scene in Greece up to Boethius' day was dominated by the new direction in Platonism initiated at Rome by Plotinus in the third century AD, and recorded and extended by his pupil Porphyry. Boethius followed the example of Marius Victorinus and Augustine in seeking a reconciliation between his Christian allegiance and this pervasive philosophy. At Athens, Proclus (*c.*410–85) was the dominant fifth-century representative of the school. As well as commentaries on several of Plato's dialogues, he wrote an extended work entitled *The Theology of Plato*, and a catechism of Neoplatonist tenets called *Elements of Theology*. Proclus was a fervent apologist for pagan religious practices, and a caustic critic of Christianity; it was this militant opposition as shown by him and by Damascius, a later

---

[26] See J. Shiel, *Mediaeval and Renaissance Studies* (1958), 217 ff.; 'Boethius' Commentaries on Aristotle', in *Aristotle Transformed*, ed. R. Sorabji (London, 1990), 249 ff. The argument certainly holds good for part of the *Organon*; see Boethius' *Second Commentary on the De interpretatione*, 2. 250.

[27] For what follows, see A. C. Lloyd, 'Athenian and Alexandrian Neoplatonism', in *The Cambridge History of Later Greek and Early Medieval Philosophy* (Cambridge, 1967), ch. 19; Chadwick, 16 ff.

head of the school, that prompted Justinian to close the doors of the Athenian Academy in 529.

The situation at Alexandria was rather different. In this cosmopolitan city the first-century Jewish scholar Philo had sought a reconciliation between the doctrines of the Old Testament and Platonist thought, and this sympathetic reception of Plato was adopted by successive heads of the Christian catechetical school, Clement and Origen; Origen's teacher, Ammonius Saccas, who also taught Plotinus, was alleged by Porphyry to have been a lapsed Christian.[28] The respect accorded to Plato's doctrines by Christians continued into Boethius' day. The writings of Bishop Cyril of Alexandria (412–44) reflect their continuing influence on Christian theology. More significantly, Ammonius son of Hermias, who was a pupil of Proclus at Athens before becoming head of the school at Alexandria, was converted to Christianity while teaching there in the second half of the fifth century, the very time when Boethius was serving his apprenticeship to his chosen discipline of philosophy. There was no danger that the young scholar would incur censure from ecclesiastical authority for his enthusiasm for the doctrines descending from Plato; as Simplicianus of Milan had put it when congratulating Augustine on studying the books of the Platonists, 'in all the Platonic books God and the Word keep slipping in'.[29]

The fundamental doctrine of Neoplatonism as taught by Plotinus in the *Enneads* is that there are three Realities, the One, the Intelligence, and the Soul. They comprise a hierarchy of Being, descending from the First Principle (the One, the Good) to the second level of divine Intellect (*Nous*) and the Forms, and from there to the third level of the World-Soul.

The One, the Good is absolute simplicity and self-sufficiency, the source of being beyond being. Words can tell us only what it is not (the *via negativa*). It does not keep perfection to itself; it creates, but without will or movement, and without diminishing itself. Plotinus occasionally terms it God, and elsewhere the Father. The Forms at the second level of being are visualized as thoughts in the mind of God.

From the One proceeds *Nous*, the divine Intelligence comprising

---

[28] So Eusebius, *Hist. Eccles.* 5. 19. [29] Augustine, *Confessions*, 8. 2.

the world of the Forms. The term used for this procession is 'emanation'; Plotinus visualizes it as the radiation of light and heat. There are two movements in such emanation. First, *Nous* is created but unformed, but then it turns back to the One in contemplation and becomes filled with being, for all things depend for their activity and power on contemplation of their Source. *Nous* is sometimes termed *Logos*; *Logos* is a force proceeding from a higher principle, representing that principle on a lower plane of being. *Nous* is thus the *Logos* of the One, and Soul is the *Logos* of *Nous*. The world of the Forms, identical with *Nous*, is no longer a group of static universals as visualized by Plato, but a living community of divine intelligence, unity in diversity.

Soul proceeds from *Nous*, and is the intermediary between the world of Intellect and the world of sense. Having proceeded from *Nous*, it returns to contemplate it. Thus formed, it regulates the entire universe. It has two levels, the higher as intelligent direction and the lower as principle of life and growth. Our individual souls are part of this World-Soul, but if they surrender to the demands of our bodies, they cut themselves off from the World-Soul. If on the other hand they remain master of the body, they can cleave to the universal soul and rise to the reality of *Nous*; in company with *Nous*, they can ascend to contemplate the One, but only fleetingly as long as they remain in the shackles of the body. (Porphyry states that Plotinus claimed to have attained this mystical experience of unity with the One on four occasions.)

All matter is evil, and is responsible for imperfection in the world. We can discover our true selves by rigorous mental and moral discipline. Then the One reveals his presence to us, and we are inspired to begin the ascent.[30]

It is clear that the doctrine of the three Realities in the hierarchy of Being could be visualized by Christians as the symbolic expression of the doctrine of the Trinity, with the One being equated with the Father, *Nous* or *Logos* with the Son, and the World-Soul with the Holy Spirit. Moreover, the soul's yearning to liberate itself from the murky world of matter, and to rise to the clear light of the true Sun, could correspond with the Christian's

---

[30] On the philosophy of Plotinus, see A. H. Armstrong in *Cambridge History*, esp. 236 ff.; R. T. Wallis, *Neoplatonism* (London, 1972).

aspiration to seek the happiness of the Beatific Vision in heaven, man's true end as formulated by Augustine. But at other points, where the Platonic-Aristotelian world-view diverges from Christian orthodoxy, Boethius allows Philosophy to remain true to her ancient spokesmen. Thus Plato's doctrine of the pre-existence of the soul in the world of the Forms, as delineated in the *Phaedo*, and the recollection (*anamnesis*) of that earlier existence is implicit especially in her poetic utterances; and again, the Aristotelian notion of the eternity of the world, as opposed to the Christian doctrine of creation *ex nihilo*, is propounded in her verses.[31]

One need not assume that Boethius personally subscribes to every doctrine propounded by Philosophy; one scholar goes so far as to argue that he charts Philosophy's entire consolation as a failure, maintaining that 'Christianity is the way out, the victor in a fruitless contest of opposing arguments'.[32] More probably, however, Boethius plays the role of a latter-day Origen in speculatively advancing the arguments of the philosophers, even at the risk of departing from Christian orthodoxy.

V. THE THEOLOGICAL TRACTATES

Though Boethius had been reared in a fervently Catholic household, and though throughout the Middle Ages he was generally hailed as a heroic Christian, scholars in the eighteenth and nineteenth centuries argued that he must either have renounced his allegiance to Christianity, or remained a nominal Christian merely to serve his secular career. His attachment to Neoplatonist doctrines persuaded them that the theological tractates traditionally ascribed to him could not have come from his pen. These critics were confounded by the discovery and publication in 1877 of a fragment of Cassiodorus which confirmed him as author in these words: 'He [sc. Boethius] wrote a book on the holy Trinity, certain chapters on dogma, and a book against Nestorius.'[33]

---

[31] For pre-existence of the soul, see the verses in 4. 1; for eternity of the world, the verses in 4. 6.

[32] See Relihan, ch. 12. He underlines his thesis with the claims, 'It is a search that fails'; 'the failure of Philosophy [is] to satisfy the needs of the prisoner'; 'the point of the *Consolation* is the limitedness of learning'.

[33] The fragment of Cassiodorus is the *Anecdoton Holderi*, discovered by A. Holder and

Of the five theological tractates represented by that description, it is arguable that the fourth, *On the Catholic Faith*, was the earliest.[34] The attribution to Boethius was once considered dubious, but scholars today are virtually unanimous in pronouncing it genuine. It is a simple statement of orthodox Christian belief. Beginning with an explanation of the Trinity, it then outlines significant moments in the Old Testament, and follows with an account of the incarnation, death, and resurrection of Christ; finally it outlines the progress of the Church. The absence of logical analysis on Aristotelian lines suggests a date of composition prior to Boethius' specialized studies in that area. The work reads like a summary of Augustine's teaching, and may be based on the catechetical instruction imparted to Boethius by his spiritual mentor John the Deacon, who may be identical with the later Pope John I.

Tractate V, *Against Eutyches and Nestorius*, which Boethius dedicated to his teacher John the Deacon, must be the earliest of the other treatises;[35] it was the outcome of a council at Rome attended by John the Deacon and Boethius. Eutyches (*c.*378–454) had maintained that there was only one nature, the divine, in the incarnate Christ; the heresy associated with the name of Nestorius (who died *c.*451) proclaimed that there were two persons in Christ, the one divine and the other human. Both views ran contrary to the Declaration of the Council of Chalcedon, that there are two natures in the one Person of Christ. Boethius was apparently dismayed by the lack of logical rigour displayed in the discussions at the Roman council; he made his contribution to the controversy by this pamphlet in which he clarified the definitions of 'nature' ('the difference which gives a thing its distinctive form') and of

published in 1877 by H. Usener. The text is accessible in CCL 95 (ed. Fridh and Halporn), v–vi; for recent discussion, see J. J. O'Donnell, *Cassiodorus* (Berkeley, 1979), 259 ff.

[34] On the Tractates in general, see J. Mair, 'The Text of the Opuscula Sacra', in *Boethius*, ed. Gibson, ch. 8, a contribution to which the discussion here is heavily indebted; H. Liebeschuetz in *Cambridge History*, 543 ff.; Chadwick, ch. 4, from whom I derive the suggestion that *De fide Catholica* is an early work. E. K. Rand's doctoral thesis sought to demonstrate that it is spurious, a view which he later recanted (*Founders of the Middle Ages* (Cambridge, Mass., 1928; repr. New York, 1959), 156).

[35] For what follows, see Mair, in *Boethius*, ed. Gibson, 207 ff.; Chadwick, 180 ff. Mair expresses doubts about Tester's dating (in the Loeb edn., 72–3) of this Tractate as early as 512.

'person' ('an individual being with a rational nature'). By these definitions he sought to expose the incoherence of the views of the Nestorians and of Eutyches, and to chart a middle course between them. The demonstration that logic was the key to sound theology commended the *opuscula sacra* as a teaching text to the leading scholars of the Middle Ages.[36]

The first two Tractates, probably composed between 519 and 523, apply the lessons of logic to the theology of the Trinity. The brief Tractate II was probably composed first. In it Boethius argues that God is a single substance, and that each of the three persons is a separate substance. Accordingly the persons cannot be predicated of God as substance, but in some other way (*alio modo*), that is, in a relative sense (*ad aliquid*). The longer Tractate I, which was dedicated to Boethius' father-in-law Symmachus, initially acknowledges Augustine's *De Trinitate* as its basis; it then proceeds by Aristotelian arguments to demonstrate that God is one, and that he is pure form. To state that the Father is God, the Son is God, the Spirit is God is not enumerating them as different, but reiterating them as the same. Tractate III is devoted to the argument that substances are good not because they participate in some goodness, but simply because they exist. It is likely that this treatise was written in response to a query (presumably from John the Deacon, to whom Tractate II is addressed) arising from the problem of the relationship between God and the three Persons.

Tractate II ends with the striking plea to John the Deacon to 'examine with some care these words of mine, and if possible, reconcile faith with reason'. Similarly in the prologue to Tractate I, Boethius tells Symmachus that 'our investigation should advance only as far as the insight of human reason can scale the heights of divinity'. (Philosophy, in the final book of the *Consolation*, emphasizes the limitation of the human mind in this regard.)[37] These expressions provide the key to the nature of Boethius' Christian commitment, and explain why he wrote *The Consolation of Philosophy* rather than a consolation of revealed religion. His Christianity is rational religion in the tradition of the early Greek Fathers such as Justin, who in his *Dialogue with Trypho* wears his

---

[36] See M. Gibson, 'The *Opuscula Sacra* in the Middle Ages', in *Boethius*, ed. Gibson, ch. 9.   [37] See 5. 4.

philosopher's cloak as he recounts his journey to Christianity, or
Clement of Alexandria, whose catechetical school made its appeal
to more discriminating pagans; in the tradition, too, of the African
Minucius Felix, whose dialogue *Octavius* (*c*.AD 220) depicts the
conversion of the pagan Caecilius Natalis by rational argument,
and above all in the tradition of Marius Victorinus and of the
young Augustine.[38]

Nor must we forget the political significance of these theological
investigations, for the assertion of Christ's two natures and of the
orthodox doctrine of the Trinity was in the Italian context a
repudiation of the monophysite beliefs which the Arian Theoderic
held dear. It is arguable that when the king appointed Boethius as
his Master of Offices, he was unaware of the existence of the
Tractates (which may in fact have lain unpublished in 522), or he
failed to appreciate the strength of Boethius' commitment to the
theological unification of the eastern and western churches. In this
sense a dawning awareness of the significance of these apparently
academic treatises may have reinforced Theoderic's deepening
suspicions of the disloyalty of his chief official, and thus hastened
Boethius' condemnation.

VI. THE *CONSOLATION*: STRUCTURE AND CONTENT

The title *The Consolation of Philosophy*, presumably chosen by its
author, appears to claim a connection with the *consolatio*, a genre
of writing which owes its formal inauguration to Crantor of Soli
(*c*.325–*c*.275 BC), and which in Latin became famous through the
treatise now lost by which Cicero consoled himself on the death of
his daughter Tullia in 45 BC. But the connections with these and
other classics of the genre such as Sulpicius Rufus' consolatory
letter to Cicero on the death of his daughter, or the Younger
Seneca's letters of comfort to Marcia and Polybius in their hours
of bereavement, and to his mother Helvia who was lamenting his

---

[38] For Justin's *Dialogue with Trypho*, see the edn. by J. C. M. Van Winden (Leiden,
1971). For the *Octavius*, see the Loeb edn. by J. H. Randall (London, 1931), and the Budé,
ed. J. Beaujeu (Paris, 1964).

own exile, are merely vestigial.[39] More probably Boethius signalled
by his title the close connection of his treatise with Cicero's
philosophical writing, which the great orator repeatedly claims
was composed as an anodyne when he was deprived of a meaningful role in affairs of state. So he wrote *The Nature of the Gods*
when he was 'at a loose end with nothing to do', because 'the state
was governed by the strategy and supervision of a single man', at a
time of mental depression occasioned by the death of his daughter.
The parallels, political and personal, with Boethius need no
elaboration, though the circumstances of Cicero's loss of a loved
one and Boethius' own impending death are different. Cicero's
Tusculan Disputations was probably the treatise chiefly in the
forefront of Boethius' mind, for its theme of the true means to
happiness closely identifies it with Boethius' final work. It is
noteworthy that Cicero states at the outset that he is now at
leisure to pursue philosophical studies, and he repeatedly alludes
to his earlier disquisition occasioned by his daughter's death to
indicate how philosophy can offer consolatory medicine for the
mind.[40] This is precisely the role which Boethius envisages for his
address of comfort to himself and to readers similarly distressed.
Cicero's *De finibus*, which investigates the highest good which
Epicureans, Stoics, and Academics variously propose for our life
on earth, is also closely relevant. It is no accident that the
Consolation emulates both *Tusculans* and *De finibus* in its five-
book structure.

Thus the *Consolation* is consolation in the wider sense of
philosophical protreptic or exhortation—not in the Aristotelian
sense of a protreptic to philosophy to satisfy that intellectual
curiosity by which 'all men by nature desire to know', but 'a
protreptic towards God', a philosophical exhortation with a
specifically religious message.[41]

---

[39] There is an excellent summary of the earlier history of the *consolatio* in J. H. D.
Scourfield, *Consoling Heliodorus* (Oxford, 1993). For the *consolatio* by Sulpicius Rufus, see
Cicero, *Ad fam.* 4. 5; the consolations by Seneca, *Dial.* 6, 11, 12. Boethius' treatise has little
formal connection with these; see T. F. Curley III, *AJP* (1987), 343–67, esp. 352.

[40] For the citations here, see Cicero, *ND* 1. 7; depression at Tullia's death, 1. 9. At *Tusc.*
1. 66 the long citation from his lost *Consolatio* indicates that Cicero consoled himself with
reflections on the immortality of the soul.

[41] For the Aristotelian dictum that all men by nature desire to know, see the opening
sentence of the *Metaphysics*. For the *Consolation* as 'a Protreptic towards God', see E. K.
Rand, *HSCP* (1904), 8, echoed by Courcelle, 18. This section of the Introduction is

The work opens with a dramatic confrontation. The prisoner is being consoled by the Muses of poetry; it is no accident that in this first book the verses precede the prose-passages, whereas subsequently the positions are reversed. The poetic Muses are depicted as his sole support in time of trial when the figure of Philosophy enters to put them to ignominious flight. It is important to stress that her condemnation of poetry does not represent the view of Boethius himself; as the work progresses, the poems are to exercise an increasingly influential role. The figure of Philosophy here is the mouthpiece of Plato, who in his *Republic* condemns poetry, and would expel poets from his ideal state as Philosophy here expels the Muses; she is the mouthpiece too of Cicero, who in the *Tusculans* echoes Plato's criticisms.[42]

Much dispute has centred on the persona of Philosophy; is she modelled on Sapientia (Wisdom) in the Old Testament, or on one or other of the abstract figures of virtue in the Greek Fathers? Boethius' resolute exclusion of overt Christian influences makes these candidates less attractive than such figures representative of traditional philosophy as Athena, or Philosophia as she appears in Augustine's *Soliloquies*.[43] As for the self-portrait of the prisoner, though Philosophy's constant allusions and hints depict his situation as that of a latter-day Socrates unjustly condemned, as that of a second Seneca who is victim of a cruel despot, as that of a second Cicero whose political influence has collapsed and transformed him into a philosopher, his querulous attitude at this stage makes him unworthy to sustain so noble a role.

After Philosophy has at last been identified by the prisoner, and she has promised him a physician's help in his moral sickness, he bitterly recounts his fall and his unjust fate. She responds by posing fundamental questions to him in order to diagnose his ailment. Does he believe that the world is guided by reason? To what end does it proceed? What is the essential nature of man? Though she finds his answers less than satisfactory, she sees in them the hope for a cure.

---

indebted to Anna Crabbe's splendid essay, 'Literary Design in the *De consolatione philosophiae*', in *Boethius*, ed. Gibson, ch. 10.

[42] Plato, *Rep.* 377D–403C, 595A–608B; Cicero, *Tusc.* 2. 27.

[43] For the various candidates, see 1. 1. 1 n. Courcelle, 17 ff.; Crabbe, in *Boethius*, ed. Gibson, 239.

Book 1 has thus performed the role of a prologue, setting the scene for the dramatic dialogue to follow. Good physician as she is, Philosophy proposes to treat the prisoner's ailment initially 'with gentle and limited remedies'. The meaning of the phrase becomes clear as the later books unfold: she will first demonstrate his past happiness and present consolations; then, using 'rather stronger medicines', she will detach him from the false goods which most men seek, and enable him to attain true happiness by leading him into the metaphysical world of the One and the Good.

In Book 2 Philosophy accordingly begins by censuring the prisoner's nostalgia for the gifts earlier bestowed on him by Fortune. A characteristically Ciceronian touch enlists the services of Rhetoric to drive home the lesson. Whereas Plato in the *Gorgias* had mounted a sharp attack on rhetoric as obfuscator of the truth, Cicero in the *De oratore* follows Aristotle in praising it as a persuasive art which helps philosophy in articulating a thesis, and again in the prologue to the *De officiis* he stresses the valuable alliance of the two.[44] A favourite technique of the rhetorician is deployed to allow Fortune when impugned by the prisoner to speak in her own defence; she claims that since inconstancy is the norm in the realm of nature, it should not be denied her when she administers human affairs. Boethius is compelled to acknowledge his own past happiness, and the present consolations afforded by his family. To these consolations Philosophy appends the less tangible comfort that at death the surviving mind no longer has need of material advantages, and she proceeds to condemn the aims which most men mistakenly imagine will bring them happiness—wealth, political power, fame (all of which the prisoner has enjoyed). Against these she sets friendship alone, which in its ideal form as described at the close of the *Nicomachean Ethics* is signalled as the most precious of earthly attainments.

The theme of Book 3 is identical with that of Cicero's *Tusculans*; it is the nature of true happiness, and where it is to be found. The true route to its attainment, Philosophy argues, is by reversion to our origins. With the repetition which is the mark of the committed pedagogue, she reiterates and extends the catalogue of false goods, which now includes bodily pleasures and physical

---

[44] See P. MacKendrick, *The Philosophical Books of Cicero* (London, 1989), 152, 254–5.

beauty as well as wealth, position, power, and fame; there are clear echoes of Juvenal's Tenth Satire, *The Vanity of Human Wishes*, here. We have now reached the mid-point of the *Consolation*; from the gentler remedy of the rejection of false goods, Philosophy is now (ch. 9) to turn to the more taxing medicine of the search for the true good. This entry into the sphere of metaphysics is introduced by a solemn prayer, the hinge on which the whole treatise turns. Philosophy's ensuing thesis is that the perfect good in which lies true happiness is God. When men attain such happiness, they themselves become divine. The defective goods sought piecemeal by men indicate that all things in the world are naturally conducive to that happiness, but they must be gathered into a unity. Here the Neoplatonist message that all things seek the highest reality, the One and the Good, becomes explicit.

Having now established where and how the true good is to be found, in Book 4 Philosophy embarks on a second salient topic: granted that God is the true good, does he apportion appropriate justice to good and evil men in this world? Drawing heavily on Plato's *Gorgias*, she argues that all men naturally seek the good, and that good men by attaining it become divine; wicked men by contrast through gratifying their desires are punished by relegation to subhuman status. Their wretchedness lies precisely in their ability to act wickedly. The dialogue moves on to the apparent irrationality in the world at large, in which the widespread operation of chance seems to be at odds with God's wise governance. This contention leads Philosophy to embark upon the longest chapter in the treatise so as to explain the relationship between Providence, the divine reason in a world that knows no change, and Fate, which carries through the divine plan on our earth of change. Man's understanding of this beneficent ordering of God can be only partial.

The third and final question in the second half of the treatise is explored in Book 5: how can man's free will be reconciled with divine Providence? But first the prisoner asks for guidance about the role of chance. Philosophy explains it on Aristotelian lines as the conjunction of unforeseen causes initiated by Providence and realized by Fate. As for free will, its activity is unconfined among heavily creatures, but diminishes at each stage as our souls descend to and become locked in things of earth. The prisoner's claim that free will is incompatible with God's foreknowledge is rejected by Philosophy. She first distinguishes four levels of cognition—sensation, imagination, reason, and understanding. This last is the faculty possessed by divine creatures alone. The apparent conflict between free will and foreknowledge can be resolved only by awareness that God's knowledge is unchanging and is always in the present. From that aspect of the divine foreknowledge all future events will necessarily happen as God sees them in the present, but of their own nature in this world some will necessarily occur, while others will be freely chosen.

By the close of Book 5, the *Consolation* has moved away from the prisoner's personal concerns. Does it give him much comfort to know that man's free will can be reconciled with divine Providence? The sequence of thought developed through the treatise is that the consolation which the prisoner can attain lies not in the mundane satisfactions of his earlier life, but in aspiring to and attaining knowledge of God, the One and the Good. That knowledge will bring with it the realization that God orders all things sweetly; a central feature of that divine economy is the freedom given to human beings to choose their way. So the prisoner can gain the spiritual freedom to shake off the shackles of earthly serfdom, and to rise to contemplation of the Father of all things.

VII. THE SOURCES

The problem of ascertaining Boethius' philosophical sources in the *Consolation* is rendered more difficult by the uncertainty of the nature of his confinement.[45] Had he access to any written works? If so, what were they? If not, what works can we assume he knew so intimately that he was capable of reproducing their thought without reference to the texts? One thing is certain: he was not in the privileged position of a Cicero, who composed his treatises with several volumes at his elbow, and was able to obtain others from a range of studious friends.

[45] The review of the sources that follows merely scratches the surface. For detailed surveys, see Courcelle, 161 ff.; J. Solowski, *Sophia* (1957), 76 ff.; (1961), 67 ff.

The questions begin with Plato. Of his twenty-four dialogues that are indisputably genuine, the *Consolation* reflects knowledge, direct or indirect, of at least half of them. It is hardly surprising, given the situation of the prisoner, that the group of dialogues which record the events leading to Socrates' death (*Apology*, *Crito*, *Phaedo*) should make their presence felt in Book 1, and the central concern of the *Phaedo* (and also the *Phaedrus*) with the immortality of the soul is reflected in the later books. There are repeated echoes of the *Republic*, the manual for the philosophic statesman which Boethius must have thoroughly digested. Elsewhere traces of the *Theaetetus*, *Sophist*, *Protagoras*, and *Meno* are observable. In two cases the evocations are more deliberate and sustained. The hymn to the Father at the centre of the work (3. 9) closely reproduces the teachings of the *Timaeus*, and the early chapters of Book 4 reflect close adaptation of argumentation from the *Gorgias*. One may suspect that at least in the case of these last two Boethius had access to the texts or to Neoplatonist commentaries upon them.

The case with Aristotle is rather different; Boethius had spent most of his scholarly life in study of his writings. It is hardly surprising that in a treatise concerned initially with ethics and subsequently with metaphysics, Boethius should have exploited his knowledge of the *Nicomachean Ethics* and the *Metaphysics*. Since the Neoplatonists had absorbed much Peripatetic doctrine, one must again enter the caveat that Boethius may have refreshed his knowledge of these and other works occasionally cited (*Physics*, *De philosophia*, *De anima*, *De caelo*) through study of Neoplatonist commentators.

Though Boethius was familiar with the *Enneads* of Plotinus and the commentaries of his disciple and successor Porphyry, it is probable that he recorded much of their doctrines, and those of other earlier Neoplatonists, from contemporary scholars. Proclus at Athens composed commentaries on Plato's *Timaeus*, *Parmenides*, and *Republic*, as well as treatises on *Providence and Evil*, works which have certainly left their mark on the *Consolation*. The influence of Ammonius at Alexandria is harder to assess; one distinguished scholar has argued that Boethius studied under him. Though hard evidence is lacking for this theory, the fact that Ammonius was a Christian as well as a Neoplatonist, and significant parallels with Ammonius' writings, suggest that he must have been accorded respectful attention by Boethius.[46]

Knowledge of Greek was not conspicuous in the schools of fifth-century Italy, but the study of the Latin Classics remained widespread. Boethius, as we have seen, cast himself in the role of a latter-day Cicero in his ambition to make the works of Plato and Aristotle known to his more thoughtful Roman contemporaries. He was closely acquainted with the corpus of Cicero's philosophical writings, and one may hazard that his knowledge of Stoic and Epicurean tenets stemmed largely from these works and from Lucretius. In the earlier part of the *Consolation*, where the focus is largely on ethics, there are numerous echoes of the *Tusculans*; less frequently the treatise reflects acquaintance with *De finibus*, *De officiis*, and *De senectute*. Our scholar-statesman also airs his knowledge of Cicero's *De republica*, though it is likely that he drew the citations from this work out of Macrobius' *Commentary on the Dream of Scipio*, which his father-in-law had edited. At later points in the *Consolation*, Cicero's *The Nature of the Gods* and *On Fate* are both exploited.

The works of the Younger Seneca, whose fate at the hands of Nero offered Boethius an apt parallel to his own situation, are constantly evoked. His poetry we must consider separately; of his philosophical writings, particularly prominent are echoes of the *Moral Epistles*, but the treatises *On the Happy Life*, *On Benefits*, and *On Providence* are also exploited. The influence of the diatribe as it is mediated through the *Satires* and *Epistles* of Horace, and also through Martianus Capella's *Marriage of Philosophy and Mercury*, a predecessor of the *Consolation* in the medley of prose and verse of Menippean satire, is also in evidence.

VIII. THE PROSIMETRIC FORM

Boethius fashioned the *Consolation* as a dialogue between the prisoner and the apparition of Philosophy, whom he regards as

---

[46] Courcelle's claim that Book 5 of the *Consolation* was wholly inspired by Ammonius has been sceptically received by critics from Dronke (*Speculum* (1969), 123 ff.) onwards, since Boethius could have drawn on Ammonius' sources Proclus and Porphyry. See D. Blank, *Ammonius On Aristotle, On Interpretation 1–8* (London, 1996), Introduction.

his teacher; he thus adopts a dual role as *auctor* and *actor*, author and participant. The dialogue form was inherited from his models Plato and Cicero; in some passages he deliberately incorporates phrases which characterize responses in Plato's dialogues.

But there is one conspicuous difference between the presentation of Boethius and that of his predecessors. The *Consolation* is composed in the prosimetric form, the combination of prose and verses earlier associated with Menippean satire.[47] This choice of medium was an indication that he sought a readership wider than the relatively small circle of enthusiasts for philosophy; he looked to the larger audience of those whose intellectual recreation lay in the traditional literary culture. A long history lay behind the competing claims of philosophy as a minority pursuit (in the Greek world it entailed the adoption of distinctive dress, food, and behaviour) and the literary, rhetorical, and aesthetic enthusiasms of the majority.[48] At Rome, philosophy had always struggled to find a place in the sun, in the face of public disapproval by political leaders. The increased Christianization of society from the later fourth century onwards led some Christian leaders, notably Marius Victorinus and Augustine, to throw their weight behind the Platonist philosophical tradition, which they baptized. Thus Augustine in his *De ordine* (composed at Cassiciacum soon after his conversion) sought to wean away Licentius, son of his wealthy friend Romanianus, from his preoccupation with poetic composition on mythological themes to take up the study of philosophy, which he doubtless hoped would lead him to fuller Christian commitment. Paulinus of Nola took a different and more subtle tack in attempting to win over the young man to the Christian life: he addressed a long verse-epistle to Licentius to indicate that poetic composition need not be renounced, but could be redirected towards the service of Christ.[49]

Other Christians in their attitudes towards the pagan literary classics were not troubled by the sense of alienation and even guilt which haunted the young Augustine, Jerome, and Paulinus. Men

---

[47] On this broad theme of Boethius' prosimetric presentation, see esp. S. Lerer, *Boethius and Dialogue* (Princeton, 1985); O'Daly, 16 ff.; P. Dronke, *Verse with Prose from Petronius to Dante* (Cambridge, Mass., 1994); Crabbe, in *Boethius*, ed. Gibson; Relihan.

[48] See H. I. Marrou, *A History of Education in Antiquity* (London, 1956), ch. 11.

[49] For Augustine's bullying, see *De ordine*, 1. 3. 8; 1. 8. 24. For Paulinus' more 'softly, softly' approach, see his *Letter*, 8 (text in CSEL 29, ed. Von Hartel (Vienna, 1894).

such as Ausonius and Prudentius took pride in the national literature, and we have noted how in Boethius' day it was common for Christian intellectuals to play an active role in the transmission of the pagan classics. Throughout the verse-passages in the *Consolation*, Boethius exhibits a close and enthusiastic knowledge of Virgil and Horace, Ovid and Juvenal, the plays of Seneca and other poets besides. We cannot know if he had the texts accessible to him in his confinement, but his easy handling of a wide variety of metres suggests a youthful formation in Classical poetry that fostered a ready recall of the passages which he evokes or imitates.

We are to conclude that Boethius deployed the prosimetric form with a variety of motives. He wished to exhibit his familiarity with the Classical masterpieces, and to acknowledge their role as moral and spiritual teachers. He exploited verses in the spirit of a Lucretius to sweeten his philosophical message; Philosophy in a telling aside, remarks to the prisoner: 'If the musical charms of song are what delight you, you must postpone the pleasure for a little while.'[50] In keeping with the technique earlier employed in Menippean satire, the verses encapsulate wholly or in part the implications of the previous prose-passages. In several of the poems the philosophical argument is illuminated with apposite examples from mythology or from history; elsewhere striking images offer an alternative vision of the truths earlier expressed more technically. The emotions rather than the rational faculties of the reader are occasionally engaged by the insertion of a hymn, which translates us like a myth of Plato into the world of mysticism.

It is an absorbing question to pose whether Boethius inherits the satirical purposes which are a prominent feature of the earlier Menippean tradition. Varro, at the birth of the Roman contribution to that tradition, Petronius in his *Satyricon*, and Seneca in his lampoon on the deification of the Emperor Claudius in his *Apocolocyntosis*, continue the Greek tradition of incorporating parody and comic literary allusion into a satirical framework, whether genial or savage.[51] With Martianus Capella, whose *Marriage of Philology and Mercury* was composed half a century

---

[50] See 4. 66.
[51] See my *Roman Novel* (Cambridge, 1970; now Bristol, 1995), 34 ff.

or so before the birth of Boethius, the satirical element is less in evidence. In a frame of extravagant fantasy, Philology ascends to heaven with her retinue of the Seven Liberal Arts to be wed to the god of eloquence; there follows an extensive and pedantic recital of encyclopedic information about each constituent of the quadrivium and the trivium.[52] Fulgentius, who is to be identified with reasonable certainty as the bishop of Ruspe in North Africa (*c.*468–533), is the first known Christian to exploit the prosimetric form. His *Mythologies* is a superficial account of the allegorical meanings of Greek myths; he employs the dialogue form, in which Calliope provides instruction, and Virgil makes a later appearance as 'a crochety schoolmaster'. A mildly satirical element is evident here, since the dialogue is 'a comic restructuring of student–teacher colloquy in earlier authors', notably Augustine and Macrobius.[53] There is no doubt that Boethius was familiar with these works of Martianus Capella and Fulgentius.

To suggest, however, that the *Consolation* extends the satirical tradition of the Menippean genre, and to argue that Philosophy's attempt at comfort of the prisoner is an egregious failure,[54] flies in the face of the experience of every reader from the Carolingian age to our own. The truth is that by Boethius' day the prosimetric form is exploited for purposes far wider than was envisaged by the Menippean satirists. So the youthful Ennodius, later to become bishop of Pavia (513–21), composes in this medley of prose and verses his *Paraenesis Didascalica* ('Instructive Counsel'), which in its poetic sections lauds such virtues as modesty, chastity, and faith.[55] The prosimetric medium is adapted to other literary genres, notably to letter-composition, where the practice had been anticipated by the Younger Pliny. Following the diffusion of the *Consolation* as a seminal work, the combination of prose and verse becomes a popular feature in the philosophical writing of the

[52] Text of Martianus Capella, ed. Willis, Teubner edn. (Leipzig, 1983); see now D. Shanzer, *A Philosophical and Literary Commentary on Martianus Capella's De nuptiis Philologiae et Mercurii I* (Berkeley, 1986); W. Wetherbee, *Platonism and Poetry in the Twelfth Century* (Princeton, 1972), 83 ff.; Relihan, 137 ff.

[53] Text ed. R. Helm (Leipzig, 1898). The citations here are from Lerer, *Boethius and Dialogue*, 56 ff.; see also Relihan, 152 ff.

[54] This is Relihan's conclusion, 191 ff.

[55] Text in CSEL 6, ed. Von Hartel. Relihan usefully provides a translation in app. C to his book.

high Middle Ages, notably in the *Cosmographia* of Bernard Silvestris and the *De planctu Naturae* of Alan of Lille.[56]

IX. THE METRICAL FORMS

The metrical range and patterning of the poems in the *Consolation* merit separate consideration.[57] The first feature of note is that Boethius nowhere exploits the form of the Ambrosian hymn with its quatrains of iambic dimeters. By his day this had become the regular liturgical medium for expression of Catholic orthodoxy, created earlier by Ambrose as a means of instilling into his congregation at Milan those doctrines of the Trinity and of Christ's divinity which were anathema to their Arian neighbours. The avoidance of this specifically Catholic and anti-Arian poetic form is a further indication, if such were needed, of Boethius' determination to present his message in secular rather than Christian dress. The Neoplatonists had for long interpreted the poems of Homer and Hesiod as didactic texts inculcating truth and virtue; though Boethius does not call Virgil and Horace to witness in precisely this way, the rich reminiscences of these and other Roman poets perform a similar role.

The enthusiasm of Boethius and his Christian contemporaries for the Roman poetry of the Golden and Silver Ages has already been noted. Boethius himself had earlier composed a pastoral poem (now lost) which was presumably written in the mode of a Virgil or a Calpurnius Siculus. He may also have composed verses of a risqué kind in the manner of Ovid, for his high-born friend Maximian accused him, one presumes jocularly, of playing the procurer in a love-intrigue—an accusation perhaps based on literary fancy rather than an actual escapade.[58] But the clearest

---

[56] For the increasingly broad exploitation of the prosimetric form, see C. D. Eckhardt, 'The Medieval Prosimetrum Genre', *Genre* (1983), 21 ff. For the use of the medium in the philosophical writing of the 11th and 12th centuries, see Dronke, *Verse with Prose*.

[57] See L. Pepe, 'La metrica di Boetio', *GIF* (1954), 227–43; Scheible, Introduction; O'Daly, ch. 2.

[58] For the pastoral poem ('condidit et carmen bucolicum'), see Cassiodorus, *Anecdoton Holderi* (CCL 96, V). For Maximian's taunt, see his *Elegy III*, with F. J. E. Raby, *Secular Latin Poetry* (Oxford, 1934), i. 124.

indication of Boethius' familiarity with a wide variety of metrical forms lies in the thirty-nine compositions in the *Consolation*.

Though it is possible to point to occasional use of specific metres to accommodate particular moods or themes, or to make meaningful connections between parts of the work, the chief impression made upon the reader by the prosody is Boethius' desire to demonstrate his facility with all the metres common in Roman antiquity—and with some half-dozen found only in post-Classical poetry.[59] The great hymn to God the Father at the centre of the work (3. 9) is aptly composed in dactylic hexameters, the regular form for hymns in pagan antiquity. The first poem of the work (1. 1), in which the prisoner laments his sorry condition, appears appropriately in elegiac couplets, and this metre is employed once later at 5. 1; the balance in positioning may be intended, but there is no obvious connection between the themes of the two poems. The most popular metre throughout is the glyconic, used on five occasions, once in each book. Though there is no common theme throughout the five, the first two (1. 6; 2. 8) establish the common lesson of the harmony in the world of nature, and the second two (3. 12; 4. 3) are closely connected formally, being poetic narratives of the myths of Orpheus and of Circe respectively; the fifth (5. 4), however, with its theme the rebuttal of the Stoic doctrine that the mind is merely the receptacle of sense-impressions, has nothing in common with the earlier four. The Phalaecian line of eleven syllables, earlier in Roman poetry employed as a vehicle for abuse or for castigation of folly, is found once in its simple form (1. 4) and on three other occasions in combination with other metres (3. 4, 3. 10; 4. 4); this group of poems alternately exhorts the reader to banish fear of tyranny (1. 4) and debased pleasures (3. 10), and censures the human behaviour which promotes tyranny (3. 4) and the madness of war (4. 4).

The poems in an identical metre with the strongest thematic coherence are four composed in anapaestic dimeters. In the first (1. 5), the prisoner laments the contrast between regularity in the realm of nature and the apparent anarchy prevailing in the fortunes of men. The theme of harmony in nature is renewed in

---

[59] For a full list of metres, see Gruber, 21 ff.

the second (3. 2), which emphasizes that all things return appropriately to their origins. The third in the series (4. 6), reverts yet again to the regularity in nature, here at the close of the poem implicitly refuting the prisoner's earlier claim of anarchy in the affairs of men by emphasis upon the Creator's universal governance. The last of the four (5. 3) offers the philosophic solution: the human mind has the capacity to observe the wise dominion of God in the round, but it cannot always fathom his particular ordinances as they affect human lives.

These and other more complex metrical variations throughout the *Consolation* offer a formidable challenge to the translator. Since the content of the poems reinforces the philosophical messages, the renderings are to adhere closely to the meaning of the Latin, but some attempt must be made to demonstrate the variety of the metrical forms which Boethius offers as relief from the technicalities of philosophical discourse. The *via media* sought in this translation is to deploy a range of verse-forms familiar to modern readers, mostly unrelated to the Latin metres but registering closely the sense of the originals.

Judgement of the merits of the poems varies widely. My view envisages Boethius more as versifier than true poet. Too often he is the prisoner of his models, assembling a medley of borrowings without ordering them into a unique vision. He shows considerable skill, however, in adapting the messages of the verses to the contexts of the philosophical arguments, and if this was his main aim he can be said to have achieved his purpose.

X. LATER HISTORY OF THE TEXT

In the centuries immediately following Boethius' death, the *Consolation* remained little read.[60] Alcuin of York, who may have brought a manuscript containing the treatise from Italy to the court of Charlemagne, is owed the credit for the initial cult of

---

[60] For the review that follows, see Courcelle, 241 ff., and the enlightening essays of Jacqueline Beaumont ('The Latin Tradition of the *De consolatione philosophiae*') and of Alastair Minnis ('Aspects of the Medieval French and English Traditions of the *De consolatione philosophiae*') in *Boethius*, ed. Gibson, chs. 11 and 13. Also H. R. Patch, *The Tradition of Boethius* (New York, 1935); E. Reiss, *Boethius* (Boston, 1982), ch. 7.

the work. The prisoner's Platonist claim that political leaders should be students of philosophy is echoed in a letter of Alcuin to Charlemagne, and in the prologue to his *De grammatica*, Alcuin contrasts the importance of the study of wisdom with the worthlessness of fame, honours, and wealth, which cause men to stray 'like a drunkard who does not know the way home'. Alcuin Christianized the treatise, and established it in the academic curriculum; the glosses on a ninth-century manuscript from Tours probably record his teaching there.[61]

Alcuin's example inspired a series of commentaries on the *Consolation*, the first known being that of Lupus of Ferrières (d. 862) on the metrical forms of the poems, preceded by a brief life of the author.[62] The Irish foundation of St Gall, where a large collection of Boethian manuscripts was subsequently assembled, was the provenance of a full commentary which attempted to establish Catholic orthodoxy for the doctrines of the treatise. But the dominant commentary of the Carolingian age was that of Remigius of Auxerre, composed in Paris between 902 and 908. This compilation, in which Lady Philosophy was Christianized as Wisdom, and the concepts of Providence, Fate, and free will were interpreted on Augustinian lines, became the staple quarry for subsequent medieval commentators.

In the tenth century, three surviving commentaries were composed with widely differing interpretations. While the *Anonymus of Einsiedeln* sought to align Boethius' doctrine with that of Plato's *Timaeus*, and the *Anonymus of Brussels* was content to follow Remigius in proclaiming Boethius as a champion of Christian orthodoxy. Bovo of Corvey struck a discordant and more realistic note. Unfortunately his commentary has survived only for the verses at the close of 3. 9, but this extract acknowledges that there are doctrines in Boethius which do not square with Christian teachings, notably the triple nature of the World-Soul, the suggestion that the stars are ensouled, and the notion that the human soul descends into the body from the other world.

[61] For the letter to Charlemagne, see Alcuin, *Ep.* 229, ed. Dümmler, in MGH, *Epp. Carol. Aev. II* (1895), 372 ff. For *De grammatica*, see PL 101. 849C ff. The image of the drunkard is taken from 3. 2 of the *Consolation*. The Tours MS is now at Orléans, Bibl. Mun. 270.

[62] See Virginia Brown, 'Lupus of Ferrières on the Metres of Boethius', in *Latin Script and Letters, A.D. 400–900*, ed. J. J. O'Meara and B. Naumann (Leiden, 1976), 63 ff.

Bovo does not dismiss the treatise as unworthy of study, but insists that the orthodox aspects acceptable to Christians must be distinguished from the pagan elements.

Bovo's animadversions may have contributed to the general neglect of the treatise in the eleventh century, but it regained popularity in the twelfth, when five new commentaries make their appearance. The most distinguished is that of William of Conches (*c.*1080–1154), pupil of Bernard of Chartres, who had instilled in him a generous spirit of Christian humanism. William's commentary was so wide-ranging in its purview that it served as a general education in the liberal arts while at the same time claiming Christian orthodoxy for the Neoplatonist content. More generally in this era, the *Consolation* haunted the imaginations of the leading philosopher-poets, Bernardus Silvestris and Alan of Lille; Bernard's goddess Natura in his *Cosmographia*, and her counterpart in Alan's *De planctu Naturae*, are reincarnations of Boethius' Philosophia.[63]

The thirteenth century, with the flowering of Aristotelian studies in the French schools, witnessed a decline in the fortunes of the Platonist treatise, which continued to be read but attracted no new commentary until the Dominican Nicolas Trevet published one shortly before 1307. This publication, which drew heavily on William of Conches with additional matter from Alfred the Great of Wessex, became so celebrated that over a hundred manuscripts of it have survived. Its popularity may have been partly attributable to Nicolas' preference for literal explanation rather than allegorical and moralizing interpretation. His work became a quarry for numerous imitators over the next two centuries; one of these successors, William of Aragon, has a claim on historians of literature, since the Preface to his commentary was taken over by Jean de Meun as Introduction to his *Li Livres de confort*.[64]

---

[63] For the five 12th-century commentaries, see Courcelle, 302 ff. William of Conches's commentary is in C. Jourdain, *Excursions historiques et philosophiques à travers le moyen âge* (Paris, 1889); see Brian Stock, *Myth and Science in the Twelfth Century* (Princeton, 1972), 249 ff. For Natura in Bernard, see Stock, 63 ff.; in Alan of Lille, Wetherbee, *Platonism and Poetry*, 188 ff. Other major works of the age notably influenced by the figure of Lady Philosophy include Hildebert of Lavardin's *Philosophia de interiore et exteriore homine* (where the *interior homo* evokes Lady Philosophy), and Adelard of Bath's *On Sameness and Difference*, in which Philocosmia plays the role of instructress.

[64] For the commentary of Nicolas Trevet and its successors, see Courcelle, 318 ff. For its exploitation of Alfred's translation, see B. S. Donaghey in *The Medieval Boethius*, ed.

The history of the influence of the *Consolation* on the vernacular
literatures of western Europe begins as early as the late ninth
century at the court of Alfred the Great. After the temporary
repulse of the Danes, Alfred imitated the example of Charlemagne, and established his court as a centre of learning. He
himself translated the *Consolation* into Old English, as well as
Orosius' *History against the Pagans*, Bede's *Ecclesiastical History*,
and the *Dialogues* and *Liber regulae pastoralis* of Gregory the Great.
In this translation of the *Pastoral Rule* of Gregory, he remarks that
'the clergy have gained little benefits from these books, because
they could not understand any of them, since they were not
written in their own language'. Alfred, whose biographer Asser
states that the king suffered from an unknown malady, regarded
the *Consolation* as a text for coping with adversity. His translation
is prefaced with detail which emanates from popular accounts
concerning the alleged circumstances of composition: Boethius,
seeing that Theoderic was attacking the Catholics, sent secret
word to Constantinople, begging Caesar to restore the Christian
faith and the ancient laws to Italy. For this he was confined in a
dungeon, and overcome with despondency. In the translation
itself, Alfred introduces Christian colouring, with Christ, angels,
and Satan making their appearance; Lady Philosophy becomes
Wisdom. Alfred's paraphrase survived in two versions, in one of
which the poems are rendered in prose, and the other in verse; it
was this second which Trevet exploited in his commentary.[65]

So far as the vernacular literatures are concerned, Alfred's
rendering of the *Consolation* stands out as an isolated phenomenon[66] until a more widespread proliferation of versions occurs in
France in the fourteenth and fifteenth centuries, during which at
least twelve translations appeared. Conspicuous among them was

A. J. Minnis (Cambridge, 1987), 1–31. For William of Aragon's Preface, plagiarized by
Jean de Meun, Minnis, in *Boethius*, ed. Gibson, 322.

[65] There is an edition of Alfred's Old English translation by W. J. Sedgefield (Oxford,
1899), who also published a modern version (Oxford, 1900). See Patch, *Tradition*;
R. Gameson, 'Alfred the Great and the Destruction and Production of Christian
Books', *Scriptorium* (1995), 180 ff.

[66] Mention must, however, be made of the bilingual edn. of Notker Labeo ('Notker der
Deutsche') in Latin and Old High German, made at St Gall *c*.987; text ed. by P. W. Tax
(Tübingen, 1986). There is no record of German vernacular versions between Notker's
and 15th-century texts; see N. F. Palmer, 'Latin and Vernacular in North Europe', in
Boethius, ed. Gibson, 364, 371 ff.

Jean de Meun's *Li Livres de confort*, completed shortly before the poet's death in 1305. Jean had already exploited Boethian themes in his celebrated *Roman de la rose* (*c.*1277), in which Reason, a latter-day manifestation of Boethius' Lady Philosophy, discourses on the role of Fortune and on the nature of true happiness, as well as on the sufferings of Socrates, Seneca, and Croesus, themes all prominent in the *Consolation*. When composing *Li Livres de confort*, Jean systematically consulted a commentary based on that of William of Conches; the Preface to his work, as has been noted, was taken over from that of William of Aragon.[67]

The example of Jean de Meun inspired Geoffrey Chaucer in England to turn his attention to the *Consolation*, though initially he did not read Boethius directly. In *The Monk's Tale*, later incorporated into *The Canterbury Tales*, the primary source for the two Boethian narratives is the *Roman de la rose*. When Chaucer made his own translation in about 1380, conventionally called *Boece*, he exploited not only Jean's *Li Livres de confort*, but also Trevet's commentary; it seems that he was working with a manuscript that contained both the original text and Trevet's glosses. Though the translation is literal, with the Latin verses rendered in English prose, *Boece* is half as long again as the original. Shortly after 1380, Chaucer produced *Troilus and Criseyde* and *The Knight's Tale*; in both the influence of Boethius has been widely acknowledged.[68]

Of the numerous translations into English which followed Chaucer's pioneering attempt, two in particular have gained celebrity. The first is that of John Walton, a metrical version made in 1410 which survived in twenty manuscripts before its first printed edition in 1525. The prologue is based on the learned and wide-ranging preface of Nicolas Trevet; the translation follows Boethius closely and accurately, with occasional additions from Trevet's commentary. When Thomas Richard saw the first

[67] On the early French versions in general, see A. A. Dwyer, *Boethian Fictions: Narratives in the Medieval French Versions of the Consolation of Philosophy* (Cambridge, Mass., 1976); G. M. Cropp, 'Le Livre de Boece de Consolacion: From Translation to Glossed Text', in *The Medieval Boethius*, ed. Minnis, 315 ff. The relevant section of the *Roman de la rose* is at 4837–6630.

[68] On Boethius in Chaucer, see the lively account in Patch, *Tradition*; Minnis in *Boethius*, ed. Gibson, 334 ff. For the glosses on Chaucer's *Boece*, see Minnis, 'Glosynge is a glorious thyng', and T. W. Machan, 'Glosses in the MSS of Chaucer's Boece', in *The Medieval Boethius*, ed. Minnis, 106 ff., 125 ff.

printed edition through the press, he added glosses chiefly derived from Trevet but included also observations of his own. The second rendering was noteworthy more for the identity of the translator than for the merit of the version, for it came from the pen of Elizabeth I, and is by no means free of errors. According to William Camden, her attachment to the *Consolation* was demonstrated when Henry of Navarre professed his allegiance to the Catholic faith in the church of St Denys; she sought the comfort of the scriptures and of Boethius. An enthusiastic translator (she worked also at Sallust, Plutarch, and Horace), she was celebrated as a fast worker, composing 'a page every half-hour'; the egregious errors were only to be expected in such a hastily composed version.[69]

Among the scholars of the Italian Renaissance, Boethius obtained a mixed reception.[70] There were three main reasons for the hostility which he provoked. The first was his sixth-century Latin, which jarred particularly on Lorenzo Valla, whose handbook *Elegantiae linguae latinae* minces no words. The second criticism arose from the mistaken notion that the introductory section of the *Consolation*, in which Lady Philosophy condemns the poetic Muses as *scaenicae meretriculae*, represented Boethius' rejection of Classical poetry. The third objection, which Valla voices in his treatise *On Free Will*, lay in Boethius' solution to the intractable problems of Providence, fate, and free will, which Valla considered too facile. The *Consolation* had more appeal to the readers of greater literary sensibility. Dante found comfort in it after the death of Beatrice, and he avows that it encouraged him to take up the study of philosophy. The episode concerning Fortune in *Inferno VII* echoes the content of the first two chapters of Book 2 of the *Consolation*, and there are numerous other correspondences in both the *Divine Comedy* and the prose works of Dante. Boccaccio, too, exploited the *Consolation*, notably in his

[69] For Walton's version, see *Early English Text Society 170* (Oxford, 1927), and Minnis, in *Boethius*, ed. Gibson, 343 ff.; for that of Elizabeth I, Patch, *Tradition*.

[70] For what follows, see Anthony Grafton, 'Boethius in the Renaissance', in *Boethius*, ed. Gibson, 410 ff., from whom the citation of Scaliger is taken. On Dante's numerous echoes of Boethius, see Edward Moore, *Studies in Dante, First Series* (Oxford, 1896), 282 ff. Dante places Boethius in the Circle of the Sun, in the company of the greatest Christian sages (*Paradiso*, 10. 124–9). See further W. Kranz, 'Dante und Boethius', *Roman. Forsch.* (1951), 72–8; L. Alfonsi, *Dante e la Consolatio Philosophiae di Boezio* (Como, 1944).

Filostrato, which with the *Consolation* inspired Chaucer in his *Troilus and Criseyde*. In the later fifteenth century, when scholars from the north began to flood into Italy, their less-demanding linguistic purism and their broader cultural outlook joined with Dante and Boccaccio rather than with Valla in acclaiming the treatise. As Julius Caesar Scaliger expressed it in his *Poetice*: 'In brilliance, learning, artistry, and wisdom, Boethius rivals all Greek and Latin authors . . . I feel that few are comparable to him. Valla teaches him to speak Latin, but Boethius teaches Valla to be wise.'

Following the Renaissance and the Reformation, the *Consolation* attracted translators in almost every country of western Europe. In Britain its popularity throughout the seventeenth and eighteenth centuries is attested by the appearance of a new translation in almost every generation. In 1609 the careful and talented rendering by 'I.T.' appeared, a version in which the rendering of the verses has won particular esteem; the author is believed to have been the Jesuit Michael Walpole, who deemed it prudent not to expose himself to the prejudices of the time by publishing under his own name. This was followed by renderings by Richard Fanshawe (the verses only, 1626–31), Sir Harry Coningsby, who translated the whole work into English verse (1664), Lord Richard Preston, whose version was written in 1695 but lay unpublished until 1712, William Causton (1730), R. and A. Foulis (1751), Philip Redpath (1785), and R. Duncan (1789). In the nineteenth and twentieth centuries there was a falling off until the advent of libraries of literary classics; in 1897 H. R. James translated it for the New Universal Library, and in 1902 W. V. Cooper contributed a version to the series of Temple Classics. More recently V. E. Watts has published an accurate translation in Penguin Classics (1969), and S. J. Tester's more literal rendering has replaced that of 'I.T.' in the Loeb series (1973); this last has the useful addition of a revised translation of the *Tractates* by Tester.

Until the nineteenth century, the *Consolation* was urged as recommended reading on every educated person. It is quoted by many poets—Heywood, Donne, Southey among them—and its verses have been imitated by Vaughan in his *Olor Iscanus*, and by Phineas Fletcher. We may leave the final word with Edward Gibbon, who regarded the *Consolation* as 'a golden volume not unworthy of the leisure of Plato or Tully, but which claims incomparable merit from the barbarism of the times and the situation of the author'. In this era of expanded higher education, the book deserves the prominence accorded it in *The Discarded Image* (1964) of C. S. Lewis, who numbered it among the few volumes which shaped his philosophy of life.

SUMMARY OF THE TREATISE

Book 1. As the prisoner grieves over his downfall and impending fate, Lady Philosophy appears before him. Initially he fails to recognize her, but once recognition dawns he pours out to her his resentment at the iniquity of Fortune. His devoted public service has ended in his condemnation; the order evident in the world of nature does not extend to the just treatment of humankind. Philosophy diagnoses his ailment; blinded by vicious emotions, he has forgotten how the world is ordered. She promises initially a gentler cure.

Book 2. Lady Philosophy denounces the prisoner's bitter indictment of Fortune, against whom he has no real complaint. Fortune herself is invoked to justify her ways with men. Hitherto she has favoured him, and the inconstancy she now shows is at one with the similar pattern in nature. Philosophy insists that his present life has its material consolations, but true happiness is not to be sought in them. She reviews the worldly goods to which men aspire, and successively rejects wealth, ambition for high position, and the pursuit of fame as avenues to happiness. Fortune benefits man more when adverse than when favourable.

Book 3. Before explaining where true happiness is to be found, Lady Philosophy reiterates that the quests for riches, high position, and fame, and additionally physical pleasure, are defective ways of seeking the true good. The true avenue is reversion to our beginnings. The prisoner's former wealth, the tenure of public office, the kingship under which he has served, the desire for fame, the pursuit of bodily pleasure, the reliance on physical strength and beauty are all false goods which fail to attain happiness.

At ch. 9, the mid-point in the treatise, Philosophy turns from condemnation of false goods to investigate the nature of the true good. The perfect good resides in God, who is identical with happiness. The defective goods sought by men must be merged into the unity of the One and the Good, which we must seek by introspection, for the truth lies within us. All things in the world are ordered by that highest Good.

Book 4.   Having established the identity of God as the true Good, Lady Philosophy now investigates whether he apportions justice in the world. Responding to the prisoner's lament that vice flourishes while virtue suffers, she claims that virtue has true power since it attains its end of the good, while vice fails and thereby relegates wicked men to the realm of the subhuman. While good men become divine, evil men are turned into animals. The perpetrator of crime is thus deserving of pity; he should be made to recognize his punishment as remedial.

The prisoner insists that the apparent irrationality in the ordering of human affairs is at odds with the governance of a good ruler. Philosophy responds by delineating the relationship between Providence, the divine reason directing the course of the world from an unchanging heaven, and Fate, which by a chain of causation carries through the design of Providence in the world of change. Man cannot fully comprehend this process, and must be content to acknowledge that every fortune visited upon us is good.

Book 5.   Before broaching the main theme of this final book, the reconciliation of divine Providence with man's free will, Providence clears the ground by arguing that there is no such thing as chance. So given that the design of Providence orders the world, how can there be scope for free will? Philosophy responds by recognizing four levels of cognition: sensation, imagination, reason, and understanding; these correspond with the four levels of existence, namely immobile life, that of the lower animals, the human, and the divine. The reconciliation between Providence and free will is achieved at the fourth level of divine understanding. God's knowledge is always in the present, not in the future or past. Though from the divine aspect all future events will be necessary, in their own nature some will be necessary but others freely chosen. In this sense the freedom of the will remains intact.

NOTE ON THE TEXT

Following the pioneering edition of *The Consolation* by
T. Obbarius (Jena, 1843), the first full recension of the manuscripts was undertaken by R. Peiper in the Teubner series
(Leipzig, 1871). The most notable edition to follow was that by
W. Weisenberger in CSEL 67 (Vienna, 1934). More recently,
L. Bieler has edited the text in CCL 94 (Turnhout, 1957; revised,
1984). Bieler has replaced Weisenberger as the standard edition,
and this translation is based on it. None the less, earlier editions
have remained influential. The annotated edition by A. Fortescue
and G. D. Smith (London, 1925; repr. Hildesheim, 1976) is
especially useful for the biblical and patristic parallels which
indicate the close correspondence between Neoplatonist and
Christian thought. The revised Loeb edition by S. J. Tester
(1973), replacing the earlier version of H. F. Stewart and F. K.
Rand, owes much to Peiper; that of J. J. O'Donnell for Latin
beginners, published in the Bryn Mawr series (2 vols., 1984),
incorporates the text of Weinberger. Recent editions published in
Germany and Switzerland are listed in the Bibliography. An
edition of the final sections of the treatise (4. 5–5. 6) has been
published in conjunction with Cicero's *De fato* by R. W. Sharples
(Warminster, 1991).

SELECT BIBLIOGRAPHY

For fuller general bibliographies on Boethius, see Bieler, XVIII ff.; Chadwick, 261 ff.; Gruber, 417 ff.; M. Fuhrmann and J. Gruber (eds.), *Boethius*, Wege der Forschung, 483 (Darmstadt, 1984), 445 ff. For literary aspects, O'Daly, 238 ff.; for specialized philosophical discussions, Sharples, 233 ff.

Editions and commentaries are ordered chronologically.

1. *Editions and Commentaries*

PEIPER, R., *Anicii Manlii Severini Boetii Philosophiae Consolationis libri V*, Teubner (Leipzig, 1871).

STEWART, H. F., and RAND, E. K., *The Theological Tractates and The Consolation of Philosophy*, Loeb Classical Library (London, 1918).

FORTESCUE, A., and SMITH, G. D., *Boethi De Consolatione Philosophiae libri V* (London, 1925; repr. Hildesheim, 1976).

WEINBERGER, W., *Anicii Manlii Severini Boethii Philosophiae Consolationis libri V*, CSEL 67 (Vienna, 1934).

GOTHEIN, E., *Boethii Consolatio Philosophiae* (Zurich, 1969).

BÜCHNER, K., Boethius, *Philosophiae Consolationis libri V*[3] (Heidelberg, 1977).

TESTER, S. J., rev. Loeb edn. (London, 1978).

GRUBER, J., *Kommentar zu Boethius, De Consolatione Philosophiae* (Berlin, 1978).

GEGENSCHATZ, E., and GIGON, O., *Boethius, Trost der Philosophie* (Latin/German) (Zurich, 1981).

BIELER, L., *Anicii Manlii Severini Boethii Philosophiae Consolatio*[2], CCL 94 (Turnhout, 1984).

O'DONNELL, J. J., *Boethius, Consolatio Philosophiae* (2 vols.; Bryn Mawr, 1984).

SHARPLES, R. W., *Cicero, On Fate, and Boethius, The Consolation of Philosophy IV 5–7, V* (Warminster, 1991).

2. *Translations*

For the major translations into English, see Introduction X; for renderings into other vernaculars, see Bieler, XXXIII ff.

3. *Other Works*

BALTES, M., 'Gott, Welt, Mensch in der *Consolatio Philosophiae* des Boethius', *Vig. Christ.* (1980), 313–40.

BARK, W., 'Theoderic vs Boethius: Vindication and Apology', *Amer. Hist. Rev.* (1944), 410–26; repr. in Fuhrmann and Gruber, 11–32.

——'The Legend of Boethius's Martyrdom', *Speculum* (1946), 312–17.

BARNISH, S. J. B., 'The Anonymus Valesianus II as a Source for the Last Years of Theoderic', *Latomus* (1983), 572–96.

BARRETT, H. M., *Boethius: Some Aspects of his Life and Work* (Cambridge, 1940; repr. New York, 1965).

BOISSIER, G., 'Le Christianisme de Boècc', *Journal des Savants* (1889), 449–62.

CHADWICK, H., *Boethius: The Consolations of Music, Logic, Theology, and Philosophy* (Oxford, 1981).

——'Theta on Philosophy's Dress in Boethius', *Medium Aevum* (1980), 175 ff.

CHAMBERLAIN, D. S, 'Philosophy of Music in the *Consolatio* of Boethius', *Speculum* (1970), 80–97; repr. in Fuhrmann and Gruber, 377–403.

COURCELLE, P., 'Boèce et l'école d'Alexandrie', *Mél. de l'école française de Rome* (1935), 185–223.

——*Late Latin Writers and their Greek Sources*, tr. H. Wedeck (Cambridge, Mass., 1969), of *Les Lettres grecques en Occident²* (Paris, 1948).

——*La Consolation de Philosophie dans la tradition littéraire* (Paris, 1967).

——'Le Personnage de la Philosophie dans la littérature latine', *Journal des Savants* (1970), 209–52.

CRABBE, A. M., 'Literary Design in the *De consolatione philosophiae*', in Gibson, 237–74.

CURLEY, T. F., 'The Consolation of Philosophy as a Work of Literature', *AJP* (1987), 343–67.

DRONKE, P., *Verse with Prose from Petronius to Dante* (Cambridge, Mass., 1994).

FAVEZ, C., *La Consolation latine chrétienne* (Paris, 1937).

FUHRMANN, M., and GRUBER, J., *Boethius*, Wege der Forschung, 483 (Darmstadt, 1984).

GIBSON, M. T. (ed.), *Boethius, his Life, Thought, and Influence* (Oxford, 1981).

HUBER, P., *Die Vereinbarkeit von göttlicher Vorsehung und menschlicher Freiheit in der Consolatio Philosophiae des Boethius* (Zurich, 1976).

JONES, A. H. M., *The Later Roman Empire, 284–602* (2 vols.; Oxford, 1964).

KIRKBY, H., 'The Scholar and his Public', in Gibson, 44–69.

KLINGNER, F., *De Boethii Consolatione Philosophiae* (Berlin, 1921; repr. Zurich, 1966).

LERER, S., *Boethius and Dialogue* (Princeton, 1985).

LIEBESCHUETZ, H., 'Boethius and the Legacy of Antiquity', in A. H. Armstrong (ed.), *The Cambridge History of Later Greek and Early Medieval Philosophy* (Cambridge, 1967), ch. 35.

MANITIUS, M., *Geschichte der lateinischen Literatur des Mittelalters I* (Munich, 1911), 22–36.

MANSI, M. (ed.), *Boethius and the Liberal Arts* (Berne, 1981).

MATTHEWS, J., 'Anicius Manlius Severinus Boethius', in Gibson, 15–43.

MOHRMANN, C., 'Some Remarks on the Language of Boethius' *Consolatio Philosophiae*', in J. J. O'Meara and B. Naumann (eds.), *Latin Script and Letters, AD 400–900* (Leiden, 1976), 54–61.

MUELLER-GOLDINGEN, C., 'Die Stellung der Dichtung in Boethius' *Consolatio Philosophiae*', *RhM* (1989), 369–95.

OBERTELLO, L. A. M., *Severino Boezio* (2 vols.; Genoa, 1974).

O'DALY, G., *The Poetry of Boethius* (London, 1991).

OLMSTED, W. R., 'Philosophical Enquiry and Religious Transformation in Boethius's *Consolation of Philosophy* and Augustine's *Confessions*', *Journal of Religion* (1989), 14–35.

PATCH, H. A., *The Goddess Fortuna in Medieval Literature* (Cambridge, Mass., 1927).

——'Fate in Boethius and the Neoplatonists', *Speculum* (1929), 62–72.

——'Necessity in Boethius and the Neoplatonists', *Speculum* (1935), 393–404.

PEPE, L., 'La metrica di Boezio', *GIF* (1954), 227–43.

PLATINGA, A., *The Nature of Necessity* (Oxford, 1974).

——*God, Freedom and Evil* (New York, 1974).

RAND, E. K., 'On the Composition of Boethius' *Consolatio Philosophiae*', *HSCP* (1904), 1–28; repr. in Fuhrmann and Gruber, 249–77.

——*Founders of the Middle Ages* (Cambridge, Mass., 1928; repr. New York, 1957), ch. 5.

RAUBITSCHEK, A. E., '*Me quoque excellentior* (Boethii Consolationis 4.6.27)', in J. J. O'Meara and B. Naumann (eds.), *Latin Script and Letters AD 400–900* (Leiden, 1976), 62.

REISS, E., *Boethius* (Boston, 1982).

REICHENBERGER, K., *Untersuchungen zur literarischen Stellung der Consolatio Philosophiae* (Cologne, 1954).

RELIHAN, J. C., *Ancient Menippean Satire* (Baltimore, 1993).

SCHEIBLE, H., *Die Gedichte in der Consolatio Philosophiae des Boethius* (Heidelberg, 1972).

SCHMID, W., 'Philosophisches und Medizinisches in der *Consolatio* des Boethius', *Festschrift für Bruno Snell* (Munich, 1956), 113–44.

SHANZER, D., 'Ennodius, Boethius, and the Date and Interpretation of Maximianus's *Elegia III*', *Rivista di filologia* (1983), 183–95.

—— '*Me quoque excellentior*: Boethius, *De consolatione* 4.6.38', *CQ* (1983), 277–83.

—— 'The Death of Boethius and The Consolation of Philosophy', *Hermes* (1984), 352–66.

SILK, E. T., 'Boethius' *Consolatio Philosophiae* as a Sequel to Augustine's *Dialogues* and *Soliloquia*', *HTR* (1939), 19–39.

SOLOWSKI, J., 'Les Sources du *Consolatione Philosophiae* de Boèce', *Sophia* (1957), 76–85.

—— 'The Sources of Boethius' *De consolatione Philosophiae*', *Sophia* (1961), 67–94.

TRÄNKLE, H., 'Ist die *Philosophiae Consolatio* des Boethius zum Vorgeschenen Abschluss gelangt?', *Vig. Christ.* (1977), 148–56; repr. in Fuhrmann and Gruber, 311–19.

USENER, H., *Anecdoton Holderi* (Leipzig, 1877).

DE VOGEL, C. J., 'Amor, quo caelum regitur', *Vivarium* (1972), 2–34.

—— 'Boethiana I', *Vivarium* (1971), 59–66; 'Boethiana II', *Vivarium* (1972), 1–40.

WALLIS, R. T., *Neoplatonism* (London, 1972).

A CHRONOLOGY OF BOETHIUS'
LIFE AND TIMES

401 Milan besieged by Alaric; Ravenna becomes residence of imperial court.

471 Theoderic becomes king of the Ostrogoths.

474 Zeno becomes eastern emperor.

476 Romulus Augustulus, last western emperor, deposed; German Odoacer proclaimed king of Italy.

early 480s Birth of Boethius

484 Theoderic consul at Constantinople.

489 Theoderic invades Italy.

c.490 Death of Boethius' father (praetorian prefect, consul 487). Adopted by Symmachus (consul 485), a leading Roman and Christian.

491 Anastasius succeeds Zeno in the East.

493 Odoacer surrenders to Theoderic; Anastasius confirms Theoderic as king of Italy.

502–22 Boethius publishes a stream of philosophical works, chiefly on Aristotelian logic.

510 Appointed sole consul.

518 Death of Anastasius; Justin I succeeds; promotes Justinian to prominence at Constantinople.

519–23 Boethius publishes *Theological Tractates*. Ecclesiastical reconciliation between East and West.

522 Boethius' two sons appointed consuls. Boethius delivers encomium to Theoderic; appointed Master of Offices at Ravenna.

523 Arrested with Albinus on charges of treason and sacrilege.

524 Confined to house-arrest at Pavia; composes *The Consolation of Philosophy*.

524–6 Executed.

526 Death of Theoderic.

535–40 Belisarius overthrows the Ostrogoths in Italy.

The Consolation of Philosophy

Book 1

Chapter 1

I who with zest* penned songs in happier days,
Must now with grief embark on sombre lays.
Sad verses flood my cheeks with tears unfeigned;
The Muses who inspire me are blood-stained.
Yet they at least were not deterred by dread;   5
They still attend me on the path I tread.
I gloried in them, in my youth's full spate;
In sad old age they now console my fate.
My woes have caused old age's sudden speed;
Additional years my sorrow has decreed.   10
White hairs upon my crown untimely came,
And trembling wrinkles sag on my spent frame.
Death finds no welcome in contented life,
But is oft summoned when distress is rife.
Alas, Death turns deaf ears to my sad cries,   15
And cruel, will not close my weeping eyes.
While fickle Fortune transient goods did show,
One bitter hour could almost bring me low;
Now she's put on her clouded, treacherous gaze,
My impious life spins out unwanted days.   20
Why did you harp, my friends, on my renown?
My steps were insecure; I tumbled down.

These were the silent reflections which I nursed in my heart.   1
My dutiful pen was putting the last touches to my tearful lament,
when a lady seemed to position herself above my head.* She was
most awe-inspiring to look at, for her glowing eyes penetrated
more powerfully than those of ordinary folk, and a tireless energy
was reflected in her heightened colour. At the same time she was
so advanced in years that she could not possibly be regarded as a
contemporary. Her height was hard to determine, for it varied; at 2
one moment she confined herself to normal human dimensions,
but at another the crown of her head seemed to strike the

heavens, and when she raised it still higher, it even broke through
3 the sky, frustrating the gaze of those who observed her. Her robe
was made from imperishable material, and was sewn with delicate
workmanship from the finest thread.* She had woven it with her
own hands, as I later heard from her own lips. But because it had
not been brushed up for so long, a film of dust covered it, like
4 those ancestral statues that are grimy with smoke. At the lower
edge of the robe was visible in embroidery the letter *Π*, and the
neck of the garment bore the letter *Θ*; between them could be
seen the depiction of a ladder, whose rungs allowed ascent from
5 the lower letter to the higher. But the robe had been ripped by the
violent hands of certain individuals, who had torn off such parts
6 as each could seize. In her right hand she carried some books, and
in her left a sceptre.

7   Her eyes lit on the Muses of poetry, who were standing by my
couch, furnishing words to articulate my grief. For a moment she
showed irritation; she frowned, and fire flashed from her eyes.
8 'Who', she asked, 'has allowed these harlots of the stage to
approach this sick man? Not only do they afford no remedies to
9 relieve his pains, but their succulent poisons intensify them. These
ladies with their thorns of emotions choke the life from the fruitful
harvest of reason. They do not expel the disease from men's
10 minds, but merely inure them to its presence. If you Muses were
up to your usual game of seducing some non-initiate by your
blandishments, I should find it less objectionable, for my own
work would not suffer. But this man must not be seduced, for he
has been nurtured on the learning of the Eleatics and of the
11 Academy.* Off with you, you Sirens! Your charms entice men to
their destruction. Leave him to be tended and healed with the help
of the Muses that attend me.'

12   At this rebuke the band of Muses rather gloomily trained their
gaze upon the ground, and blushes proclaimed their shame as they
13 dejectedly left the chamber. My eyes were suffused and blinded
with tears. I could not identify this woman who wielded such
imperious authority. I was struck dumb, and with downcast eyes I
14 began silently to await her next course of action. Then she drew
nearer, and sat at the foot of my couch. She gazed on my face,
which was heavy with grief and bowed to the ground with sorrow,
and she lamented my distress of mind in these lines:

Chapter 2

'Dull-witted* is his mind, alas!
    Sunk in steep depths below,
Abandoning its native light
    It purposes to go
Into the darkness of despond,   5
    As baneful troubles grow
And swell to heights immeasurable
    When earthly tempests blow.

Of old he roamed without restraint
    Beneath the open sky;   10
Made frequent tracks through heaven's domain
    And often would descry
The brightness of the roseate sun,
    The cold moon would espy,
The planets on their wandering course   15
    Charting with mastery.*

And deeper causes he had plumbed:
    Why winds' blasts rouse the main;
What breath impels the fixed stars' sphere;
    Why does the sun's bright train,   20
Once risen from the crimson east,
    The western waves attain?
What warms the gentle hours of spring
    Earth's rosy blooms to gain?

Next, who ensures, at year's ripe term,   25
    The autumn's fruitful stream,
Which bears its weight of pregnant grapes?
    Such issues were his theme.
His custom was to scrutinize
    Dame Nature's hidden scheme;   30
Her varying causes to propound,
    Her sources to redeem.

Now prostrate, mental vision dulled,
    His neck with chains close bound,
Perforce he trains his downward gaze   35
    Upon the insensate ground.

'However,' she added, 'this is no time for complaints, but for   1
healing.' She then turned her gaze keenly and wholly on me. 'Tell   2
me,' she asked, 'are you the man whom once I nurtured with my

milk and reared on my solid food until your mind attained full
3   maturity? That armour which I then bestowed on you should have
afforded you invincible strength if you had not cast it off earlier.
4   Do you recognize me? Why are you silent? Is it through shame or
stupefaction? I only wish it were shame, but I see that it is
stupefaction that possesses you.'

5   Then, on seeing that I was not merely silent but utterly
speechless and struck dumb, she placed her hand gently on my
breast, and said: 'But his condition is not dangerous. He is
suffering from loss of energy,* a weakness common to duped
6   minds. He has forgotten for the moment who he is, but he will
soon remember once he has identified me first. To help him in
this, I must spend a moment wiping his eyes, for the darkness of
his mortal concerns has clouded them.' With these words she
puckered her dress, and dried my eyes, which were bathed in
tears.

Chapter 3

Then darkness left me.* Dispelled was the night;
Vitality of old renewed my sight.
As when the north-west wind sweeps headlong by,
Foul weather gathers, rain-clouds clothe the sky,
The sun lurks hidden, night enshrouds the earth   5
Before the stars reach their allotted berth.
Then from the Thracian cave the north wind's flight
Assaults the darkness, frees the imprisoned light,
And Phoebus' sudden brilliance with his rays
Presents his orb to our astonished gaze.   10

1   In just this way the clouds of my melancholy were dispelled. I
drank in the clear air of heaven; recovery of my wits had enabled
2   me to identify my healer's face. Thus as I eyed her with
unblinking gaze, I recognized the one whose dwelling I had
attended from my youthful years, my nurse Philosophy.
3   'Teacher of all the virtues, why', I asked, 'have you come
gliding down from the pole of heaven to visit me in the solitude of
my exile? Can it be that you too are to be hounded by false
charges, and to stand trial with me?'

'What?' she rejoined, 'Was I to abandon you, my own pupil? 4
Was I to refuse to share your ordeal, to bear the burden which you
have shouldered through the odium which my name aroused? It 5
would have been sacrilege for Philosophy to forsake you, and to
leave you, an innocent man, unaccompanied on your journey. Was
I in other words to recoil from the charge laid against me, to
tremble as if this were a novel experience to undergo? Do you 6
imagine that this is the first time that philosophy has been assailed
by perils in the court of corrupt behaviour? You surely know that
in days of old, before the time of my dear Plato, there were many
occasions when I launched full-scale warfare on presumptuous
stupidity? That in Plato's own day I stood side by side with his
mentor Socrates, when he triumphed over an unjust death?*
Thereafter the mobs of Epicureans, Stoics, and the other schools 7
each did their best to plunder his inheritance. As part of their loot
they dragged me off, in spite of my protestations and resistance;
they ripped apart the gown that I had woven with my own hands,
and they departed bearing the ragged pieces which they had torn
from it. They imagined that all of me had passed into their hands;
and because they bore traces of my clothing about them, foolish 8
men regarded them as my devotees, and more than one of them
were brought to ruin through being misled by the uninitiated.

'Perhaps you have not learnt of the flight of Anaxagoras, of the 9
poison forced on Socrates, of the torturing of Zeno,* for these took
place abroad; but at any rate you have been able to acquaint
yourself with such figures as Canius, and Seneca, and Soranus,*
for the tradition about them is still fresh and famous. They were 10
dragged down to disaster for no other reason than that they were
schooled in my ways, and showed themselves utterly at odds with
the unprincipled. So it is no occasion for surprise if on the ocean of 11
life we are buffeted by storms which whistle about our ears, for
our chief aim is to displease the wicked. In spite of the huge 12
numbers of their army, we are to regard them with contempt, for
they have no leader to guide them; rash and rampant error alone
bears them off on their random course. If ever they mount their 13
battle-line against us and press us too strongly, our leader* draws
back her forces into our citadel, while the enemy engage themselves in plundering our worthless baggage. From our eminence 14
we jeer at them as they loot all our tawdriest possessions; we are

safe from the mad mêlée raging all round, protected by the rampart which their lawless stupidity is not permitted to approach.'

Chapter 4

'He who keeps composure* in a life well-ordered,
Who thrusts underfoot fate's arrogant incursions,
Confronts with integrity both good and evil fortune,
Succeeds in maintaining an undefeated outlook—
He will not be moved by the wild threats of ocean   5
Spilling out and churning up waves from deep recesses;
Nor by Vesuvius, exploding from its forges,
Issuing its smoking fires over wide expanses;
Nor by the thunderbolt, which often blazing fiercely,
Reduces to rubble the loftiest of towers.   10
Why, then, do wretched men stand awe-struck at tyrants?
Savage though they be, their mad rage has no real power.
If we renounce all fear and expectation,
Intemperate anger will be stripped of all its weapons.
But he who all atremble is fearful or desirous,   15
Through lack of inward staunchness or self-mastery,
Has thrown away his shield, and deserted his station.
He forges the chains which confine his shackled progress.

1   'Do you get the message?' she asked. 'Has it penetrated your mind, or is it a case of the donkey listening to the lyre?* Why are you weeping, with the tears running down your cheeks?

Out with it, nor hold it fast within your breast.*

If you seek the physician's help, you must uncover the wound.'
2   Then I pulled myself together* and replied with some vehemence. 'Do I need to keep reminding you? Is not Fortune's harsh and cruel treatment of me self-evident? Does not the very
3   appearance of this place tug at your heart? Is this the library, the room in my house* which you chose indisputably as your own? Were you not often closeted with me there, discoursing on
4   knowledge of things human and divine? Did I comport myself and look like this when in your company I probed the secrets of nature, when you traced for me with your rod the paths of the

stars? When you shaped my character and the course of my entire life according to the patterns established in the heavens? Are these the rewards I win for following your injunctions?

'It was you who through Plato's mouth enacted this principle:* 5 affairs of state would be blessed if students of philosophy directed them, or if those who controlled them happened to be students of philosophy. Through the mouth of that same man you warned 6 why it was essential for philosophers to take charge of public affairs: if the government of cities was left to unprincipled malefactors, it would bring plague and ruin upon the good.

'So this was the authority I followed. I sought to apply in the 7 administration of affairs what I had learnt in sequestered leisure. You, I am sure, and God who established you in the minds of 8 philosophers, are well aware that I have devoted myself to no political office without having the common interests of all good men at heart. As a result, harsh and implacable dissensions arose 9 with men of no principle. In keeping with my freedom of conscience, I never shirked offending those with greater power, in the defence of what was right.

'How often did I confront and thwart Conigastus, when he 10 sought to plunder the wealth of each and every defenceless citizen! How often did I compel Trigguilla,* prefect of the royal house, to desist from injustices on which he had embarked or in fact committed! How often did I expose my position to dangers, in order to protect poor wretches whom the barbarians with unbridled greed were constantly harassing with one unfounded charge after another! No man has ever dragged me away from the path of justice to commit injustice. When provincials lost their 11 wealth through looting by individuals or through taxation by the state, my grief was no less than that of the victims.

'During a period of harsh famine, the public purchase of grain* 12 was proclaimed. This oppressive and indefensible measure seemed likely to bring Campania to its knees through starvation. I took up the cudgels in the public interest against the Praetorian Prefect; I fought the case before the king, and succeeded in having the public purchase annulled. When Paulinus, a man of consular rank, 13 saw his wealth guzzled by the hopes and ambitions of hounds in the palace, I delivered it from their gaping jaws. To save Albinus,* 14 another consular, from suffering punishment on a charge which

had not reached the courts, I exposed myself to the hatred of
15 Cyprian,* the man who had denounced him. You may say that I
seem to have provoked quite vehement opposition. True, but I
should have obtained greater security from the rest of the court,
for in my passion for justice I held nothing back so that I could
secure greater safety among them.

16   'Who are the informers who have brought me down? One of
them, Basilius, had previously been dismissed from the king's
service. What drove him to denounce me was financial need, for he
17 was heavily in debt. As for Opilio and Gaudentius,* they had been
condemned to exile by royal decree for countless wide-ranging
frauds. They refused to submit to this penalty, and tried to protect
themselves by seeking sanctuary in a shrine. When the king
discovered this, he decreed that unless they quitted Ravenna by
the appointed day, they would be expelled with foreheads
18 branded. What imaginable penalty could be more severe than
this? Yet it was under their signatures that the accusation was
19 lodged on that very day against me. So was this what my talents
deserved? Did the condemnation which my accusers had earlier
merited transform them into just men? And did Fortune feel no
shame, if not at the indictment of an innocent man, at least at the
worthlessness of my accusers?

20   'Perhaps you wish to hear the substance of the charge against
me? The allegation is that I sought to safeguard the existence of
21 the senate. Would you like to hear how I did this? I am accused of
hindering the informer from presenting evidence to charge the
22 senate with treason. You are my teacher; what is your judgement
on this? Am I to deny the charge, to avoid bringing shame on you?
In fact, however, I did seek, and shall never cease to seek, the
continued existence of the senate. So should I plead guilty? But
these efforts of mine to hinder the informer did not succeed.
23 Should I then pronounce it a crime to have sought the safety of the
senatorial order? Indeed, the senate by passing its decrees against
24 me had already declared my deed to be criminal. But such
ignorance as they have shown is always self-deceiving, and
cannot alter the merits of the case. I follow the injunction of
Socrates,* and regard it as impious either to hide the truth or to
25 give entry to falsehood. But I leave you and the philosophers to
assess the facts; I have committed the sequence of events, and the

truth about them, to paper for later scrutiny, so that they cannot be hidden from posterity.

'I see no point in referring to the fraudulent documents which 26 support the accusation that I hoped to restore Roman liberty. Had I been allowed access to the declaration of the informers themselves, its falsity would have been exposed; in all such cases this procedure carries the greatest force. I ask you, what remnant of 27 freedom can one hope for? I only wish that some such possibility existed. I could in such circumstances have met the charge with the words of Canius.* When Gaius Caesar, son of Germanicus, charged him with being implicated in a conspiracy against him, Canius remarked: "Had I known of it, you would not!" Grief has 28 not so addled my brain in this affair as to cause me to complain that evil men have mounted criminal attacks on virtue, but I find it utterly astonishing that they have achieved their aim. Doubtless 29 evil intentions are a feature of human frailty, but it is quite outrageous that a criminal's plot against an innocent man should prevail while God looks on. There is certainly justice in the 30 question posed by one of your devotees:* "If God indeed does exist, what is the source of evil? But if he does not exist, what is the source of good?"

'Suppose I had granted that the wicked ones who seek to shed 31 the blood of all honourable men and of the entire senate were justified in wishing to bring me down as well, for they had realized that I was championing those honourable men and the senate. But 32 surely I did not deserve like treatment from the senators as well? When the king was at Verona—I am sure that you remember this, for you were always present in person, guiding my words and actions—in his eagerness to sound the death-knell on the entire senate, he strove to divert the charge of treason laid against Albinus on the whole senatorial order. You remember with what disregard for my own danger I defended the innocence of the entire body. You know that I speak the simple truth, and that I 33 have never indulged in idle boasting. There is a sense in which self-justification within us is diminished when it obtains the reward of fair fame by advertising what one has done.

'But you see the outcome of my innocent behaviour. Instead of 34 being rewarded for genuine virtue, I am punished for a crime that I did not commit. Was there ever any crime in which even frank 35

admission of guilt found judges so unanimous in passing harsh sentence, that none of them were softened by reflecting on man's proneness to error, or on the uncertainty of fortune to which all
36 are subject? If I were charged with planning arson of a temple, or with sacrilegiously cutting the throats of priests, or with plotting the murder of all honourable men, sentence would have been passed on me as I stood in the dock, having confessed or having been found guilty. But here I am, five hundred miles away,* condemned to death and loss of property, unable to speak a word in my own defence, and all for my overzealous support of the senate! Surely no one could be rightly condemned on a charge like this!

37   'Even those who have laid this accusation realize its triviality, for in order to blacken it by compounding it with some crime, they have lyingly claimed that ambition for high office led me to stain
38 my conscience with sacrilege.* But you were dwelling in my heart; all longing for mortal things you drove from the abode of my mind. With your eyes upon me, it would have been impious for me to make a home for sacrilege. Every day you dinned into my
39 ears and thoughts the dictum of Pythagoras: "Follow the god."* It would not have been fitting for me to seek the support of most worthless spirits, when you were moulding me to attain the
40 excellence which would make me godlike. There are other facts too in my favour which protect me from any suspicion on this charge: the innocent confines of my house, my many friends who are beyond reproach, and also my august father-in-law* who is as
41 worthy of veneration as you yourself. But my accusers—a monstrous situation, this—make their heinous charge plausible by citing you; I shall seem to have been an accomplice especially in this offence, because I am steeped in your teachings, and schooled
42 in your manners. So it is not merely that my veneration for you has gained me no advantage; you too, though innocent, are to be
43 scourged because of what I have done. And further, my evil plight is greatly intensified by the fact that most people look not at the merits of a case, but at its chance outcome. They consider the stamp of success as the sole criterion of prudent forethought, and so the first casualty of failure is one's good repute.

44   'It irks me to think of the common gossip and the range of contrasting judgements now circulating. I make bold to say only

that the final burden imposed by hostile Fortune is the general belief that wretches charged with some offence deserve all the punishment which they get. For myself, I have been parted from 45 my possessions, stripped of my offices, blackened in my reputation, and punished for the services I have rendered. By contrast, 46 images appear before my eyes of criminals in their dens, wallowing in sensual joys, the most abandoned of them plotting renewed false accusations, while good men are prostrate with fear as they survey my danger. I see evildoers, one and all roused by their impunity to venture on wicked deeds, and by rewards to see them through; I see innocent men deprived not only of safety, but also of the right to defend themselves. This is what stirs my cry of lament.

Chapter 5

'Creator of the starry sphere,*
Seated upon your timeless chair,
You move the sky in swift gyration,
Ordering with law each constellation.
So now the hornèd moon entire   5
Reflects in full her brother's fire,
And gleaming, shrouds the lesser stars;
Soon, close access to Phoebus mars
And dissipates its crescent light.
The evening star at fall of night   10
First makes its frigid presence known,
But then, as Lucifer at dawn,
Relinquishing its earlier reins,
Pale presence with the sun maintains.

You, as cold winter strips the trees,   15
Draw in the light on shorter lease;
You, when the heat of summer lours,
Abbreviate night's fleeting hours.
Your power adjusts the changing year.
Leaves that through Boreas disappear   20
Return when the mild Zephyr blows.
The seeds that Arcturus first sows
As tall crops Sirius roasts dry.*
Nought can your ancient law deny
Or fail its function to perform;   25
All things you govern with fixed norm.

But human acts you do not school;
You justly spurn to wield your rule.

Else, why does slippery Fortune range,*
Encompassing such violent change?   30
Harsh pains, owed villainy as its due,
Instead the innocent pursue.
With wicked ways ensconced on high,
We blameless souls unjustly lie,
Our necks pressed down by guilty men;   35
Virtue's bright sheen is hidden then
In blinding darkness. Probity
Endures crushing iniquity.
Sworn lies and specious deceit
Attract no danger or defeat;   40
Once they decide upon their goal,
It is their pleasure to control
Great kings, whom countless nations dread.

O God, who nature's parts hast wed,
Cast eyes upon this wretched earth;   45
Man, in creation no mean worth,
Is buffeted on Fortune's main.
These headlong waves, we pray, restrain;
To earth that steadfast law apply
With which you rule the boundless sky.'   50

1   Philosophy greeted these yelps of sustained pain with a calm
2 demeanour of indifference to my complaints. 'Earlier, when I
observed your downcast tears, I at once realized that you were
living unhappily in exile. But if you had not expounded it in your
own words, I should never have grasped how distant was your
3 place of banishment. But this distance you have travelled from
your native land* is the outcome not of expulsion, but of your
going astray; if you wish to regard it as expulsion, such expulsion
was self-induced, for no other person could lawfully have imposed
4 such exile. You must reflect on the land from which you are
sprung. It is not governed by the rule of the masses like the Athens
of old, for "There is but one lord and one king",* and he prefers
his citizens to throng around him rather than to be in exile. To be
guided by his reins, to obey his just commands is perfect freedom.
5 You must surely be acquainted with the most ancient law of your
city, which ordains that one who opts to make his home there

cannot lawfully be banished from it?* Indeed, if a person resides
within the protection of its rampart, he need never fear sentence of
banishment; but once he ceases to desire a home there, he likewise
ceases to deserve it. So what engages me is the sight not so much 6
of this residence as of your demeanour. What I look for is not
library walls adorned with ivory and glass, but your mind's abode;
for I have installed there not books, but what gives books their
value, the doctrine found in my writings of old.

'What you say about your services to the common good is true; 7
indeed, considering the great number of your achievements, your
account was spare. You mentioned the allegations made against 8
you; the world knows whether they are false or true. You were
right to assume that you needed make only passing reference to the
crimes and deceits of those who laid charges against you, for they
are all on the lips of the people at large, and are better and more
fully known to them. You have also sharply rebuked the role of the 9
senate. In addition, you have expressed regret at the charges made
against me, and you have lamented the damaging harm done to my
reputation. Finally, in the white heat of your resentment, you 10
inveighed against Fortune; you complained that your merits have
not won commensurate rewards, and at the close of your fierce
verses, you prayed that the peace which prevails in the heavens
might also govern the earth. This welter of disturbed emotions 11
weighs heavily upon you; grief, anger, and melancholy* are tearing
you apart. So in your present state of mind, you are not as yet fit to
face stronger remedies. For the moment, then, I shall apply 12
gentler ones, so that the hard swellings where the emotions have
gathered may soften under a more caressing touch, and may
become ready to bear the application of more painful treatment.'

Chapter 6

'When Apollo,* with his rays,
Roasts the Crab's oppressive days,*
Seeds in plenty which you sow
In the furrows will not grow.*
Robbed of any hope of grain,   5
Acorns from the oaks obtain!*

Should you wish to pick spring flowers
From the crimson-laden bowers,
Never purpose there to go
When the savage north winds blow,　　　　　10
Shrieking fiercely o'er the plain,
Lifting vertically the grain.

Do you wish to harvest wine?
Do not therefore strip the vine
With greedy hands in days of spring;　　　　15
Bacchus' preference is to bring
Gifts when later in the year
Autumn makes its presence clear.

To each season God assigns
Duties meet for his designs;　　　　　　　20
He prohibits changes made
To the sequence he has laid.
Headlong rupture of that chain
Unhappy outcome will obtain.

1　'So will you first allow me to ask you a few simple questions, so as to probe and investigate* your mental state? By this means I can decide upon your cure.'

2　'Ask away at your discretion', I replied, 'and I shall answer you.'

3　Then she asked: 'Do you think that the course of the world is random and haphazard, or do you believe that it is guided by reason?'

4　'I should certainly refuse to believe', I answered, 'that such unerring movements are the outcome of random chance. I know that the creator God superintends his creation. The day will never come when I detach myself from the truth of that statement.'

5　'I accept what you say', she rejoined, 'because this was also the substance of your verses a moment ago, in your lament that mankind alone was excluded from God's care. You did not budge from your conviction that all else is governed by reason.

6　How odd! I find it utterly astonishing that you are sick, when your beliefs are so wholesome. But let me probe deeper, for I suspect

7　some defect here. So tell me: in your assurance that God governs the world, how do you envisage him wielding the reins?'

8　'I can scarcely grasp what you are asking', I replied, 'let alone answer your question.'

9　'I was certainly not mistaken', she commented, 'in assuming some defect in your make-up. It is like a gap in a fortified rampart, through which the disease of emotional disturbance has permeated into your mind. Tell me this: do you remember the final purpose 10 of the world, the goal to which the whole order of nature proceeds?'

'I was told it earlier,' I replied, 'but my distress has clouded my recollection.'*

'But you do know, I take it, the source from which all things 11 have come?'

'Yes,' I answered, 'God is the source.'

'So how can it be that you know the beginning of things, and 12 not their goal? However, these emotional upheavals to which you 13 are prone are powerful enough to unbalance a person, but they cannot undermine and utterly uproot him. Now please tell me this 14 as well: Do you remember that you are a man?'

'Of course I remember!' I replied.

'So can you define what a man is?'   15

'Are you asking if I am aware that I am a mortal creature endowed with reason?* Yes, I know that, and I proclaim it.'

'But are you aware of being anything more?' she asked.   16

'No, nothing more.'

'Now I know', she said, 'the further cause of your sickness,* and 17 it is a very serious one. You have forgotten your own identity. So I have now fully elicited the cause of your illness, and the means of recovering your health. Forgetting who you are has made you 18 confused, and this is why you are upset at being both exiled and stripped of your possessions. Then, since you are unaware of the 19 goal to which creation proceeds, you imagine that wicked and unprincipled individuals are powerful and blessed. Moreover, since you have forgotten the reins that control the world, you believe that the changes of fortune which have befallen you are random and unguided. These are serious symptoms, which bring on not only sickness, but also death. But thanks be to the source of health, for nature has not wholly forsaken you; your true 20 conviction of the government of the world provides us with the nourishment to restore you to health, for you believe that the universe is guided by divine reason, and is not subject to random chance. So have no fear; this tiniest of sparks will cause life's heat to be resuscitated in you.

21   'But it is not yet time for stronger remedies. As all know, it is
the nature of the human mind, once it dispenses with true beliefs,
to adopt false ones, from which there develops a cloud of
emotional disturbance which distorts the true vision previously
held. So I shall try for a little while to break up this cloud with
gentle and limited remedies, so that once the darkness of deceiving
emotions is dispersed, you can acknowledge the brightness of the
true light.'

Chapter 7

'When black clouds envelop*
Stars which shone bright,
They can no longer
Pour forth their light.

If the stormy south wind,   5
Assaulting the sea,
Stirs up the salt-surge,
The waves that lay free
And were glassy, encalmed
As unclouded days,   10
Are fouled with dredged mud
And opaque to our gaze.

Rocks torn from high crags
Oft stem a stream's force,
As it pours down the mountains   15
In wandering course.

Your case is like these.
If you wish to behold
The truth in clear light,
And to take the straight road,   20
Forgo empty joys,
Dismiss every fear,
Renounce idle hope,
Let grief come not near.*

The mind is befogged,   25
Imprisoned in chains,
When emotions like these
Wield monarchical reins.'

Book 2

Chapter 1

She fell silent* for a little while, and her quiet reticence riveted my attention. Then she resumed her discourse. 1

'If I have fully grasped the causes and the nature of your 2 sickness, you are wasting away because you are yearning and pining for your earlier fortune. The interpretation which you have put on your changed circumstances has corrupted your mental faculties. I well know the manifold deceits of that monstrous lady, 3 Fortune;* in particular, her fawning friendship with those whom she intends to cheat, until the moment when she unexpectedly abandons them, and leaves them reeling in agony beyond endurance. But if you recall what she is, her ways and her worth, you 4 will realize that you neither had, nor have lost, anything of worth through your association with her. I imagine that you need no 5 urging at all to recognize this, for in her very presence, even as she fawned on you, you would assail her with manly words, and attack her with sentiments gathered from my shrine. But no sudden 6 change of circumstances occurs without causing some mental turmoil, which is why even you for the moment have abandoned your usual serenity.

'But now it is time for you to sample and imbibe a soothing 7 medicine with a pleasant taste. Once you have absorbed it, it will prepare the way for stronger draughts. So let me now apply the 8 persuasion of sweet-sounding rhetoric,* which walks on the right path only when it does not abandon our precepts, and let it alternate with music, that native servant of our dwelling, between lighter and graver measures.

'What is it then, mortal man, that has plunged you into 9 melancholy and grief? You have, I believe, undergone a strange and unfamiliar experience. You think that Fortune has changed towards you, but you are mistaken. Her ways and her nature are 10 always the same. What she has done is to manifest towards you the fickleness which reflects her characteristic constancy. She was no different when she fawned on you and made sport of you with the

11 enticements of a bogus happiness. You have experienced the ambivalent features of the blind goddess.* While she keeps her true self still hidden from others, she has revealed herself fully to you.

12 'If you approve of her, enjoy the way she behaves, and do not complain. If her treachery appals you, despise her and cast her off as she plays her destructive games, for what is now the cause of your great grief should in fact have been the source of composure. Why? Because she has abandoned you, and none can ever feel sure

13 that she will not abandon them. Surely you do not believe that purely ephemeral happiness is of value? Are the attentions of Fortune dear to you, when you cannot trust her to remain, and

14 once she departs she will cause you grief? If you cannot keep her with you as you would like, and her swift departure spells a man's undoing, what else does her fleeting figure signify but a portent of

15 future disaster? It is not enough to keep an eye on what lies immediately before you; the prudent person assesses the future outcome. The threats of Fortune become less frightening, and her blandishments less desirable, precisely because she switches so readily from one to the other.

16 'A final point. If once you have bowed your neck beneath her

17 yoke, you must bear philosophically all that is enacted on her playing-field. When you have freely chosen her as your mistress, it would surely be inequitable if you attempted to lay down terms for her stay or her departure? Refusal to bear with your lot would

18 make it more bitter since you cannot change it. Suppose you spread your sails before the winds; your course would then be dictated not by your own inclination, but by the direction from which they blew. Again, if you sow seeds in your fields, you must balance the barren years against the fruitful harvests. Having entrusted yourself to Fortune's dominion, you must conform to

19 your mistress's ways. What, are you trying to halt the motion of her whirling wheel?* Dimmest of fools that you are, you must realize that if the wheel stops turning, it ceases to be the course of chance.

'When Fortune's haughty hand her changes rings,
And, like Euripus' tidal currents,* swings,
She harshly grinds down kings long viewed with dread,
And lifts with guile the vanquished person's head.
To wretched tears she pays no heed or care,   5
But grimly smiles at groans she's made men bear.
Such is her sport; she demonstrates her power:
The prostrate man rides high within the hour.'

Chapter 2

'But I should like to raise with you a few arguments in Fortune's   1
own words,* so consider whether her demand is just. "Why, good   2
man, do you indict me day after day with your complaints? What
harm have I done you? What possessions of yours have I
purloined? Appoint any judge you like so as to dispute with me   3
the possession of riches and of offices, and if you succeed in
demonstrating that all such things belong to any human being, I
will readily grant that the things which you are demanding back
were already yours.

'"When nature brought you forth* from your mother's womb, I   4
adopted you; you were naked then, and bereft of everything. I
nurtured you with my resources, and—this is what now makes you
so angry with me—I bent over backwards to spoil you, and to give
you a pampered upbringing. I hedged you round with the
glittering panoply of all those riches rightfully mine. It now   5
suits me to withdraw my gifts. You owe me a debt of gratitude
for having enjoyed possessions not your own; you have no right to
complain as if you have lost what was indisputably yours. So why   6
moan and groan? I have not laid violent hands on you. Wealth and
position and all such things are at my discretion. These handmaids
of mine acknowledge their mistress; they come with me, and they
retire when I depart. I can assert with confidence that if those   7
possessions whose loss you lament had really been yours, you
would certainly not have lost them.

'"So am I alone to be forbidden to exercise my rights? The   8
heavens are allowed to engender bright days, and then to shroud
them in dark nights.* The year is permitted at one time to adorn

the face of the earth with blossoms and fruits, and at another to plague it with rain-clouds and freezing cold. It is the sea's right at one moment to smile indulgently with glassy waters, and at another to bristle with storms and breakers. So when people's wishes are unfulfilled, will they confine me to that consistent

9 behaviour which is alien to my character? This power that I wield comes naturally to me; this is my perennial sport. I turn my wheel on its whirling course, and take delight in switching the base to the

10 summit, and the summit to the base. So mount upward, if you will, but on condition that you do not regard yourself as ill-treated if you plummet down when my humour so demands and takes its course.

11   ' "You were surely acquainted with my ways? You must have heard how Croesus,* king of the Lydians, after being only recently an object of fear to Cyrus, became thereafter a pitiable figure when consigned to the flames of the pyre, but was then delivered by a

12 shower of rain sent by heaven? It can hardly have escaped you that Paulus shed tears of pity over the disasters which overwhelmed King Perseus* his prisoner? What else do the groans of tragedy lament but the overthrow of prosperous kingdoms by the random

13 blows of Fortune? As a youngster you must surely have learnt of the two jars,* one containing evils, the other blessings, which lie

14 on Jupiter's threshold? So now, even though you have had more than your share of blessings, even though I have not wholly abandoned you, even though this very fickleness of mine gives you just cause to anticipate a better future,* are you bent on pining away? And do you aspire to a law of your own which governs your life, when you are a citizen of the common kingdom of the world?" '

> 'If from her bounteous horn,* with generous hand
>   The goddess Plenty gave
> Gifts countless as the grains of shifting sand
>   Stirred by the snatching wave,
> Or numerous as the bright orbs in the sky*   5
>   Born of the star-decked night,
> The human race would not forbear to cry
>   And mourn their wretched plight.
>
> Though God is pleased to grant them their petitions,
>   To shower them with gold,   10

To crown with glittering office their ambitions,
  Such blessings leave them cold.
Relentless greed devours those earlier gains,
  Reopens wide its jaws;
Can headlong lust be curbed by any reins,   15
  Be bounded by fixed laws?

Thirst for possessions* blazes all the more,
  The more those gifts extend;
With anxious sighs, believing he is poor,
  The rich man hates to spend.'*   20

Chapter 3

'So if Fortune were to argue a case like this against you, you would   1
not be able to utter a word in reply—or if you *can* adduce some
justification for your complaint, now is the time to come out with
it, for the opportunity is yours.'

  Then I said: 'True, these are plausible arguments. Thickly   2
smeared as they are with the sweet honey of rhetoric and music,
they afford momentary pleasure as we listen to them. But when
people are unhappy, awareness of their misery runs deeper, so
once these words cease to echo in our ears, the grief implanted in
our hearts outweighs them.'

  'I grant that,' she rejoined. 'The fact is that as yet, such words are   3
no cure for your sickness. At this stage they serve merely as a
poultice for the pain which stubbornly resists all healing. When the   4
time is ripe, I shall apply remedies to penetrate deep within the skin.

  'But you should not count yourself as wretched—or have you
forgotten the number and extent of your blessings?* I pass over   5
the fact that as an orphaned child you were looked after by people
of the greatest distinction; and when you were chosen to marry
into the leading family in the state, you gained the affection of
your in-laws from the start, even before the marriage-alliance was
cemented. This is the most precious form of kinship that exists.
Was there a single person who did not proclaim that you were   6
supremely blessed through the lustre of your wife's family,
through her chaste demeanour, and through the prospect of
male children to follow? I make no mention of those distinctions   7

which even men of mature years fail to attain, but which you gained in your youth. I prefer to pass over the honours which you shared with others. What I dwell with pleasure on is that crowning

8 moment of happiness which was uniquely yours. If the enjoyment of human affairs brings any measure of content, can the recollection of that day be blotted out by the weight of oppressive ills, however great? I refer to the day when you saw your two sons conveyed as twin consuls from your home, escorted by a throng of senators, and applauded by the common folk. That day your sons were seated on the curule chairs in the senate-house, as you delivered the encomium* to the king, and you won high praise for your originality of thought and your power of utterance. That day, seated in the Circus between the two consuls, you did more than satisfy the expectation of the encompassing crowd when you bestowed the largesse appropriate to a triumph.

9 'I am sure that you hoodwinked Fortune then, as she fawned and doted on you as her favourite. You emerged with a gift which she had never previously bestowed on any private individual. So

10 are you willing to compute the score with her? This is the first time that she has cast a malevolent eye on you. Tot up the number and extent of your happy days against the unhappy ones, and you cannot deny that your life up to now has been blessed.

11 But even if you refuse to acknowledge your previous good fortune because those seeming joys of earlier days have vanished, you still have no reason to count yourself wretched; for what you now

12 think of as harrowing days are likewise passing away. It is not as if you are a stranger to the stage of life, treading the boards suddenly for the first time! You surely cannot believe that there is any regularity in human affairs, when the swift passage of time

13 so often reduces men themselves to dust and ashes? It is true that only rarely can we place trust in the permanence of Fortune's gifts; but the closing day of human life brings an end also to such fortune as remains. So what difference do you think it makes, whether you abandon Fortune by dying, or whether she abandons you by making off?

> 'When Phoebus* in his rose-red car climbs higher,
>   And starts to flood the sky with light,
>   The constellations, gleaming white,
> Grow pale and dim before his thrusting fire.

When quickened by the warm west wind, the bower   5
   Turns crimson with the vernal rose;
   If Auster,* wild and rainy, blows,
The thorns are stripped of every handsome flower.

Often the ocean sparkles, calm and bright;
   Its waves immobile, placid lie;   10
   But often, too, the sea churns high,
When Boreas'* seething storms rage at their height.

Since in this world inconstancy is sure,
   And rampant changes are the rule,
   Then trust in fleeting goods, you fool!   15
Expect men's transient fortunes to endure!

One thing is fixed, by eternal law arranged;
Nothing which comes to be remains unchanged.'

Chapter 4

Thereupon I remarked: 'Your observations are true, nurse and   1
repository of all the virtues; I cannot deny the meteoric success of
my career. But this is precisely what roasts me more fiercely as I   2
contemplate it, for of all Fortune's blows, the unhappiest aspect of
misfortune is to have known happiness.'*

'But your suffering', she rejoined, 'is the penalty for your   3
mistaken belief; you cannot rightly blame the course of events
for that. If indeed the hollow claim to unsubstantial happiness is
important in your eyes, you must reflect with me on the numerous
and extensive blessings which you enjoy. I put it to you: if God   4
allows you to preserve whole and intact that possession which is
the most precious in the entire range of your fortune, can you
reasonably make issue of your wretchedness, when you continue to
enjoy all that is of greater worth?

'Consider first the undiminished vigour of your father-in-law   5
Symmachus, that glory of the human race beyond price. You
would readily give your life to be that total personification of
wisdom and the virtues that he embodies. Without thought for the
indignities which he himself suffers,* he laments over yours.
Then, too, your wife lives on, making no show of her talents, a   6
woman whose modesty and chaste life are beyond compare. To
sum up all her attributes in a single phrase, she is the image of her

father. Yes, she lives on, but she loathes her present life, and persists in it for your sake alone; in her longing for you, she wastes away in tearful grief. In this one respect—even I go so far as to

7 grant you this—your happiness is diminished. Need I mention your sons of consular rank, those boys who already at their early age show glowing evidence of the talents of their father or

8 grandfather? You are truly fortunate, if only you would acknowledge your blessings;* for while men are concerned above all to preserve their lives, no one doubts that the blessings which even

9 now you enjoy are dearer than life itself. So come now, dry your tears. Fortune does not yet direct her hatred against all your household. The storm which has gathered over you is not too hard to endure, for your anchors still hold fast,* and their grip is such that they do not allow present consolation or future hope to disappear.'

10 'I pray that they do hold fast,' I said, 'for so long as they remain in place, I shall survive whatever the conditions. But you do observe the depths of my decline from my proud offices?'

11 'We have made some progress', she observed, 'if you are no longer wholly disgusted with your present lot. But I find your self-indulgence hard to bear when you complain so mournfully and neurotically that something is lacking to your happiness.

12 Does any individual* enjoy such total blessedness that he does not find fault in some respect with the nature of his condition? Human welfare is a cause of worry, for it never wholly prospers,

13 and it never remains constant. One man has abundance of wealth, but is ashamed of his inferior origins; another is celebrated for his noble birth, but would prefer to lie low, since he is beset by

14 domestic poverty. One man is richly endowed with both nobility and wealth, but laments his life as a bachelor; a second is happily married but childless, and nurses his wealth merely for some outsider to inherit; a third is blessed with a family, but the failings

15 of a son or daughter cause him distress, and awaken his tears. So no person is easily reconciled to his allotted condition; every human person faces drawbacks, whether unknown because not yet

16 experienced, or grim because already encountered. Moreover, the most fortunate people are also the most squeamish; being unused to any hardship, unless everything comes to them on the nod they are floored by the slightest difficulties. Even trifling reverses

detract from the sum of happiness of those who are most privileged.

'How many people exist, do you reckon, who would think that 17 they were in heaven if they enjoyed the merest fraction of the fortune which is still yours? This very locality, which you label your place of banishment,* is the hearth and home of people who dwell here, So nothing is wretched unless you account it so, and 18 conversely, the lot of all who bear it with tranquillity is blessed. Is 19 any person so fulfilled that once he caves in to depression, he would not wish to change his condition? How numerous are the 20 drops of gall which mar the sweet taste of human happiness! That happiness may seem pleasurable to the person who still enjoys it, but it cannot be prevented from vanishing at will. So what is 21 crystal-clear is how wretched is the happiness which mortal possessions bring, for those content with life do not possess it for ever, and it does not satisfy in its entirety those who live in distress.

'So why, mortal men, do you pursue happiness outside 22 yourselves, when it lies within?* Error and ignorance derange you. I shall briefly outline for you the hinge on which the greatest 23 happiness turns. Is there anything more precious to you than yourself? Nothing, you will reply. Well then, as long as you are in command of yourself, you will possess what you would never wish to lose, and what Fortune can never withdraw from you. So that 24 you may acknowledge that true happiness cannot reside in this realm of chance, you must grasp this argument: If happiness is the 25 highest good of a rational nature, and if what can be taken from you in any way cannot be the highest (for what cannot be taken away ranks higher than what can), it is obvious that the fluidity of Fortune cannot hope to win happiness.

'A second point. The man who embarks on this transitory 26 happiness either knows or does not know that it can change. If he does not know, how can he be happy in his state of blind ignorance? If he does know, he must inevitably fear the loss of what he is in no doubt can be lost, and therefore his enduring anxiety does not permit him to be happy. Or does he perhaps think that he can disregard the prospect of losing it? In that case again it 27 is a trifling good, since the loss of it is so readily borne.

'Now you are that same person who I know held the rooted 28

conviction, instilled by numerous proofs, that the minds of men are in no wise mortal;* and since it is obvious that the happiness which chance brings ends with the body's death, there can be no doubt, assuming that such happiness can confer well-being, that when death signals the end the whole human race is plunged into
29 misery. Yet we know that many have come to enjoy such well-being not only in death, but even in pain and torture.* So how can that happiness whose cessation does not make us wretched induce well-being in us by its presence?

> 'The careful man* who plans to found
> A lasting home upon firm ground
> Avoids collapse; he must stand fast
> Against the east wind's sounding blast;
> Must spurn the threatening, wave-tossed deep,   5
> Must shun the exposed mountain-steep,
> The greedy, thirsting sands forgo.
> For south-west winds with wanton show
> In all their force attack the height;
> Loose sand can't bear a tottering weight.   10
> If dangerous hazards loom close by,
> Don't choose a site to please the eye.
> Play safe. Above all, don't forget
> To build your house on rock deep-set.
> Enclosed by your walls' silent strength,   15
> You'll live untroubled for the length
> Of all your days; and by and by
> Smile at the anger of the sky.'

Chapter 5

1 'But now that the warming applications of my arguments are penetrating more deeply below your skin, I must, I think, make the
2 dressings stronger. So let us suppose that Fortune's gifts were not transitory and fleeting; what is there in them which you could ever possess, or which when scrutinized and pondered is not tawdry?
3   'Are riches truly your possession, or by their nature valuable?
4 Which of them in particular? Gold and money in abundance? But their sheen is more attractive when they are doled out rather than gathered in,* for avarice always breeds hatred, whereas generosity

brings men fair fame. Now none of us can retain what is passed on 5
to another, so money becomes valuable only when bestowed on
others by the practice of giving, thus ceasing to be possessed.
Indeed, if all the money in the world were concentrated in the 6
hands of a single person, the rest would be rendered penniless.
The human voice can fill the ears of many at once without
diminution, but men's riches cannot pass to more than one
unless they are fragmented; and when that happens, they must
impoverish those who relinquish them. So how restrictive and 7
poverty-stricken are these riches, which cannot be possessed in
their entirety by the many, and which do not pass to any single
person without leaving the rest in want!

'Or is it the sparkle of jewels that attracts men's eyes? Yet if 8
their brilliance is something out of the ordinary, their brightness is
the property of the jewels, not of the men who own them. Indeed,
I am utterly astonished that men admire them, for can anything 9
justifiably appear beautiful to a rational nature endowed with life,
if it lacks the movement and physical frame of a living creature?
Admittedly jewels can claim a measure of beauty at the lowest 10
level, as being the work of the Creator with their own distinctive
quality, but they rank below human excellence, and should in no
way deserve the admiration of men.

'But perhaps it is the beauty of your estates that delights you? 11
Such delight is well-founded, for they are a beautiful feature of the
most beautiful creation. At times we similarly take pleasure at the 12
sight of a shimmering sea, or we marvel at the sky, the constellations, the moon, and the sun. But do any of these things belong to
you? Do you presume to boast of the lustre of any such elements?
Is your beauty enhanced by spring blossoms? Does the swelling 13
fecundity of summer fruits attach itself to you? Why are you 14
ravished by such empty joys? Why do you embrace external goods
as if they were yours? Fortune will never award you what the
world of nature has set apart from you. Undoubtedly the fruits of 15
the earth are intended to nurture living creatures, but if you desire
mere natural sufficiency to satisfy your needs, there is no point in
seeking abundance from Fortune. Nature is content with few 16
possessions, and the humblest; should you seek to overload her
sufficiency with superfluities, the additions will become distasteful
or harmful.

17   'Do you think it also a fine thing to cut a resplendent figure with
a varied wardrobe? If your clothes are eye-catching, what will win
my admiration is the quality of the cloth, or the skill of the tailor.

18   Or is it perhaps a long retinue of servants that keeps you happy?
But if on the one hand they have corrupt manners, they will be a
baleful burden on your house, and fiercely hostile to the master
himself;* and if on the other hand they are honest, how can the

19   honesty of others be credited to your resources? All these examples
make it crystal clear that none of the possessions which you count
as yours actually belong to you. So if on the one hand they manifest
no beauty worth acquiring, why should you grieve at losing them,

20   or be glad at keeping them? And if on the other hand they are
naturally beautiful, how is that relevant to you? You might have
appreciated them on their own account, without making them part

21   of your possessions. It was not that their value lay in having
become part of your riches, but that you preferred to count them
among your wealth because they seemed valuable.

22   'What do you men long for so much when you make this outcry
against Fortune? I imagine that you are trying to dispel want by

23   acquiring an abundance. But the effect you achieve is the very
opposite, for to protect your wide range of costly goods, you need
a number of aids. There is truth in the saying that "if you have a
lot, there's a lot you haven't got".* And the converse is also true,
that those who measure their riches according to natural need
rather than superfluous show are short of very little.

24   'Have you men no resources within you that you call your own,
seeing that you seek your goods in things external and distinct

25   from you? Has the world become so topsy-turvy that a living
creature, whom the gift of reason makes divine, believes that his

26   glory lies solely in possession of lifeless goods? Other creatures are
content with what they have; but you, who are godlike with your
gift of mind, seek to embellish your surpassing nature with the
grubbiest of things, and in so doing you fail to appreciate what an

27   insult you inflict on your Creator. He sought to make the race of
men superior to all earthly things, but you have subordinated your

28   dignity to the lowliest objects. For if every good belonging to an
individual is truly more valuable than the person to whom it
belongs, then on your own reckoning you men rank yourselves
below the tawdriest things, when you pronounce them to be your

goods. Such an outcome is fully deserved, for the status of man's 29
nature is this: it excels all other things only when aware of itself,
but if it ceases to know itself, it falls below the level of the beasts.
This is because lack of self-knowledge is natural in other living
creatures, but in humans is a moral blemish.

'How rampant is this error entertained by you humans in 30
thinking that anything can be enhanced by external adornment!
This cannot be the case. Whatever the lustre possessed by such 31
appendages, it redounds to their own praise, whereas the object
itself, however much cloaked and concealed, remains as unsightly
as ever below.

'I surely cannot be mistaken when I claim that nothing which 32
harms its possessor can be good? Of course not, you reply. Yet 33
riches have often harmed their owners. Individuals who are
thoroughly evil, and who are accordingly all the greedier for
what does not belong to them, believe that they alone are pre-
eminently worthy to own all the gold and precious stones in
existence. You yourself are apprehensive at present, fearful of the 34
club and the sword,* but if as a traveller on life's path you had first
set out with empty pockets, you could face the highwayman with a
song on your lips.* Outstanding blessings indeed are those 35
conferred by riches, for once you have acquired them, you cease
to feel safe!

> 'Happy indeed, those earlier days*
> When faithful fields made men content;
> No idle luxury sapped their ways;
> Acorns at hand, when day was spent,
>
> Sated their hunger. None then knew   5
> The liquid honey to apply
> To Bacchus' gifts; nor to imbue
> The sheen of silk with Tyrian dye.
>
> Men slumbered restful in the glade;
> Their drink the gliding river gave,   10
> The towering pine afforded shade.
> Not yet did sailors cleave the wave
>
> Coursing the sea's unfathomed road,
> Their eyes trained on the unknown strand,
> As strangers, voyaging abroad   15
> To gather goods from every land.

No trumpet's savage blare as yet
Called men to war. No blood was shed,
Provoked by men with rabid hate,
To dye the bristling cornfields red.   20

Why should such hostile rage ignite,
Inciting warfare to begin,
When savage wounds oppressed men's sight?
No gain from bloodshed could they win.

Would that our age could now return   25
To wholesome manners, as of old;
But fires more fierce than Aetna's burn
In men's hot lust to have and hold.

Who first, alas, forced spade to yield
Treasures from which harsh dangers spawn—   30
Rich bars of gold by earth concealed,
And gems which choose to lurk unknown?'

Chapter 6

1 'What comment should I make on positions of honour and power, which you men in ignorance of true worth and power exalt to the heavens? Once these positions fall into the hands of unscrupulous individuals, what Aetnas with belching flames, what floods would 2 unleash such havoc? At any rate, as I think you can recall, your forbears sought to rescind the consular authority which had launched the beginning of freedom, because of the arrogance of consuls; it was this same arrogance which had earlier led your 3 ancestors to expunge the title of king* from the state. On the other hand, on the rare occasions when such positions are bestowed on men of integrity, their sole recommendation is the integrity of those who wield them. So high position does not confer honour on the virtues; rather, virtue confers honour on high positions.

4   'And what is this desirable, glorious power which you men seek? Being living creatures of the earth, you presumably give thought to those you see as your subjects, and to your own role as masters? Imagine your reaction if you saw a colony of mice, and one of them was claiming lawful dominion over the rest; that would be good for 5 a belly-laugh! Yet if you consider physique alone, can you lay eyes on anything feebler than that of humans? Why, even mere flies, if

they bite you or creep into some inward part, can kill you! How 6
can a person exercise rights over any other, except over his body
and that which ranks below his body, namely his fortune? You can 7
exercise no dominion whatever, can you, over a free mind? Or
disturb from its natural serenity a mind at one with itself through
the steadying influence of reason? When the tyrant thought that by 8
torture he would force a free man to betray his associates in the
conspiracy against him, the free man bit through his tongue,* and
threw it in the face of the storming tyrant. In this way that sage
made a virtue out of the tortures which the tyrant believed were
instruments of cruelty.

'Is there any treatment which a person can inflict upon another 9
such as he may not himself sustain at another's hands? The story 10
goes that Busiris, who used to murder his guests, was himself
slaughtered by his guest Hercules.* Regulus had fettered a 11
number of Carthaginian prisoners-of-war, but later he himself
surrendered his hands to the chains of his victors.* So when a man 12
cannot ensure avoiding at another's hands what he can mete out to
another, can you imagine that he wields any power?

'A further point: if there were some natural and intrinsic good 13
in these positions of rank and power, they would never fall into the
hands of wicked men, for contraries do not associate with each
other; nature rejects the fusion of opposites. Since there is no 14
doubt that the most wicked of men frequently administer high
offices, it is likewise clear that positions which lend themselves to
association with the wicked are not good by their nature. The same 15
claim can be even more justifiably made about all the gifts of
Fortune, which every scoundrel attains in abundant measure.

'I think that we can visualize these matters in another light as 16
well. No one doubts that the brave man is one in whom bravery
resides, and it is clear that it is the person endowed with swiftness
who is a swift runner. In the same way, what makes musicians is 17
knowledge of music, that of medicine makes physicians, and that
of rhetoric, rhetoricians. The nature of each art produces what is
proper to it; it is not embroiled in the opposite effects, but
spontaneously rejects what is opposed to it. Yet riches cannot 18
snuff out insatiable greed; power cannot impart self-control to the
man whom wicked desires hold fast in bonds that cannot be
broken. High position bestowed on scoundrels does not merely fail

to make them worthy of it; indeed, it betrays and flaunts their
19 unworthiness. Why does this happen? It is because you men like to
attach alien titles to things which differ from them; the names are
readily rebutted by what the things themselves bring about. So
neither the riches nor the power mentioned earlier, nor the high
position which we are discussing now can by rights deserve the
names they bear.

20   'In short, we can draw the same inference about Fortune in
general. Clearly she has nothing worth seeking, nothing inherently
good, for she never attaches herself to good men, and those whom
she joins she does not make good.

> 'We know what destruction* was wrought by savage Nero;
> Flames engulfed the city; senators were slaughtered.
> The emperor earlier disposed of his brother,
> And bloodied his hands with the murder of his mother.
> As his gaze wandered over her dead body,   5
> No tears stained his face; an impassive critic,
> He graded the corpse as in a beauty competition.
>
> Yet he with his sceptre ruled so many peoples:
> Those which the sun-god, emerging from the orient,
> Beholds, till he plunges his rays beneath the ocean;*   10
> Those which the cold north gales oppress severely,
> Those which the dry heat of the furious south wind
> Scorches, as it bakes the burning sands of waste land.
>
> Here I pose the question: could that sovereign power
> Not have overturned the mad course of vicious Nero?   15
> Grievous, indeed, we must judge that bitter outcome,
> The unjust sword adding strength to savage poison!'

Chapter 7

1 'You yourself', I remarked, 'are aware that ambition for material
things had little or no influence with me; rather, I sought the
opportunity for public service so that virtue would not languish in
silence.'

2   'And yet', she observed, 'the one thing that can entice naturally
outstanding minds which have not put the finishing touches to
the perfection of their virtues is precisely the desire for glory and
the reputation for outstanding achievements in the service of the

state.* But this is how you must measure its triviality and total ₃ unimportance. As you have learnt from the proofs of the astronomers,* it is certain that the entire circumference of the earth is a mere pinprick when measured against the dimension of the heavens; in other words, if we compare the earth with the size of the heavenly sphere, it is seen to be utterly insignificant. And ₄ tiny as this region of ours is in the universe, only about a quarter of it is inhabited by living creatures known to us, as you have learnt from Ptolemy's demonstrations.* Then, if you mentally subtract ₅ from this quarter all the areas occupied by seas and marshlands, and also the huge tracts of land laid waste by drought, only the narrowest confines will barely remain for human occupation. So ₆ hemmed in and circumscribed as you are within this tiny microcosm of a microcosm, are your minds intent on publicizing your reputations and in glorifying your names? What renown and splendour can your fame possess when confined within such petty and restricted limits? Moreover this paddock, which serves as your ₇ modest dwelling-place, is inhabited by numerous nations which differ in their languages, customs, and manner of life, and because of difficulties of travel, varieties of language, and infrequency of trade, the fame not just of individual persons but even of cities cannot penetrate to them. Thus in the days of Marcus Tullius, as ₈ he himself points out in some passage,* the glory of the Roman state had not as yet reached beyond the mountain-range of the Caucasus, though by then Rome was at its zenith, inspiring fear in the Parthians and in the other nations of that region.

'So are you aware how confined and circumscribed is the fame ₉ which you struggle to extend and spread abroad? Do you imagine that any individual's repute will reach the regions where the glory of the Roman state cannot penetrate? Bear in mind as well the ₁₀ divergent characters and customs of different nations; what some of them regard as praiseworthy others condemn as punishable. So ₁₁ it is in no way in the interests of anyone who aspires to fair fame to see his name proclaimed among numerous nations. Each person ₁₂ must therefore settle for a reputation widespread among his fellow-citizens, and for that glorious immortality of fame to be restricted within the boundaries of a single nation.

'How many men, highly famed in their own day, have been ₁₃ expunged from our memory because the poverty of written

records has brought oblivion? And writings themselves are of little avail, for in the long run they and their authors are buried by the
14 passage of time. Yet you men imagine, as you contemplate your
15 future fame, that you are perpetuating your immortality. But if you address your minds to the boundless extent of eternity, what
16 reason have you to celebrate a lasting fame? Compare the length of a moment with the period of ten thousand years; the first, however minuscule, does exist as a fraction of the second. But that number of years, or any multiple of it that you may name, cannot even be
17 compared with a limitless extent of time, the reason being that comparisons can be drawn between finite things, but not between
18 finite and infinite. So fame which survives over any length of time, however extensive, if compared with unbounded eternity, is seen to be not just trifling but wholly non-existent.

19 'But your sole criterion of right behaviour is to bow to popular whim and gossip. You disregard the sovereign role of conscience and virtue, and demand your rewards from the common gossip
20 of others. Hear how one man made fun of the pettiness of such arrogance. He had roundly abused some fellow who had mendaciously assumed the title of philosopher, not to practise genuine virtue, but for arrogant self-esteem; and he added that he would at once know if the other were a true philosopher if he bore mildly and tolerantly insults heaped upon him. For a moment or two the other donned the mask of patience, and bowed before the insults. Then he sneered, and said: "So now at last do you realize that I am a philosopher?" Whereupon the first man bitingly answered: "I should have known it, if you had kept your mouth shut."*

21 'I refer now to outstanding individuals who seek glory through virtue. I ask you, what concern have they with reputation once
22 their bodies have relaxed in death? If on the one hand men's death spells total annihilation (though the arguments we advance forbid such belief), glory is wholly non-existent, since the one to whom it
23 is said to belong has passed from life. If on the other hand the mind is happily self-aware, is loosed from its earthly prison, and in freedom makes for heaven, it surely scorns all earthly business, and in the enjoyment of heaven rejoices at having been removed from things of earth.

'One who seeks fame, and nought but fame, with fierce intent,
    And thinks it of the utmost worth,
Should train his eyes upon the boundless firmament
    Then contemplate this puny earth.

He will feel chagrin that his wide celebrity   5
    Such narrow precincts fails to fill.
Why vainly seek, proud souls, to cheat mortality,
    Whose yoke your necks belabours still?

Although your glory through far distant nations goes,
    Where men's tongues celebrate your name,   10
And though your noble house with signal honours glows,
    Still, death despises such high fame.

Death lumps together lowly and high-born as one;
    She ranks the highest with the base.
Where are the bones of trusty Fabricius now gone?   15
    Brutus, stern Cato have no place.*

The meagre glory that outlives men marks you down
    As ciphers, in few letters read,
Does bare acquaintance with illustrious names alone
    Impart real knowledge of the dead?   20

So you men all lie buried, doomed to be unknown;
    No glory celebrates your name.
Should you believe extended life will surely dawn
    Through tidings of your earthly fame,
Mere lapse of time this expectation will dethrone.   25
    A second death waits you to claim.'

Chapter 8

'But I would not have you think that I am waging pitiless war 1
against Fortune. There comes a time when she does not deceive,
and thus deserves well of men—I mean when she manifests her
true self, removes her mask, and proclaims her ways. Perhaps you 2
do not yet grasp what I am saying. What I am eager to explain is
something remarkable, and in consequence I can scarcely find
words to express my meaning. My opinion in fact is that adverse 3
Fortune benefits people more than good, for whereas when good
Fortune seems to fawn on us, she invariably deceives us with the
appearance of happiness, adverse Fortune is always truthful, and

4 shows by her mutability that she is inconstant. The first deceives, the second instructs; the first, with her manifestation of deceitful blessings, shackles the minds of those who enjoy them, whereas the second frees them through making them realize the frailty of happiness. So one can see that the first is puffed up, inconstant, and ever lacking self-awareness; the second is sober, girt for action,
5 and wise through her handling of adversity itself. The result is that good Fortune with her enticements diverts men from the path of the true good, whereas adverse Fortune often yanks them back
6 with her hook to embrace true goods. You must surely believe that we are to regard it as no trivial blessing that this harsh and repulsive Fortune has laid bare the attitudes of friends loyal to you? She has separated those of your associates whose regard is unwavering from those who show ambivalence. On her departure,
7 she robbed you of her own kind, but left you with yours. How much would you have paid for this awareness when you were unscathed and in your own estimation blessed? Though now you lament the loss of your wealth, you have found your true friends, the most precious of all riches.*

'Why does the world with steadfast faith*
Harmonious changes put in train?
Why do the ever-warring seeds
Eternal treaties yet maintain?

Why does the sun in golden car   5
Inaugurate the rose-red day,
Appoint the moon to rule the night,
Once Hesperus* has led the way?

And greedy sea confine its waves
Within the boundaries it has set,   10
Forbidding the encroaching lands
Extend their coastlines further yet?

The power that constrains this chain
Of nature's orderings is Love.
Love governs lands and seas alike,   15
Love orders too the heavens above.*

Should Love once slacken its tight rein
And cease to order near and far,
The mutual love which all things show
Will in a moment turn to war.   20

With beauteous motions Nature's parts
In fond compact invigorate
The fabric of the universe,
Which else they'd strive to dissipate.

Such love embraces nations, too;   25
In hallowed pacts it them combines.
With chaste affections man and wife
In solemn wedlock it entwines.

Love's laws most trusty comrades bind.
How happy is the human race,   30
If Love, by which the heavens are ruled,
To rule men's minds is set in place!'

Book 3

Chapter 1

1 Philosophy had by now ended her song. As I listened eagerly, its sweetness had held me spellbound, and I remained dumbstruck with my ears still pricked, so it took me a moment to respond.

2 'You are indeed the greatest comfort for weary spirits,' I said. 'What refreshment you have brought me with the depth of your judgements and the sweetness of your songs! I no longer count myself unable to bear the future blows of Fortune. So far from dreading those remedies which you said would sting a little more, I am eager to hear them,* and I pressingly demand them.'

3 Then she replied: 'Yes, I became aware of that when you seized on my words so silently and hungrily. I anticipated this reaction from you, or to put it more truthfully, I myself elicited it. The medicines remaining for you to take are the kind which are bitter

4 on the tongue, but sweet when swallowed. As for your saying that you are keen to hear them, your enthusiasm would grow white-hot if you realized the goal to which I intend to lead you.'

'What goal is that?' I asked.

5 'The goal of true happiness,' she replied. 'You too dream of it, but your mind cannot focus on it because of the shadowy figures obtruding on your sight.'*

6 'Lead on, I beg you,' I said. 'Do not hesitate for a moment, but show me what true happiness is.'

7 'I shall do so,' she replied, 'and gladly, for your sake. But first I shall try to depict and express in words something more familiar to you, and once you have that in mind, you can turn your gaze in the other direction, and acknowledge the beauty of true happiness.'

> 'He who intends to sow* in virgin soil,
> Will first remove the brushwood with much toil,
> Brambles and ferns with scythe he will restrain;
> Thus Ceres enters, laden with fresh grain.

Sweeter tastes honey, labour of the bees,   5
If bitter flavour first the tongue displease.

More welcome is the stars' celestial gleam,
Once Notus' rainy tempests* cease to scream.

Day with its rosy horses dawns more bright,
Once Lucifer dispels the gloom of night.*   10

There is a moral here for you to learn:
Deceitful are the goods you first discern.
Withdraw your neck, and leave their yoke behind;
Then truth at once will infiltrate your mind.'

Chapter 2

Then Philosophy for a moment cast down her eyes. It was as   1
though she were retreating within the venerable abode of her mind
as she began.

'Mortal creatures have one overall concern. This they work at   2
by toiling over a whole range of pursuits, advancing on different
paths, but striving to attain the one goal of happiness.* This is the
good which once attained ensures that no one can aspire to
anything further. Indeed, it is the highest of all goods, and gathers   3
all goods within itself. If any good were lacking to it, it could not
be the highest good, since some desirable thing would be left
outside it. Thus it is clear that happiness is the state of perfection
achieved by the concentration of all goods within it. All mortals, as   4
I have said, strive to attain it by different paths; for this longing for
the true good is naturally implanted in human minds, but error
diverts them off course towards false goods.

Some believe that the highest good lies in going short of   5
nothing, so they strive to attain abundant riches. Others identify
it as the good most worthy to command respect, so they seek the
veneration of their fellow-citizens by attaining high position. Then   6
there are those who decide that the highest good lies in the
exercise of the greatest power, so they either aspire to the kingship
themselves, or seek close connections with those on the throne.
People who think that fame is a fine thing make haste to spread
abroad their name when it is celebrated in the arts of war or peace.
But the greatest number measure the benefit of a good by the joy   7

and delight it brings; they think it the height of blessedness to
8   wallow in pleasure. There is another category of person for whom
the aims and causes of these goods are interlocked. For example,
some aspire to riches for the power and pleasure they bring, while
others seek power to obtain money, or to make their name known.
9   So human acts and aspirations are centred in these and other
such goods. For example, renown and popular favour are seen to
confer a species of fame. A wife and children are sought for the
delight which they bring. The most sacred category of good, that
of friendship,* lies in the province of virtue rather than of
Fortune. The other kinds are cultivated to obtain power or
10 pleasure. As for the goods of the body, we see that they are
related to those I mentioned earlier, for strength and stature are
seen to lend power, beauty and fleetness of foot bring fame, and
11 good health makes for pleasure. Clearly what men seek in all these
goods is nothing but happiness, for each person reckons that what
he aims for above all else is the highest good. Now we have already
defined the highest good as happiness. So each and every one
envisages that state of happiness as that which he desires above all
others.
12 'So before your eyes are laid, so to say, the forms which human
happiness takes: riches, distinctions, power, fame, pleasures. By
pondering these and nothing else, Epicurus concluded* that for
him pleasure was the highest good, because it is to the mind that
13 all those other things seemingly bring delight. But I return to
those pursuits which men favour; though their memory is clouded,
their minds none the less are trying to rediscover their proper
good, but like a drunkard they do not recognize the path which
would bring them back home.*
14 'Take those who strive to go short of nothing: are they really
going astray? There is surely no condition capable of achieving
happiness to compare with an abundance of all possessions, for
this makes you wholly self-sufficient and independent of what
15 other people have. Again, are people wrong when they regard the
best as worthiest of venerable respect? By no means, for what
almost all men strive to acquire is not anything cheap or
16 despicable. And is not power to be numbered among the goods?
We are surely not to regard as weak and effete the quality generally
17 agreed to surpass all else. Again, is renown to be accounted

worthless? We cannot ignore the fact that it is the supremely
excellent that also wins the fairest fame.

'There is surely no need to stress that happiness knows no 18
trouble or melancholy, that it is exposed to no griefs or worries.
This is clear since even in the most insignificant things, men seek
to own and enjoy what they love. What they wish to acquire and 19
accordingly long for are riches, high positions, kingships, fame,
and pleasure; and the reason why they want them is because they
believe that these are the means by which they will gain self-
sufficiency, respect, power, renown, and joy. So in their differing 20
pursuits men seek what is good, and this readily indicates the
scope of nature's power; for though their aspirations vary and are
at odds with each other, all are at one in choosing the good as their
goal.

'It is my whim on pliant strings*
To hymn these themes in tuneful song:
The strength which potent Nature brings
To reins which guide the world along;
The laws by which her providence   5
Preserves the world's unbounded sphere;
How she enchains the elements
Enmeshed in bonds that must cohere.

Though Punic lions proudly wear*
Their handsome chains, accepting food   10
Which human hands for them prepare,
As cowed by their harsh lord, they brood,
Inured to bear his savage blows,
Yet pride, long dormant, then revives
Should blood besmear their bristly jaws.   15
Deep roars awake their earlier lives;
Constraining bonds they fiercely burst,
No halters now their necks engage;
With bloodstained teeth they mangle first
Their tamer, roused to furious rage.   20

The bird who whistled without end*
While she sat perched on branches high,
Now in a cage's depths is penned.
Though people sport with her, and vie
In fond devotion to provide   25
Cups smeared with honey, and rich fare,
Once she green-shaded groves has spied,

As she hops in her prison there,
Her food she spatters all around
And tramples it beneath her feet.   30
'The woods!' she whispers with sweet sound,
The woods alone she longs to greet.

A sapling bends its topknot low*
When downward dragged with might and main,
But should your hands their grip withdraw,   35
Its top looks up to heaven again.

Phoebus at evening takes his bath
And sinks below the western sea,
Then turns his car on hidden path
To rise with regularity.   40

All things in nature thus retrace
The paths acknowledged as their own;
They gladly then regain their base.
Assigned to them is this alone,
To seek as end their starting-place,   45
And make the world a stable zone.'*

Chapter 3

1 'You too as earth-bound creatures have a dreamlike notion,
however hazy, of your beginning,* and your gaze is trained on
that true end of happiness. It is by no means clear to you, but you
have some sort of conception of it. This is because a natural
tendency guides you towards it and towards the true good,
2 whereas manifold error draws you away from it. Put this question
to yourself: can men attain their destined end through the means
3 which they think will bring them happiness? If indeed money,
distinctions, and the rest are so productive that with them no good
seems to be lacking, I too must confess that some men achieve
4 happiness by acquiring them. But if those possessions cannot
realize their promise, and do not contain the greater number of
goods, it is surely crystal-clear that the appearance of happiness
which men see in them is false.

5   'So first I enquire of you as one who until recently possessed
abundance of riches: when you had all that money, was there never

a time when you were worried and disturbed in mind through some wrong you sustained?'

'I have to admit', I answered, 'that I cannot recall ever feeling 6 free from one worry or another.'

'And this was occasioned by the absence of something which 7 you wanted, or the presence of something which you did not want.'

'Just so,' I said.

'So you regretted the presence of the one, and the absence of the 8 other?'

'Yes,' I admitted.

'Now if a person longs for something,' she asked, 'is he short of it?' 9

'He is,' I said.

'And if he is short of something, he is not wholly self-sufficient?'

'He is far from it,' I answered.

'So in your own case you felt this lack in spite of your abundant 10 wealth?'

'Yes, of course,' I said.

'So wealth cannot free you from want, and make you self- 11 sufficient, in spite of its apparent promise to do so. Then there is a 12 further point which I think is especially worth considering: money of its nature has no means of preventing its being taken from its owner against his will.'

'I grant that,' I said.

'Of course you do, since every day some stronger person 13 extracts it from an unwilling victim; for what lies behind the grievances aired in court, except the attempt to recover money seized by force or fraud from people against their will?'

'True enough,' I remarked.

'So each and every one needs some external protection to keep 14 his money safe?'

'No one would deny that,' I said.

'Yet a man would not need such protection if he had no money 15 to lose?'

'That is undeniable,' I said.

'So the position is now reversed: the riches which people 16 thought made them self-sufficient compel them instead to require external protection. How then does wealth succeed in banishing 17

want? Rich men can surely go hungry, and experience thirst? And
don't people with money feel the winter cold in their bones?

18   'You will reply: "But wealthy people have the resources to
satisfy their hunger, to slake their thirst, and to ward off the cold."
True, want can be assuaged in this way by riches, but it cannot be
wholly dispelled, for it sits there with its mouth open, making
incessant demands, and even if it is gorged with riches, it must still
19   remain there, waiting to be satisfied. I need not mention that
nature demands very little, whereas greed is never satisfied. So if
riches cannot dispel want, and if indeed they create their own
need, why should you men imagine that they provide sufficiency?

> 'The miser may wax rich with streams of gold,*
> Unsatisfied, though hoarding wealth untold,
> His neck bent low with pearls from India's shore,*
> His rich fields ploughed by oxen, score on score.
> Yet gnawing care attends him all his days;   5
> At death his fickle wealth without him stays.'

Chapter 4

1   'It is true that public office bestows honour and respect on
incumbents, but do magistracies improve the minds of those
2   who hold them, by inculcating virtues and banishing vices? As a
matter of fact, such tenure of offices highlights rather than
removes depravity. Hence the resentment we feel that the most
depraved individuals have often attained them. So Catullus calls
Nonius an excrescence,* even though he occupied the curule
3   chair. Do you observe what deep disgrace attaches to the wicked
through their tenure of high positions? Their unworthiness would
be less glaring if they did not gain fame through such advance-
4   ment. I am sure that you yourself could never have been induced
to hold office with Decoratus,* once you became aware that he had
5   the mentality of a worthless man about town and informer. The
truth is that we cannot regard men as worthy of respect because of
6   the offices they hold, if we deem them unworthy of such offices. If
on the other hand you observe that a man is endowed with
wisdom, you could surely not regard him as unworthy of respect,
or of the wisdom with which he is endowed?'

'Of course not,' I replied.

'This is because virtue has a native worth which it at once 7 confers on those with whom it is associated. But honours bestowed 8 by the common folk cannot impart such worth, so clearly those distinctions do not have the splendour possessed by true worth.

'What is particularly notable here is this. If a man becomes 9 more contemptible the more he is despised by people at large, tenure of offices makes evil men even more worthless, because it cannot win respect for those whom it exposes to the public gaze. And the offices themselves suffer thereby, for wicked incumbents 10 make them like themselves, by defiling them with their own pollution.

'I would have you realize that the true respect I mentioned 11 cannot be won by these unsubstantial honours. So consider this case: suppose a man who had been consul several times chanced to visit uncivilized nations. Would his eminence win him respect 12 there among the barbarians? Yet if high position implanted such respect as a law of nature, it would not detract from the tenure of it amongst people anywhere, just as fire does not lose its heat wherever it is. But such respect is not a quality inherent in offices, 13 but rather is attached to them by the delusory beliefs of men; so when they journey abroad among people who do not regard them as distinctions of worth, the bubble is pricked there and then.

'This is the outcome among foreigners, but do those offices 14 endure for ever amongst the communities where they originated? Take the praetorship;* once it was a powerful office, but nowadays 15 it is an empty title, weighing heavily on the resources of senators. Again, once upon a time the person charged with the public corn-dole was held to be *magnus*, but today what meaner position is there?* As I remarked a moment ago, things which have no 16 inherent nobility at one time gain lustre, and at another lose it, according to the views of those who wield them.

'So if exalted positions cannot make men worthy of respect, 17 and if moreover they are tarnished through contagion with worthless men, if they lose their gloss with changes in the times and the world regards them as tawdry, what splendour worth seeking do they possess in themselves, let alone impart to their incumbents?

'Nero lived,* hated by all folk,
Savage, extravagant, and vain,
And though he strutted with disdain
In snowy pearls and crimson cloak,*

On hallowed senators he would heap   5
Inglorious offices of state.
So who would think those honours great,
When those who grant them are so cheap?'

Chapter 5

1 'But cannot kingships and intimacy with kings make men more
2 powerful? Surely this is so, since the happy life of kings persists
without end? Yet antiquity is full of examples, as is the present
age, of kings whose state of happiness was exchanged for disaster.*
How glorious, I suppose, is such power, when we find that it does
not succeed even in preserving itself!

3   'Let us assume, however, that the power which resides in
kingships does beget blessedness. Yet if it were lacking in some
respect, this would surely detract from that blessedness, and inflict
4 misery? Now however widely human empires extend, inevitably
there are further nations over which an individual king does not
5 govern. At that point, beyond which the power which makes men
happy ceases to extend, lack of power makes its presence felt,
which causes men to be wretched. In this sense, then, kings must
inevitably bear a greater share of misery.

6   'That tyrant who had experienced the dangers of his station
compared the fears felt by a king to the terror of a sword poised
7 overhead.* So what sort of power is it which cannot banish
gnawing anxieties, or avoid the stinging pricks of fears? Kings
themselves would prefer to live untroubled lives,* but this they
8 cannot do, so instead they boast of their power. But do you regard
as powerful the man whom you see aspiring to what he cannot
achieve? Do you pronounce him powerful when he is flanked by a
bodyguard, when his own fears outweigh those of his terror-
stricken subjects, and when the power he parades lies in the hands
of his menials?

9   'Need I adduce the cronies of kings, when I prove that kingship

itself embodies such frailty? Those friends often fall victim to the royal power, both when it is secure and when it is brought low. Nero forced his friend and tutor Seneca to choose his own form of death.* As for Papinian, who had long held sway among those at court, he was impaled by Antoninus on the swords of his own soldiers.* Yet both these men sought to renounce their power, and Seneca even tried to consign his wealth to Nero, and to seek a life of retirement. But neither man gained his wish, because the very weight of their position dragged them down to their destined fall. What sort of power, then, is it, when those who have it fear it, when even those who aspire to it are insecure, and when those eager to renounce it cannot escape it?

'As for those friends who are won over not by your merit but by your worldly success, do they shield you? No; the friend gained in prosperity will be a foe in time of misfortune.* And what plague does you more effective harm than a friend turned foe?

> 'If power is what you seek,*
> Then curb your fierce anger;
> Don't let lust be your master,
> Don't submit to its foul reins.
> Although remote India   5
> May quail at your dictates,
> Although furthest Thule*
> Is enslaved in your service,
> If black cares are not routed,*
> If sad plaints are not banished,   10
> Such impotence lacks power.'

Chapter 6

'As for glory, how often it deceives, and how worthless it is! So with justice the tragic poet cries out:

> O bubble reputation, countless men,
> Born as mere nothings, you have raised on high!*

For numbers of men have often emerged with high repute through the mistaken assessments of the mob. Can anything be imagined more disgraceful than that? Men falsely celebrated must themselves blush to hear their praises sung. Even if such praises were

3 gained on merit, how could they add to the wise man's self-awareness, seeing that he measures his worth not by common gossip, but by the truth of self-knowledge?

4   'Now if getting your name celebrated abroad seems desirable in itself, it follows that failure to have achieved this is adjudged
5 ignoble. But since, as I maintained a moment ago,* there must inevitably be many nations which a single individual's reputation cannot reach, the upshot is that the man you reckon to be famous
6 appears a nonentity in a neighbouring part of the world. In this connection, I consider mass popularity to be not even worthy of mention, for it does not proceed from ripe judgement, and never remains consistent.

7   'As for noble birth, surely everyone sees how empty and worthless that title is!* If it lays claim to renown, such renown belongs to another, for obviously noble birth is the species of
8 praise which derives from the status of one's parents. Now if praise brings fame, clearly the famous are those who win praise; so if you have no renown of your own, that which belongs to another
9 does not make you illustrious. If there *is* any good attached to noble birth, I think it resides in the obligation which rests on noblemen not to fall away from the excellence of their forbears.

> 'All men on earth from one source take their rise;*
> One Father of the world all things supplies.
> To Phoebus, rays; horns to the moon on high,
> To earth its men, as starlight to the sky.
> To lodge in bodies, souls from heaven He leads;   5
> All mortals thus are sprung from noble seeds.
> Why boast so loud of forbears and proud race?
> Reflect on your beginnings, and God's place
> As source of all. No man's bereft of worth,
> Save if through vices he betrays his birth.'   10

Chapter 7

1   'Need I speak of bodily pleasures, when the pursuit of them is full
2 of anxiety, and over-indulgence in them brings remorse? How grievous are the illnesses, and how hard to bear the pains which they frequently inflict on the body as reward, so to say, for the

wickedness of those who enjoy them! I boast no knowledge of the 3
delight which their impact brings, but whoever is willing to recall
his low inclinations will know that the outcome of pleasure is
melancholy. If such pleasures can make men blessed, there is no 4
reason why beasts of the field cannot likewise be called blessed, for
they devote themselves to speedy fulfilment of their bodily needs.*
Most honourable of all pleasures should be the joy which a wife 5
and children bring, yet the reality was mirrored all too truly when
it was said that someone had found that his children turned the
screw on him.* I need not remind you that you yourself have had
experience at other times, and are concerned now, with how much
the fortunes of your children gnaw at you, whatever their
situation. In this matter I approve the epigram of my dear protégé 6
Euripides, who remarked that the misfortune of the childless man
is a happy one.*

> 'All pleasures take this road:
> Those who indulge they goad.*
> Then, like the bees that swarm,*
> Having yielded honey's charm,
> They flee; but on the heart   5
> A lasting sting impart.'

Chapter 8

'Thus it is beyond doubt that these paths to happiness turn out to 1
be byways, and cannot guide a man to the goal that they promise.
Indeed, I shall point very briefly to the ills in which they are 2
enmeshed. What, then, is your choice? Will you seek to amass 3
money? In that case you will rob its owner. Or would you like to be
a luminary? You will go on your knees before the one who confers
positions, and in your longing to excel all others in status, you will
demean yourself by abject begging. Or is it power for which you 4
long? Then you will be exposed to the plotting of your subjects,
and dangers will overhang you. Or would glory be your aim? Then 5
you are beset by every sort of hardship, and you lose all peace of
mind. Or would you opt for a life of pleasure? But who would not 6
scorn and spurn one who was a slave to that most tawdry and frail
of things, the body?

7 'As for those who boast of their physical attributes, how mean and fragile is the possession on which they rely! Can you outmatch elephants in bulk, or bulls in strength? Can you surpass tigers* in

8 fleetness of foot? Contemplate the extent and the stability of the heavens, and then at last cease to admire worthless things. Even so, you should marvel at the heavens not so much for those

9 features as for the innate reason by which they are guided. By contrast, how short-lived is the sheen of the body's beauty,* how

10 transient, more ephemeral than blossoms in spring! If, to quote Aristotle,* men had the use of Lynceus' eyes, enabling them to see through solid obstacles, would not the celebrated physique of Alcibiades,* so very handsome on the surface, seem totally ugly once his inner parts came into view? So what makes you handsome is not your native appearance, but the weak eyes of those who gaze

11 at you. You men can put whatever inflated value you like on the blessings of the body, so long as you realize that this object of your admiration, such as it is, can be reduced to nothing by the mere onset of tertian fever.*

12 'All this can lead you briefly to conclude that since these things cannot produce the goods which they promise, nor attain perfection by the assemblage of all goods, they are not what one might call the paths which lead to blessedness, nor do they in themselves make men blessed.

'What ignorance, alas,* draws wretched men
　From treading the straight line?
Do you seek gold in verdant foliage, then,
　Or pluck gems from the vine?
Do you lay hidden nets on mountain peak,　　　　　5
　To crown your feast with fish?
Do you the deep Etruscan waters seek,
　To hunt goats as you wish?

Not so. Men even plumb those hidden caves
　Which in deep waters lie,　　　　　　　　　　10
Where snowy pearls abound beneath the waves,
　And purple murex-dye.*
Men know which shores the tender fish provide,
　Which prickly urchins* show,
But where the hidden goods they seek reside,　　15
　Blind, they care not to know.

> The good which lies beyond the star-decked sky
>   Sunk in the earth they seek;
> What condemnation apt for such stupidity,
>   What curses should I speak?   20
> For riches and high office let them strain
>   (Great labour this implies),
> Once these false goods they finally attain,
>   True goods then recognize.'

Chapter 9

'So far I have sketched the outline of false happiness, and on this I 1 will say no more. My next step is to indicate what true happiness is.'

'I do recognize,' I rejoined, 'that wealth cannot ensure suffi- 2 ciency, nor kingship power, nor high offices due respect, nor glory fair fame, nor pleasures joy.'

'And the reasons for this, have you grasped them as well?' 3

'I think that I have a sort of keyhole vision of them, but I would rather hear you state them more clearly.'

'The explanation is readily accessible. What in nature is simple 4 and undivided is split by human error, which diverts it from the true and perfect towards the false and imperfect. Do you believe that if something lacks nothing, it has no power?'

'Of course not,' I replied.

'You are right,' she said, 'for if a thing somehow lacks strength, 5 it must to that extent need the support of something else.'

'True enough,' I observed.

'And so sufficiency and power are by nature one and the same.' 6

'Yes. It seems so.'

'Now do you regard anything that falls into that category as 7 despicable, or is the opposite true, that it is of all things worthy of respect?'

'Most worthy, beyond a doubt.'

'So let us subjoin reverence to sufficiency and power, and thus 8 consider the three to be a unity.'

'Yes, indeed, for we are seeking to proclaim the truth.'

'Now do you think that this combination of qualities lies 9

10 hidden, and is something cheap, or does it stand out brightly with the fairest fame? You must reflect on this, in case what we acknowledged as short of nothing, and as most powerful and worthy of honour, seems to lack fame, being unable to confer it upon itself, and is accordingly to some extent more contemptible.'

11 'I am bound to admit,' I said, 'that its very nature ensures that it also obtains the greatest renown.'

12 'So it follows that we must declare fame to be identical with the previous three.'

'That is so,' I said.

13 'So if something lacks nothing outside itself, and can achieve everything by its own power, and commands both fame and respect, is it not beyond all doubt also supremely happy?'

14 'I cannot even imagine how any unhappiness can infiltrate itself into something like that, so I must grant that as long as those earlier qualities abide, it is full of happiness.'

15 'Now these considerations make it inevitable that though sufficiency, power, renown, respect, and pleasure are different terms, they do not differ at all in substance.'

'Yes, that conclusion must follow.'

16 'So what is one and simple by nature is fragmented by man's wrong-headedness. In his attempt to acquire a part of the thing which has no parts, he obtains neither a segment of it, for none exists independently, nor the whole, for which he has no desire whatever.'

17 'How does that come about?' I asked.

'The person who seeks riches to avoid poverty,' she replied, 'has no concern with power, chooses to live a tawdry and hidden existence, and also withdraws from the many pleasures of nature

18 so as to avoid the loss of the money he has gathered. But by acting in this way he fails to obtain even sufficiency, for power forsakes him, distress pricks him, tawdriness makes him contemptible, and obscurity keeps him out of sight.

19 'Again, the person whose sole aim is power, squanders his resources, despises pleasures and positions without power, and

20 attaches no importance to fame. You can realize how many things he forgoes, for on occasion he lacks life's necessities, he is gnawed by worries, and since he is unable to dispel them, he also ceases to attain the power which was his primary aim.

'One can reach similar conclusions about high positions, fame, 21 and pleasures. Since each and every one of these is identical with the rest, whoever seeks one of them independently of the others does not lay hold even of the things which he desires.'

'But what if someone were eager to attain the sum of them at the 22 same time?' I asked.

'True, he would be seeking the aggregate of happiness, but would he not fail to find it in those pursuits which we have shown do not confer what they promise?'

'He will certainly not find it there,' I agreed.   23

'So there is no way in which happiness is to be found in those pursuits which were believed individually to bestow desirable things.'

'I grant that,' I replied. 'No truer word could be spoken.'

'So now', she said, 'you are acquainted with both the form 24 which false happiness takes, and its causes. Now turn your mind's eye in the opposite direction, for at once you will see there the true happiness which I have promised.'

'But even a blind man can see it clearly,' I said. 'You 25 identified it a moment ago when you sought to clarify the false causes of it. If I am not mistaken, true and perfect 26 happiness is what makes a person self-sufficient, powerful, venerable, famous, and joyful. To help you realize that I have 27 inwardly digested this, I recognize without ambiguity that what can truly achieve any of these ends is total happiness, for all of them are one and the same.'

'My pupil,' she said, 'how blessed you are in promising that 28 belief, especially if you add just one thing!'

'What is that?' I asked.

'Of those mortal and transient things, do you think that there is 29 any which can endow such happiness?'

'In my view, certainly not,' I answered, 'and you have shown this so conclusively that no further demonstration is needed.'

'So such things seem to impart to mortals mere appearances of 30 the true good, or certain incomplete goods, but they cannot bestow the true and perfect good.'

'I agree,' I said.

'So now that you have acknowledged the nature of that true 31 happiness, and on the other hand those things which counterfeit happiness, it now remains for you to recognize the source from which you can seek the true happiness.'

'Yes, indeed,' I said. 'I have been eagerly awaiting this for some little time.'

32   'But since', she added, 'as my dear Plato maintains in his *Timaeus*,* support from heaven should be invoked even in the smallest matters, what do you propose that we do now, so that we may deserve to discover the abode of that supreme good?'

33   'We must invoke the Father of all things,' I replied, 'for if this were not done, we should not base our search on the appropriate first step.'

'Well said,' she replied. With that she hymned the following verses:

> 'Father of earth and sky,* You steer the world
> By reason everlasting. You bid time
> Progress from all eternity. Yourself
> Unshifting,* You impel all things to move.
> No cause outside Yourself made you give shape   5
> To fluid matter, for in You was set
> The form of the ungrudging highest good.*
> From heavenly patterns You derive all things.*
> Yourself most beautiful, You likewise bear
> In mind a world of beauty, and You shape   10
> Our world in like appearance. You command
> Its perfect parts, to form a perfect world.*
>
> Its elements You bind in harmony.*
> Dry cold with fluid flames closely conspires,
> So rarefied fire may not fly out above,   15
> Nor earth be dragged by weight to depths below.
> The soul which stirs all things You intertwine
> In threefold nature as its middle part;*
> You distribute it through harmonious limbs.
> The soul, thus split, then concentrates its course   20
> Within two orbits,* as it journeys back
> Upon itself, encircling the mind
> That lies deep down. The soul turns round the heavens,
> Which mirror in this way its very self.*
>
> Through causes of like nature You send forth   25
> Both human souls and those with lesser lives.*
> Installing them aloft in weightless cars,

You plant them through the heavens and on the earth.
Your genial law prompts them to turn to You,
To journey back when guided by their fire.   30

Let my mind rise to your august abode,*
And there, dear Lord, survey the source of good.
Then grant that, once I have attained the light,
My inward eye I may direct on You.
Disperse the fog and the encumbering weight   35
Of this earth's bulk, and shine forth, clear and bright;
For in the eyes of all devoted men,
You are calm brightness and the rest of peace.*
Men aim to see You as their starting-point,
Their guide, conductor, way, and final end.'*   40

Chapter 10

'So now that you have seen what is the shape of the imperfect   1
good, and also that of the perfect good, I think that I must now
show you the region in which the perfection of happiness is set.

'Any consideration of this must, I think, first investigate   2
whether any good of this kind, as defined by you a little earlier,
can exist in this world. We shall thus ensure that we are not
beguiled by some vacuous mental image which is remote from the
true reality lying before us. Now it cannot be denied that the   3
perfect good exists, and that it is, so to say, the source of all goods,
for everything said to be imperfect is so described because it is less
than perfect. The logical conclusion is that if in any class of   4
objects something imperfect appears, that class must also contain
something perfect; for if such perfection is removed, one cannot
even imagine how that which is called imperfect has come into
existence. The universe does not take its rise from things which   5
were curtailed or incomplete; rather, it issues from things which
are intact and fully developed, and it disintegrates into this parlous
and sterile world of ours.* Now if, as we demonstrated a little   6
earlier, there is what we may call imperfect happiness in a good
that is brittle, there can be no doubt of the existence of some
unalloyed and perfect happiness.'

'That conclusion,' I said, 'is as solid and as true as it can
possibly be.'

7　'Now as for the abode of that happiness,' she went on, 'ponder it in this way. The belief which human minds share demonstrates that God, the source of all things, is good; for since nothing better than God can be imagined,* who can doubt that if something has
8　no better, it is good? Reason in fact establishes that God's goodness is such as to demonstrate further that perfect good
9　resides within him. Were this not the case, he could not be the source of all things, for there would be something more pre-eminent, which would be in possession of perfect good, and would be seen to take precedence ahead of him, since all perfect things
10　clearly take precedence over things less complete. So to prevent the argument advancing into infinity, we must allow that the highest God is totally full of the highest and perfect good. Now we have established that the perfect good is true happiness, so true happiness must reside in the highest God.'

'I grant that,' I said. 'No possible counter-argument can be raised against it.'

11　'But do realize, I beg you,' she added, 'how solemn and sacrosanct is your approval of my statement that the highest God is entirely full of the highest good.'

'How do you mean?' I asked.

12　'Well, you are not to imagine that the Father of all that exists has either obtained from an external source that highest good with which he is said to be filled, or that he possesses it naturally in such a fashion as to make you think that the substance of happiness which is possessed is distinct from the substance of
13　God who possesses it. If you believe that he obtained it from outside, you could well think that what bestowed it was more pre-eminent than the recipient, whereas we must fittingly claim that he
14　is the most outstanding of all things. If on the other hand the highest good is naturally innate in him but logically distinct, an able thinker may pose the question, since we are claiming that God is the origin of all things: "But who combined these different
15　elements?" And finally, if something differs from something else, it is not identical with that from which we know it is different. So what is by nature different from the highest good is not the highest good. But this would be a sacrilegious thought to entertain about God, seeing that all agree that nothing is more outstanding than he
16　is.* For since there is absolutely nothing whose nature is superior

to the source from which it comes, I make bold to conclude with infallible reasoning that the origin of all things is in its own substance the highest good.'

'You are absolutely right,' I said.

'But we have already conceded that the highest good is 17 happiness.'

'Indeed we have,' I replied.

'And so,' she said, 'we must acknowledge that God is happiness itself.'

'I cannot refute your earlier assertions', I said, 'and I do see that this rider necessarily follows.'

'Now consider,' she added, 'whether the same conclusion is also 18 reached even more demonstrably from this: there cannot be two highest goods which differ from each other. Indeed, it is clear that 19 if two goods differ, the one is not the other, and accordingly neither can possibly be perfect, since each lacks the other. Now clearly if something is not perfect, it is not the highest. So it is 20 totally impossible for highest goods to differ from each other. But we have concluded that both happiness and God are the highest good, so the highest divinity must itself be the highest happiness.'

'No possible conclusion', I said, 'could be truer in fact, surer in 21 logic, or worthier of God.'

'Then too', she said, 'I shall follow the example of the 22 geometricians who often add riders (they call them *porismata*)* to theorems which they have proved. Like them I shall present you 23 with this corollary: since men become happy by achieving happiness, and happiness is itself divinity, clearly they become happy by attaining divinity. Now just as men become just by 24 acquiring justice, and wise by acquiring wisdom, so by the same argument they must become gods once they have acquired divinity. Hence every happy person is God; God is by nature 25 one only, but nothing prevents the greatest possible number from sharing in that divinity.'*

'What a beautiful and valuable observation that is,' I said, 26 'Whether you prefer to call it a *porisma* or a corollary!'

'But nothing is more beautiful than a further conclusion, which 27 reason advocates must be appended to what went before.'

'What conclusion?' I asked.

'Now that happiness is seen to embrace many things,' she asked, 28 'do all of them combine to form a single body of happiness with some variation in its parts, or is there some one thing among them which embodies the whole substance of happiness, to which the rest are related?'

29   'Perhaps you could clarify the matter', I rejoined, 'by citing those other things.'

'Have we not pronounced happiness to be a good?' she asked.

'Indeed we have,' I replied. 'The highest good.'

30   'You can complement all of them with happiness,' she said, 'for happiness is regarded also as the highest sufficiency, the highest
31   power, the highest respect, and renown, and pleasure. So are all these things—the good, sufficiency, power, and the rest—limbs, so to say, of the body of happiness, or are they all associated with it, with the good leading them?'

32   'I understand', I replied, 'what you are proposing for enquiry, but I am eager to hear your own solution to it.'

33   'Then take note of the distinction to be made here. If all those things were limbs of the body of happiness, they would also differ from each other, for while the parts comprise one body, they are
34   by nature different. But all those qualities we mentioned have been shown to be identical with each other, and therefore they are certainly not limbs of a body, for otherwise happiness would be seen to be a combination of a single limb, which is an impossibility.'

35   'That is certainly beyond doubt,' I rejoined. 'But I am keen to hear the rest of what you have to say.'

36   'In fact it is clear that the other qualities are associated with the good. Sufficiency is sought because it is thought to be a good, and the same inference can be made about respect, and fame, and
37   pleasure. So the good is the sum and cause of all that should be sought, for if a thing contains no good either in reality or in
38   appearance, in no way can it be sought after. And contrariwise, even things not good by nature are sought out as genuinely good so long as they appear to be so. The conclusion is that goodness is rightly considered to be the sum of all things worth pursuing, the hinge on which they turn, and the reason why they are sought.

39   'What men desire most of all when they seek something is that which motivates their action. For example, if a man goes in for horsemanship in the interests of his health, it is not so much the

equestrian exercise which he seeks as the resultant physical well-being. And so, since all things are sought to obtain the good, what all men desire is the good itself rather than the things which men seek. But we have already agreed that happiness is the reason for desiring all other things, and this makes it crystal-clear that the substance of happiness and of the good itself is one and the same.' 40 41 42

'I cannot see why anyone would disagree with that.'

'But we have shown that God and true happiness are one and the same.' 43

'We have indeed,' I said.

'Therefore we can safely conclude that God's substance too lies in the good itself, and nowhere else.

'All captives, shackled in your wanton chains
By lusts which dupe the minds which they invest,
Come, journey here, where peace from toil obtains,
The haven which abides in tranquil rest,
Sole refuge which for wretched souls remains.* 5

Green emeralds and pearls with snowy gleam
—Mixed yield of Tagus from its golden sand,
From Hermus' ruddy banks, from Indus' stream
Which borders on the equator's torrid land—
Such do not light men's sight, nor eyes redeem; 10
In deeper darkness, blind in mind, men stand.*

The pleasures that men's minds are roused to love
Are nourished by the earth in caverns deep;
The guiding light which powers the realm above
Sees nothing of the soul's dark fall so steep. 15

If you can once set eyes on that blest light,
You'll then deny that Phoebus' rays are bright.'

Chapter 11

'I agree with that,' I said, 'for your entire discourse holds fast, linked together with the strongest of arguments.' 1

Thereupon she asked: 'What value will you place on it once you grasp what the good itself is?' 2

'A value beyond measure,' I replied, 'for then it will be my fortune to know God as well, for he is the good.' 3

4   'I mean to make this clear with the most valid reasoning', she
said, 'so long as the conclusions reached a moment ago hold good.'
     'They will do so,' I said.

5   'Did we not show,' she went on, 'that the things sought by most
men were not true and perfect goods, for the reason that they
differed from each other? And since each lacks what the next one
has, it could not confer the full and absolute good? And that the
true good emerges when those aims are gathered into a single
shape, so to say, and effective force, so that sufficiency is identical
with power, renown, and pleasure? And indeed unless all are one
and the same, they have no claim to be counted among things
worth seeking?'

6   'Yes,' I said, 'that has been proved, and cannot possibly be
doubted.'

7   'So things which when separate from each other are remote
from the good, but which begin to be good once they become one
and the same, attain goodness by the acquisition of unity?'
     'It seems so,' I said.

8   'Now do you grant that everything good is good by sharing in
the good,* or do you totally reject this?'
     'It is as you say.'

9   'So on the same grounds you must allow that the one and the
good are the same,* for things which in the course of nature do not
differ in their outcome are the same substance.'
     'I cannot gainsay that,' I said.

10   'So you are aware', she continued, 'that everything that exists
continues to remain in being as long as it is a unity, and that it
perishes and breaks up when it ceases to be one?'
     'How so?' I asked.

11   'Take the case of living creatures,' she said. 'When soul and
body unite and continue to exist, men call this a living being; but
when its unity is dissolved by the separation of the two, it clearly
12   dies, and is no longer a living being.* Then too as long as the body
itself survives in the one shape with its limbs united, it is regarded
as a human figure; but if its parts become scattered and separated,
and thus split the body's unity apart, it ceases to be what it had
13   been. It will likewise be absolutely obvious to a person who
observes other objects that each and every one continues to exist
as long as it is a unity, but perishes as soon as it ceases to be one.'

'The more examples that occur to me,' I said, 'the more the principle seems to be exactly the same.'

'Now is there anything', she asked, 'which in the course of its 14 natural behaviour abandons its zest for living, and longs to embrace death and corruption?'

'If I think of living creatures', I replied, 'which possess some 15 natural faculty of choice and rejection, I cannot envisage any situation such as induces them, as long as no external pressures are put on them, to abandon their efforts to remain alive, and to hasten voluntarily to their own destruction. For each and every 16 living creature struggles to maintain its safety, and to avoid death and destruction.* But I am considerably hesitant to express any 17 opinion about plants and trees, or about inanimate things in general.'

'But', she said, 'there is no reason for possible doubt about them 18 either; for to begin with you notice that plants and trees grow in places that suit them,* so that there, in so far as their nature allows, they can avoid soon withering and dying. Some sprout on 19 plains, others on mountains; some grow in fens, others cling to rocks; others again grow in profusion in barren sand, and these would wither away if anyone tried to transplant them elsewhere. Nature in fact dispenses what is appropriate to each, and takes 20 pains to ensure that they do not die for so long as they can possibly survive.

'Then again, don't they all thrust their mouths, so to speak, into 21 the earth, imbibe nourishment through their roots, and dispense energy throughout their pith and bark?* Are not the softest parts 22 such as the pith always kept shielded inside under a tough outer covering of wood, while at the very outside the bark confronts inclement weather, like a champion bearing the brunt of harsh attacks? Think, too, how attentive nature is in ensuring that all 23 plant life is reproduced by the proliferation of seed.* Can anyone 24 fail to be aware that all these means are devices, so to say, for ensuring not merely their temporary survival species by species, but also their virtually permanent existence?

'As for objects considered inanimate, do not all of them too in 25 like fashion seek what belongs to them? Why is fire borne upwards 26 by its lightness, and earth forced downwards* by its weight, if not that such locations and movements are appropriate for each?

27 Moreover, each individual thing is kept in being by what is suited
28 to it, whereas hostile elements destroy it. Hard objects such as
stones cling most tenaciously to their component parts, and resist
29 easy fragmentation, whereas fluid elements such as air and water
readily yield to agents which separate them, but then rapidly
coalesce with the parts from which they have been sundered; and
as for fire, it escapes all division.

30   'Here we are discussing not voluntary movements of the
conscious soul, but the thrust of nature; for example, unthinking
31 digestion of foodstuffs, or unconscious breathing in sleep. Even in
living creatures desire for survival stems not from repeated
32 decisions of the soul, but from nature's basic instincts. Often
compelling circumstances prompt the will to embrace the death
which nature greatly fears, and on the other hand, the will from
time to time restrains the act of procreation, by which alone the
continued existence of mortal things persists, whereas nature
33 always craves it. In this sense the love of self proceeds not from
the soul's prompting, but from natural instinct, for Providence has
endowed the objects of her creation with what is the greatest
incentive to survive, namely the natural desire to go on living for
34 as long as possible. So there is no possible ground for you to doubt
that all existing things naturally seek stable survival, and avoid
destruction.'

35   'I admit', I said, 'that I now regard as beyond doubt what for
long has seemed uncertain to me.'

36   'Now what strives to exist and to survive', she went on, 'desires
to be a unity, for if such unity is dissolved, the very existence of
anything will not continue.'
        'True enough,' I said.

37   'So all things long for unity,' she added.
        'Yes,' I said.
        'But we have demonstrated that unity is identical with the
good.'
        'We have indeed,' I said.

38   'So all things seek the good, and you can define the good as that
which is desired by all things.'*

39   'No truer concept can be formulated,' I said, 'for either all
things have no connection with any single thing, and without unity
at their head, as one might put it, they are left stranded to flounder

aimlessly without a guide; or alternatively, if there is any one thing towards which all things hasten to make their way, this will be the highest of all goods.'

'My pupil,' said she, 'how happy this makes me! You have 40 implanted in your mind the signpost to the very centre of truth. And this has brought home to you the point which a little earlier you said you did not know.'*

'What was that?' I asked.

'The end of all things,' she replied. 'It is surely that which is 41 desired by all, and because we have concluded that this is the good, we must now proclaim that the end of all things is the good.

> 'He who with deep reflection tracks the truth,*
> Determined not to stray along false paths,
> Must turn the beam of his mind's eye within,
> Compel his far-flung thoughts to circle home,
> Must draw his mind away from search abroad   5
> To lodge it in its treasure-house within.
> Then what the cloud of error has long hid
> Will shine more brilliantly than Phoebus' rays.
>
> The body's weight imparts forgetfulness,*
> Yet does not banish all light from the mind.   10
> For sure a spark of truth holds fast within,
> Which learning fans and coaxes into flame.
> Or how, when challenged, could you answer true,
> If embers were not lodged deep in your hearts?
> Indeed, if Plato's Muse sounds forth the truth,   15
> What each man learns, forgetful he recalls.'*

Chapter 12

At this point I said: 'With Plato I emphatically agree. Your 1 reminder has brought these things home to me for a second time. To begin with, the contamination of the body made me lose my memory, and thereafter I lost it again when I was downcast with the weight of grief.'

She then observed: 'If you reconsider what we earlier agreed, 2 you will not be far from recalling what some little time ago you confessed that you did not know.'

'What was that?' I asked.

3   'The controls', she replied, 'which govern the universe.'

'I do remember', I said, 'that I confessed my ignorance. But now, though I have some inkling of your explanation, I should like to hear it more clearly from your lips.'

4   'A little while ago', she remarked, 'you thought it wholly beyond doubt that the universe is governed by God.'

'Indeed,' said I, 'I regard this as beyond doubt at this moment, and it will always be my belief. Let me explain briefly the grounds
5   on which I reached this conclusion. Since the universe is composed of such varied and opposing parts,* it could never have merged into a unified pattern if one individual had not joined
6   the diverse parts together. Moreover, when combined, these diverse natures at such odds with each other would split and tear themselves apart unless there were one individual to hold
7   together what he has interlinked. Indeed, the pattern in nature could not maintain itself, and its parts could not preserve such orderly progression in their locations, their timing, their effects, the distance between them, and their characteristics, if there were not one individual to order this range of changes while remaining
8   fixed himself. Whatever causes created things to remain in being and in motion I call God, the conventional term which all men use.'

9   Then she said: 'Since this is how you feel, I think that little remains for me to do to ensure that you return in safety and
10   happiness to your homeland. But let us examine the arguments which we have mounted. Did we not bracket sufficiency with happiness, and did we not agree that God is happiness itself?'

'We did indeed.'

11   'So to control the universe he will require no external aids, for if he was short of anything, he would not possess full sufficiency.'

'Inevitably so,' I answered.

12   'So God orders all things through himself alone?'*

'That is undeniable,' I replied.

13   'Now God, as was demonstrated, is the good itself.'

'So I recall,' I said.

14   'So he orders all things through the good, since we have agreed that he is the good and he governs all things through himself. He is, so to say, the helm or rudder by which the frame of the universe is held steady and remains undamaged.'

'I emphatically agree,' I said, 'and a moment ago I was 15 anticipating what you were about to say, though my suppositions were vague.'

'I believe you,' she said, 'for as I see it you are now focusing 16 your eyes more keenly to discern the truth. But what I am going on to say will be just as obvious to you.'

'What is that?' I asked.

'Since God', she resumed, 'is rightly believed to steer all created 17 things with the rudder of the good, and since all these same things, as my teaching has shown, surge by natural instinct towards the good, it is surely beyond doubt that they submit willingly to guidance, and that of their own accord they accede to the will of him who orders them, being compliant and submissive to their ruler.'

'That must be so,' I said, 'for such a dispensation, if indeed it 18 were a yoke borne by unwilling subjects rather than a guarantee of the welfare of compliant ones, would appear to be an unhappy one.'

'So nothing which conforms with its own nature tries to oppose 19 God?'

'Nothing at all,' I said.

'And if such an attempt were made,' she went on, 'would it have 20 any success, do you think, in the face of the one who we agreed is most powerful in his blessedness?'

'It would have absolutely no success,' I replied.

'So there is nothing which would either seek or be able to 21 obstruct the highest good?'

'I do not think there is,' I replied.

'So God is the highest good which governs all things power- 22 fully, and orders them sweetly.'*

Then I remarked: 'What gives me such pleasure is not just the 23 way your arguments have turned out, but much more the words you employed to express them. Now at last I am ashamed of the stupidity which has inflicted such wounds on me.'

'One of the stories', she said, 'with which you are familiar tells 24 of the Giants who laid siege to heaven;* appropriately enough, they too were put in their place by a kindly but firm hand. Now 25 how about making the arguments themselves collide head on? Perhaps such a clash will cause a splendid spark of truth to fly out.'*

'Then proceed at your discretion,' I said.

26 'Surely no one doubts', said she, 'that God has power over all things?'

'There is not a man Jack in his right mind', I replied, 'who could possibly doubt it.'

27 'Now if someone has power over all things', she added, 'there is nothing that he cannot do?'

'Nothing at all,' I said.

28 'But God cannot commit evil, can he?'

'Certainly not,' I replied.

29 'And so evil is a nothing, for there is nothing that he cannot do, but he cannot commit evil.'*

30 'Are you making sport with me?' I asked. 'You are weaving a labyrinth of arguments from which I cannot find my way out. At one moment you go in where you intend to come out, and at another you come out where you intend to go in. Or are you

31 weaving some fantastic circle of divine simplicity? A moment ago you began with happiness, stating that it was the highest good, and

32 you said that it was situated in the highest God. In your discourse you maintained that God himself is both the highest good and total happiness; in the course of this you offered as a kindly concession the view that no person would attain happiness without

33 likewise becoming divine. You further stated that the form of the good itself was the substance of God and of happiness, and you taught that unity itself was identical with the good sought by the

34 whole of creation. You also argued that God governs the entire universe with the rudder of the good, that all things willingly obey

35 him, and that evil has no existence in the world. These arguments you advanced without adducing any external authority; rather, you drew on the internal proofs proper to our discipline,* each deriving its credibility from its predecessor.'

36 Then Philosophy said: 'This is no game we are playing; far from it. Through the kindness of God, to whom we prayed a little while

37 ago, we have dealt with the issue which is the greatest of all. The form of the divine substance is such that it is not diffused into things outside itself, nor does it admit anything itself from outside. As Parmenides describes it,

'Tis like the substance of a perfect rounded sphere,*

rotating the mobile sphere of the universe, while maintaining its own immobility.

'You need not be surprised if we have mounted arguments not 38 adduced from outside, but set within the boundaries of our subject, for you have learnt from Plato's prescription that the language we use must be germane to the topics under discussion.*

> 'How blest is he who could discern
> The bright source of the good,*
> How blest, for he could slip the chains
> Of earth, which weigh men down!
>
> Of old, the Thracian poet mourned   5
> His wife's unhappy death;*
> His tearful lays had earlier
> Forced woods to shift at speed;
> Made streams to linger in their course;
> Caused hinds to show no fear   10
> As with fierce lions they bedded down;
> The hare was not afraid
> On sighting the oncoming hound
> Which Orpheus' song had soothed.
>
> But now a fiercer flaming fire   15
> Burned in the poet's breast;
> The measures that subdued all else
> Could not assuage their lord.
> With plaints against the cruel gods,
> He visited hell's halls;   20
> In harmony on sounding strings
> He sang alluring songs;
> His goddess-mother's noble springs*
> Inspired his utterance.
> So did his sorrow unconfined,   25
> And love redoubling grief.
> He stirred the cave of Taenarus*
> With tears and his sweet pleas,
> Imploring mercy from the lords
> Of shadowy realms below.   30
>
> The three-formed guardian* of the gate
> Was lulled by this new song.
> The goddesses who take revenge
> On human wickedness
> By terrorizing guilty men   35
> Bedewed their cheeks in grief.*

No longer did the spinning wheel
Whirl Ixion's head around,
And Tantalus, long dogged by thirst,
Rebuffed the inviting stream.   40
The vulture took his fill of song,
And Tityus' liver forsook.*

At last the ruler of the shades
In pity cried: "He wins!*
That spouse on husband we bestow,   45
His comrade bought by song.
But this condition must obtain,
This law confines our gift:
Until he quits the realm of hell
He must not turn his gaze."   50

Yet who for lovers can prescribe?*
Love has its greater law.
Alas, his dear Eurydice
Quitting Night's boundary
Orpheus beheld, lost, was undone.   55
This tale is meet for you
Who purpose to direct your minds
Up to the day above.
For he who, conquered, turns his eye
Into hell's cave below,   60
Forfeits such merit as he won,
By gazing on the dead.'

Book 4

Chapter 1

Philosophy, still wearing that dignified and serious expression, had 1 just ended this gentle and sweet song, and was rehearsing some further words when I cut her short, for I had not yet forgotten my deep-seated sense of grief. I said: 'Lady, you are our guide to the 2 true light, and your earlier injunctions have clearly emerged as both divine considered in themselves, and beyond dispute by reason of your arguments. Though resentment at the injury I suffered made me forget your observations of late, they were not wholly unknown to me earlier. But the consuming cause of my 3 depression is this, that in spite of the existence of a good ruler over the world, it is at all possible for evils to exist, or to go unpunished. You surely concede that this fact alone merits considerable astonishment, but it leads on to a greater problem: since wicked- 4 ness rules and flourishes, virtue not only goes unrewarded, but is also subservient, trodden underfoot by the feet of criminals, and pays the penalty which crimes should pay. That this should 5 happen when a God reigns who is omniscient and omnipotent, and who wills only the good, must cause boundless surprise and complaint from all.'*

She replied: 'Indeed, it would be a source of astonishment 6 beyond measure, more grisly than any portent, if your suggestion were correct that in the carefully ordered house of so powerful a master, worthless vessels were tended while valuable ones lay neglected.* But such is not the case; for if the conclusions which 7 we have just reached remain valid and are not uprooted, you will realize on the authority of him of whose kingdom we now speak that the powerful men are in fact always the good, while the wicked are always the abject and the weak; that vices never go unpunished, nor virtues unrewarded; that the good always achieve success, and the wicked suffer misfortune.* There are many such

considerations which will lay your complaints at rest, and establish
8 you on firm foundations. Now since through my earlier instruction
you glimpsed the shape of true blessedness, and further recognized where it lies, once I have run through all the preliminaries
which I think are necessary, I shall show you the way which will
9 bring you back home. I shall also equip your mind with wings to
enable it to soar upward. In this way you can shrug off your
anxiety, and under my guidance, along my path, and in my
conveyance you can return safely to your native land.

'For I have wings equipped to fly
Up to the high vault of the sky.*
Once these are harnessed, your swift mind
Views earth with loathing, far behind;
Climbs through the sphere of boundless air,   5
Surveys the clouds below it there;
Up through the sphere of fire can go,*
Ablaze with aether's supple flow;
Then to the starry halls can run,
Merge with the pathways to the sun,   10
Or join the frozen Ancient's car
As escort for the fiery star;*
Or stellar orbit* retraverse,
Where glints of dappled night disperse.

Then, with your journeying replete,   15
Your mind must quit the topmost seat,*
Swift Aether's frame below depress,
Then venerable Light possess.
The Lord of kings here sceptre wields,
Reins ruling all to none he yields.   20
The whole world's gleaming arbiter,
Himself unmoved, guides that swift car.*

If to this place you can return
For which forgetfully you yearn,*
"I mind my native land," you'll say,   25
"My origin. Here shall I stay."
But should it be your wish to find
Benighted earth now left behind,
Tyrants you'll see in exile there,*
Whose frowns the wretched nations fear.'   30

Chapter 2

At this I exclaimed: 'My goodness, what giant promises you make! 1
I don't doubt that you can redeem them, but now that you have
excited me, don't keep me waiting!

'Well then,' said she, 'the first thing you will be able to grasp is 2
that power always lies with the good, whereas all strength forsakes
the wicked;* the one thesis is the corollary of the other. For since 3
good and evil are opposites, once it is agreed that the good is
powerful, the weakness of evil becomes clear. If on the one hand
evil emerges as feeble, the strength of good is obvious. But to 4
ensure that your confidence in my argument is more overwhelm-
ing, I shall develop it on both fronts, and thus make good my
assertions from the two sides alternately.

'The outcome of human actions is entirely dependent on two 5
things, will and capability.* If one of these two is absent,
nothing can be accomplished. For if the will is lacking, people 6
do not even embark on action which they have no wish to carry
out; on the other hand, if they are incapable of doing it, it is vain
to will it. It follows from this that if you observed someone 7
wanting to acquire something but totally failing to get it, you can
be certain that what he lacked was the ability to attain what he
desired.'

'That is obvious', I said, 'and indeed wholly undeniable.'

'As for the man who you see has achieved his wish, you will 8
surely be convinced that he had the capability?'

'Absolutely,' I replied.

'In fact we must account each person strong in what he can 9
achieve, and weak in what he cannot.'

'I agree,' I said.

'You do remember', she went on, 'that our conclusion from our 10
previous arguments was that the entire thrust of the human will as
directed to various pursuits is to hasten towards happiness?'*

'Yes, I recall that this was established as well,' I replied.

'And do you not remember that happiness is the good itself, and 11
that all men desire the good when happiness is their aim?'

'Remembering is not the right word,' I said. 'I have that firmly
fixed in the forefront of my mind.'

12 'So all men, good and bad alike, strive with identical effort to attain the good?'

'Yes, that follows,' I said.

13 'Now it is clear that men become good by acquiring the good?'

'Yes, that is sure.'

'So good men attain what they go after?'

'It seems so.'

14 'Now if evil men were to attain the good which they seek, they would not be evil.'

'That is the case.'

15 'So since both seek the good, but good men attain it while evil men certainly do not, can there be any doubt that good men have capability, whereas evil men are weak?'

16 'If anyone does doubt it', I observed, 'he cannot be looking at reality, nor at the outcome of the arguments.'

17 She went on: 'Then again, imagine that the two men are addressing the same natural objective. One successfully completes it while fulfilling his natural role; the other is utterly unable to exercise that role, but against his nature he imitates the one who has attained the objective, rather than implements it himself. Which of the two do you regard as the stronger?'

18 'I can hazard what you are getting at', I said, 'but I should like to hear the point put more clearly.'

19 'I take it', she said, 'that you will not deny that the process of walking is natural to humans?'

'Of course not,' I replied.

20 'Nor do you doubt that such is the natural role of the feet?'

'That too I accept,' I said.

21 'So if one person capable of proceeding on foot were to walk, but another lacking this natural faculty of using his feet tried to walk by resting on his hands,* which of the two can rightfully be regarded as the stronger?'

22 'Continue with what follows,' I said. 'No one could possibly doubt that a person able to exercise his natural faculties is stronger than the one who cannot.'

23 'Now the highest good is the aim of good and evil men alike, but good men seek it by natural exercise of the virtues, whereas evil men try to acquire it through desires of one kind or another, and

not through the natural faculty of attaining the good. Or do you disagree?'

'Certainly not,' I said, 'and indeed the conclusion from this is 24 obvious as well: the arguments which I have accepted necessarily establish that good men are powerful, but evil men weak.'

'You do well to anticipate,' she said. 'Doctors are often 25 optimistic that this is the mark of a constitution now restored and resistant.

'Since I see that you are most eager to grasp this issue, I shall 26 assemble the arguments thick and fast. Notice, then, how blatant is the weakness of men who are corrupt. They cannot even attain the end to which their natural instinct leads and virtually frogmarches them. So how would they fare if they were abandoned by this 27 potent aid of nature's guidance, which is virtually invincible? Reflect too on the crippling paralysis which grips the wicked. The 28 rewards which they seek but fail to grasp and hold are "no paltry and playground prizes".* They fail in their quest for the supreme crown of reality, for the wretched creatures do not succeed in attaining that outcome for which alone they struggle day and night, whereas the power of good men is conspicuous in this respect. The person you would regard as the accomplished hiker is 29 he who by making his way on foot could reach the point at which further progress was impossible; similarly you must concede full power to him who attains the goal of the desirable ends beyond which lies nothing further. And the converse follows, that those 30 who wholly fail to attain this end are clearly bereft of all power. Why is it that they abandon virtue and pursue vices? Is it because 31 they do not recognize things that are good? If so, what is more effete than the blindness of ignorance? Or are they aware of what they should pursue, and lust sends them helter-skelter sideways off the path? In that case too lack of self-control makes them frail, and they cannot wrestle with vice. Or do they abandon the good 32 and turn to vice wilfully and in full knowledge?* If that is the case, they cease not just to be powerful, but to exist at all, for people who abandon the goal which all existing things have in common likewise cease to exist.

'This claim of ours may perhaps sound surprising to some, that 33 wicked men, who form the majority of mankind, do not exist, but that is the actuality. I am not denying that evil men are evil, but I 34

am claiming that in the pure and simple sense they do not exist.
35 You could say that a corpse is a dead man, but you could not call it
a man pure and simple; in the same way, I grant that corrupt men
are wicked, but I refuse to admit that they exist in an absolute
36 sense. Whatever maintains its due order and preserves its nature,
exists; if it abandons its nature, it ceases also to exist, for its
existence is bound up in its nature.

37   'But evil men, you will say, have power. I would not deny this
myself, but their power stems not from their strength but from
38 their weakness; for they can perform evil things, whereas had they
been able to continue doing good things, they could certainly not
39 have performed evil ones. The capability which they do have
shows more clearly that they have no power; for if, as we
concluded a little earlier, evil is nothing, it is obvious that
wicked men have no power, because they can perform only evil
deeds.'

'Yes, that is clear.'

40   'Now I would have you understand the thrust of this ability of
theirs. A short while ago we laid it down that nothing is more
powerful than the highest good.'

'Indeed we did,' I said.

'But the highest good', she went on, 'cannot achieve evil.'

'It certainly cannot.'

41   'So is there anyone,' she asked, 'who imagines that men are
omnipotent?'

'Only a madman could think that!' I replied.

'Yet men can do evil.'

'Yes,' I said, 'and I only wish they could not!'

42   'So since he who has control over good things can do all things,
whereas those who control evil things cannot do everything, it is
43 clear that those who can do evil things are less powerful. In
addition, we have demonstrated that all power is to be reckoned
among desirable things, and all desirable things are related to the
44 good as to the high point of their nature. But the capacity to wreak
evil cannot be related to the good, and so is not something to be
desired. Yet all power is desirable, so it is clear that capacity for
evil is not power.

45   'All this makes plain the power of good men, and puts beyond
doubt the weakness of evil men. The truth of that saying of

Plato's* becomes clear: only the wise can implement their desires, and wicked men can follow their inclinations but cannot fulfil their longings. They do what they like in the belief that they will 46 achieve the good which they desire by means of the things which give them pleasure. But they fail totally to attain the good, because shameful deeds are not conducive to happiness.

'You see kings seated high on lofty thrones,*
In gleaming purple bright, fenced by grim arms,
Speechless with rage, threats on their louring brows.
Draw back this veil of arrogant, empty show,
Then see close chains which bind the lords within. 5
Lust with its poisonous greed excites their hearts;
Wild anger whips up storm-waves in their minds;
Grief plagues these captives,* slippery hope torments.*
The king you see by many lords possessed,
His aims frustrated, by harsh masters pressed.' 10

Chapter 3

'So do you see the clinging mire in which shameful deeds wallow, 1 and the glow with which moral virtue shines? This makes it clear that good men never lack rewards, and that crimes never go without their punishment; for in all activities, the purpose for 2 which each deed is performed can reasonably be regarded as its reward. For example, the crown of victory is the purpose of running on the racetrack, and therein lies the reward.* Now we 3 have demonstrated that happiness is the good for which all actions are performed, and so the good itself lies ahead as the general reward, so to say, for all actions. This reward, however, cannot be 4 isolated from good men, for no one will justly be called good if once he lacks the good. Worthy manners therefore are not 5 deprived of their own rewards. So wicked men can rage as much as they like, but the wise man's crown will not tumble or wither, for no outsider's wickedness can pluck from honest hearts the glory that is theirs. Now if a person derives that glory from an 6 external source, some other person, even the donor himself, could deprive him of it; but since it is bestowed on the individual by his own worth,* he will forgo his reward only when he ceases to be good.

7   'Finally, since every reward is sought because it is believed to be a good, is anyone to imagine that the one who possesses the good

8 goes without his reward? What reward do we mean? Why, that which is most beautiful and greatest of all. Think back to that splendid gift of the "corollary" which I presented to you a short

9 while ago,* and come to this conclusion: since the good itself is happiness, clearly all good men become happy precisely because

10 they are good. Now we have agreed that those who are happy are gods; and so the reward of good men—a reward which no time can eradicate, no man's power can diminish, no man's wickedness can overthrow—is to become gods.*

11   'In view of this, wise men could not possibly be in doubt about the punishment irremovably attached to the wicked. Since good and evil, and likewise punishments and rewards, are wholly contrary to each other, what we see accrue as reward to the good man must find its corresponding opposite in the punishment

12 of the evil man. Therefore just as goodness itself becomes the reward for good men, so wickedness itself is the punishment for

13 bad men.* Now any person who is punished is in no doubt that he is suffering evil. So if wicked men are willing to look at themselves, can they regard themselves as unpunished, when wickedness, the worst of all evils, has not merely attended them but has also harshly devastated them?

14   'Observe now the nature of this punishment which attends the wicked, by contrasting it with the situation of the good. A little while ago* you learnt that every existing thing is a unity, and that unity itself is the good. The conclusion drawn from this is that

15 everything that exists is also good. In this sense whatever departs from the good ceases to exist, so evil men cease to be what they had been before. Of course, the very appearance of the human frame which they still possess shows that they were men; thus by resorting to wickedness they have lost their human nature as well.

16 Since goodness alone can raise a person above the rank of human, it must follow that wickedness deservedly imposes subhuman status on those whom it has dislodged from the human condition.*

'What follows from this is that you cannot regard as a man one

17 who is disfigured by vices. A man who in seizing the possessions of

others is consumed by greed is comparable to a wolf.* The
aggressive and restless man who devotes his tongue to disputes
can be considered a dog.* The underhand plotter who rejoices in 18
stealthy theft can be likened to young foxes.* The man of
ungovernable temper who roars his head off can be regarded as
having a lion's disposition.* The fearful man who does not stand 19
his ground and trembles when there is nothing to fear can be
compared with hinds.* The idle sluggard who is a slave to sloth
lives a donkey's life.* The fickle, capricious person who passes 20
from one thing of interest to another is no different from the
birds.* The one who steeps himself in foul and unclean lusts
lingers over pleasures like a filthy sow.* In this sense he who 21
abandons goodness and ceases to be a man cannot rise to the status
of a god, and so is transformed into an animal.

'The Ithacan leader's billowing sails,*
His ships that roamed the sea,
The east wind beached upon the isle
Where dwelt divine Circe.
That beauteous one, who claimed descent   5
From Phoebus' orb that warms,
Distils for each of her new guests
Cups charged with magic charms.

Her touch, so masterful with herbs,
Transformed all men she knew.   10
The likeness of a boar cloaked one;
An Afric lion too
With sabre tooth and monstrous claws
Where man had been, stood by;
A third, now partner with the wolves,   15
Howled when he sought to cry.
An Indian tigress took the shape
To which the fourth was changed;
A meek and gentle tigress this
As through the halls she ranged.*   20

Although the winged Arcadian god*
Pitied their lord's reverse,
Discharged him, steeped in diverse ills,
From Circe's monstrous curse,
By then the oarsmen of his ships   25
Had drunk the poisoned wine,
Were crunching acorns, and not bread,

For they had turned to swine.
True voices and true shapes were lost;
Bereft of human norms,   30
Their minds alone endured unchanged
To mourn their monstrous forms.

That hand of Circe was too weak,*
Her plants less power impart,
Though human limbs they could transform,   35
They could not reach the heart.
Concealed within its citadel
Man's true strength dwells inside;
The poisons which dehumanize
Within him now reside.   40
These potions deeply penetrate;
Though bodies feel no pain,
The deadly wounds which they inflict
Impact upon the brain.'

Chapter 4

1 'At this I remarked: 'I quite see that there is some justification for
saying that though wicked men preserve the appearance of human
bodies, they are transformed into beasts so far as the quality of
their minds is concerned. But I only wish that those brutal and
criminal minds were not permitted to go on the rampage, and to
cause the destruction of good men.'

2 'But they are not so permitted,' she replied, 'and this will be
shown in due course. However, if the discretion which people
think is granted them were removed, the wicked would be relieved
3 to a great extent of the punishment which they merit. What may
perhaps seem incredible to some is that evil men must be
unhappier when their aspirations are fulfilled than if they cannot
4 achieve them;* for if it is wretched to desire to do evil things, it is
still more wretched to have acquired the power to do so, for
without that power their wretched aspiration would lack the
5 strength to succeed. So since each stage contains its own wretchedness, those who you see have the desire, the power, and the
actual performance of evildoing must be oppressed by a threefold
misfortune.'

'I grant you that,' I said, 'but I earnestly wish that they would 6 soon be rid of that misfortune by being deprived of the opportunity to commit crime.'

'They will be rid of it sooner than perhaps you would wish,' she 7 replied, 'or sooner than they themselves imagine; for in this life's brief compass nothing comes so late that the mind finds waiting for it tedious,* especially as the mind is immortal. Those great 8 expectations entertained by the wicked, and the ambitious design of their crimes, often come to nothing through a sudden and unexpected end. This in fact is what sets a limit on their wickedness; if wickedness makes man unhappy, then extended depravity must make people unhappier still.* If death did not 9 bring a final end to their wickedness, I should regard them as supremely unhappy, for if our inference about the misfortune which depravity brings is true, clearly the wretchedness acknowledged as eternal must be without end.'

'That is a remarkable conclusion,' I said, 'and one difficult to 10 concede, but I recognize that it very much accords with what was granted earlier.'

'Your assessment is correct,' she said, 'whereas the person who 11 finds it hard to assent to my conclusion should reasonably either demonstrate that there is some flaw in the previous argument, or that the combination of premises does not validate the necessary conclusion. Otherwise, as long as the previous contentions are granted, there is no reason whatever to challenge the conclusion. In fact what I am going to submit next may seem no less 12 surprising, but this too inevitably follows from what we have already accepted.'

'What is that?' I asked.

'That the wicked', she replied, 'are happier if they suffer 13 punishment than if no deserved punishment constrains them.* I 14 do not here labour the point which might occur to anyone, that debased behaviour is corrected by retribution and restored to the right path by fear of punishment, and further, that this serves as an example to the rest to avoid what is blameworthy. I think that there is another sense in which the wicked when they go unpunished are unhappy, even if we take no account of such correction, and no thought is given to the example it sets.'

'What other sense is there besides these?' I asked. 15

'Have we not agreed', she demanded, 'that the good are happy, and the wicked wretched?'

'We have indeed,' I replied.

16 'So if an element of good is bestowed on someone's misery, is that person not happier than he whose wretchedness is uncompounded and stark, without the admixture of any good?'

'It seems so,' I said.

17 'Now suppose the wretched man who lacks every good has a further evil attached to him in addition to those which make him wretched. Is he not to be regarded as much unhappier than the one whose misfortune is lightened by some share in the good?'*

'But of course,' I replied.

18 'Now it is clear that punishment of the wicked is just, and that their escaping punishment is unjust.'

'Who would deny it?'

19 'But no one', she said, 'will deny the additional point that what is just is good, and on the other hand that what is unjust is evil.'

20 'That's as clear as daylight,' I replied.

'So when wicked persons are punished, they have an element of good attached to them, namely the punishment itself, which is good because it is just; and again, when they avoid punishment, some further evil is present in them, namely their getting off scot free, which you have conceded is an evil by virtue of its being unjust.'*

21 'I cannot deny that.'

'So the wicked are much unhappier when accorded unjust impunity than when punished with just retribution.'

22 At this I said: 'These observations of yours follow from the conclusions reached a moment ago. But the question I pose to you is this: Do you not leave room for any punishments of souls after the death of the body?'

23 'Yes indeed. There will be considerable punishments, some of which I believe are imposed with punitive harshness, but others with a kindly process of cleansing.* But I have no intention of discussing these now.

24 'So far it has been my aim* to enable you to realize that the power of the wicked, which seems to you most inappropriate, is non-existent; to get you to see that those who you complained go unpunished never avoid punishment for their base conduct; and to

ensure that you learn that their freedom to act, which you prayed would quickly come to an end, does not last long; that if it were protracted it would be unhappier still, and if it were eternal, it would be supremely unhappy; and further, that the wicked are more wretched when acquitted with unjust impunity than if they were punished with just retribution. What follows from this 25 declaration is that they are oppressed with heavier punishments at the very time they are thought to get off scot free.'

Then I said: 'When I reflect on your arguments, I think that no 26 truer words were spoken. But if I revert to the judgement of men, there is surely not a single individual who does not regard them not merely as unworthy of belief, but even as not worth listening to.'*

'You are right,' she answered. 'That is because their eyes are 27 accustomed to darkness, and they cannot raise them to the light of clear truth. They are like those birds whose vision is enhanced at night and blinded by daylight.* In concentrating their gaze not on the order of nature but on their own emotions, they imagine that freedom to commit crimes or impunity for committing them is a blessing.

'But note what the immortal law ordains: shape your mind to 28 better things, and you will not need a judge to bestow a reward, for you set yourself among the more outstanding features of creation; turn your affections towards the worse, and you need to look for 29 no outsider to impose retribution, for you have relegated yourself to the region of baser things. It is as though your gaze were trained alternately on the filthy earth and the sky, with nothing else in sight; on the evidence of your eyes alone, you would appear at one moment to be down in the filth, and at the next among the stars. But the common herd does not gaze at the stars above. So what are 30 we to do? Should we join those whom we have shown to be brute 31 beasts? Imagine a man who has become wholly blind, has forgotten that he had been sighted, and believes that he lacks nothing to attain human perfection; would we who have sight share that blind man's belief? Yet the common herd will not even assent to the 32 argument that those who inflict injustice are unhappier than those who suffer it, though this rests on equally strong foundations of reasoning.'

'I should like to hear that reasoning,' I said.

33   'Surely you do not deny', she said, 'that every wicked man deserves punishment?'

'Certainly not.'

34   'And it is clear on many grounds that wicked men are unhappy?'

'Yes,' I said.

'So you do not doubt that those who deserve punishment are wretched?'

'No; I quite agree,' I replied.

35   'Now if you were sitting as judge,' she asked, 'on whom would you think that punishment should be inflicted—on the person who had committed an injustice, or on the one who had suffered it?'

'I have no doubt', I replied, 'that I would render satisfaction to the victim by making the perpetrator suffer.'

36   'So in that case the aggressor would seem to you to be more wretched than the victim of the injustice.'

'Yes, that follows,' I said.

37   'So for this reason, and others rooted in the fact that base conduct by its nature makes men miserable, it is clear that when an injustice is inflicted on anyone, it is not the victim but the perpetrator who is wretched.'

'It seems so,' I replied.

38   'But nowadays advocates claim the opposite.* They try to arouse the pity of judges on behalf of those who have suffered some grievous and painful injury, whereas the pity would be more justly owed to those who inflict it. Those perpetrators ought to be brought to court not by angry accusers, but rather by kindly sympathizers, as if they were sick men brought to a doctor* to have the disease of their guilt excised by the surgery of punish-

39   ment. If this happened, the task of defence lawyers would become wholly superfluous, or if they chose to be of use to society, they

40   would switch to the role of prosecutor. As for the scoundrels themselves, if the will of heaven allowed them to glimpse through some tiny chink the virtue which they had renounced, and if they saw that the pains of punishment would be the means of their abandoning their filthy vices, they would not regard them as pains, because they were balanced by attainment of goodness.* They would reject the efforts of defence lawyers, and entrust themselves wholly to their accusers and judges.

41   'What follows from this is that there is no place whatever for

hatred in the minds of the wise. Only an utter idiot would hate good men, and it is irrational to hate the wicked; for if vice is a 42 species of mental disease comparable to illness in the body, since we regard those who are physically ill as wholly undeserving of hatred and deserving rather of pity, then men with minds oppressed by wickedness, a condition more dreadful than any sickness, should all the more be pitied rather than hounded.*

'Why take delight in rousing mass disorder?*
Why raise your hands to tempt the hand of Fate?*
If Death is what you seek, that harsh Recorder
Herself draws close; her swift steeds do not wait.
Snakes, lions, tigers, bears, and boars gnaw men,   5
But men with swords their fellow-humans mar.
Is this because men's manners differ, then,
That they launch unjust battles and fierce war,
Wishing to die from wounds of give and take?
No justice lies in savagery gone mad.   10
To man's deserts you would due payment make?
Then rightly love the good, pity the bad.'

Chapter 5

At this point I interjected: 'I quite realize what happiness or 1 wretchedness is bound up with the merits of honourable or dishonourable men, but as I see it there is an element of good 2 and evil in the popular conception of Fortune.* Not even one of your wise men would prefer a life of impecunious and shameful exile to residence in his own city with abundant riches, respected status, and powerful influence. Wisdom's tasks are more perspicu- 3 ously and clearly carried out when the happy existence of rulers is, so to say, transmitted to the folks dependent on them;* and especially so when imprisonment, execution, and the other ordeals enjoined as punishment by the laws fall on misbehaving citizens against whom they were in fact instituted. So I am utterly 4 astonished at the reversal of this norm, as a result of which good men are oppressed by punishment for crimes, while evil men grab the rewards for virtues, and I long to hear from you a possible explanation for such a welter of injustice. I should of course be less 5 surprised if I believed that universal confusion was the result of

the workings of chance; but as it is, the existence of God's
6 governance compounds my astonishment. Since he often dispenses kindnesses to good men and harsh treatment to the bad,
but then on the other hand extends harsh treatment to the good
and grants the bad their dearest wishes,* what apparent difference
is there between this and the random process of chance, unless
some reason for it is established?'

7   'It is hardly surprising', she remarked, 'that people regard events
as random and chaotic if they are unaware of the planned order of
the world. As for yourself, though you do not grasp the final end*
of this great dispensation, you must not doubt that all things
happen as they should, because a good ruler orders the world.

> 'He who does not know that the stars of Arcturus*
> Glide along close to the highest hinge of heaven,
> Or why so slowly Boötes guides his Wagon,
> Plunging his fires so late into the ocean,
> Whereas he unfolds his rising very swiftly—*   5
> He will stand amazed at the laws of high heaven.
> If the horns of Phoebe, at her full, glow fainter,
> Shaded by the cones of the all-enshrouding darkness,
> And if she, when eclipsed, then does uncover
> Stars which her gleaming orb earlier had hidden,   10
> Then mass perplexity disturbs all the nations;
> Bronze gongs are wearied by perpetual beating.*
>
> Yet no one shows wonder that the blasts of Corus*
> Batter the coastline with the thundering sea-waves,
> Nor that the snow-mass, hardened by the cold blast,   15
> Later is melted by the glowing heat of Phoebus.
> For here below to discern a cause is easy,
> But hearts are confused by the hidden laws of heaven.
> All events which time brings forth only rarely,
> Happenings whose suddenness stuns the fickle masses,   20
> These would surely cease to seem surprising,
> Once the clouded error of ignorance departed.'

Chapter 6

1 'True enough,' I remarked. 'But since it is your task to unravel the
causes of things that lie hidden, and to explain the processes which

lie veiled in darkness, please expound the conclusions you draw from this, for that strange situation which I mentioned* troubles me a great deal.'

Philosophy smiled briefly, and said: 'The topic to which you 2 challenge me is the greatest of all to investigate; it is virtually inexhaustible. It is the sort of subject in which when one doubt is 3 excised countless others spring up like the Hydra's heads,* and there would be no limit to them if one did not restrain them by applying the most penetrating fire of the mind. The problems 4 which it frequently raises for investigation include the single nature of Providence, the chain of Fate, the suddenness of chance events, God's knowledge and predestination, and the freedom of the will.* You yourself can assess how burdensome 5 these problems are. But it is a part of your healing that you should come to know these things as well, so I shall try to give some consideration to them, however much we are constrained by the narrow limits of time. If the musical charms of song are what 6 delight you, you must postpone that pleasure for a little while, to allow me to weave together the interconnected arguments in due order.'

'Do as you wish,' I said.

Then as though she was making a fresh start, this is how she 7 proceeded: 'The birth of all things, the entire development of natures subject to change, and all that is in any way stirred to motion, derive their causes and order and shapes from the unchanging steadfastness of the divine mind. This mind, estab- 8 lished in the citadel of its own oneness, decides upon the complex plan of the course of events. This plan, when envisaged in the total clarity of the divine intelligence, is called Providence; but as related to the things which that intelligence moves and orders, it has been labelled Fate* by men of old. That the two concepts are 9 different will readily become clear if we mentally consider the force of each. Providence is the divine reason itself, established within the highest originator of all things, who disposes them all, whereas Fate is the order imposed on things that change, through which Providence interlinks each and every object in their due arrangement. Providence indeed embraces all things alike, how- 10 ever different and however boundless, whereas Fate organizes the separate movement of individual things, and allocates them according to place, shape, and time. Thus when this arrangement of the temporal order is a unity within the foresight of the divine mind, it is Providence, whereas when that unity is separated and unfolded at various times, it is called Fate.

11   'Though the two are distinct, the one depends on the other, for the order of Fate emerges from the indivisibility of Providence.*

12   Comparison can be made with the craftsman who first envisages in his mind the shape of the object which he is to create. He sets to work on it, and stage by stage he produces what he had earlier visualized as a unity, and at a single moment.* In the same way, God by Providence orders what is to be done in a unified and unchanging manner, but by Fate he carries through these arrange-

13   ments in a manifold way within the bounds of time. The work of Fate may be performed by divine spirits which are the handmaids, so to speak, of Providence; or else the chain of Fate may be knitted together by the World-Soul, or by the obedience of the whole of nature, or by the motions of the stars of heaven, or by the power of angels, or by the diverse skills of demons, or by some or all of these.* But what is absolutely clear is that the unmoving, undivided pattern of events as they unfold constitutes Providence, whereas Fate is the movable nexus and the ordering in time of what God's undivided nature has planned to be carried out.

14   'Hence all that is subordinate to Fate is likewise subject to Providence, to which Fate itself is subject;* but there are some things under the aegis of Providence which transcend the chain of Fate.* Such things are planted immovably close to the supreme Godhead, so that they lie outside the regime of changeability

15   managed by Fate. Imagine a series of concentric circles revolving round the same axis; the innermost one lies closest to the single nature of the central point, and itself acts as a sort of axis round which the other circles lying outside it can turn.* The outermost circle travels round in a wider circle, and the further it departs from the undivided middle point, the more widespread is the area over which it extends. Should anything ally and attach itself to the mid-point, it is absorbed into its undivided nature, and it ceases to separate and to spread in all directions. Similarly, whatever distances itself further from the highest Mind becomes enmeshed in the broader chains of Fate, whereas the closer to the axis of the world which a thing approaches, the freer it becomes from the

control of Fate. If in fact a thing clings fast to the unchanging 16
nature of the divine Mind, it becomes motionless, and it also
passes beyond the necessity imposed by Fate. As the power of 17
reasoning relates to the intellect, as becoming is to being, as time is
to eternity, as a circle is to its mid-point, so is the shifting chain of
Fate related to the unchanging oneness of Providence.

This chain of Fate moves the heavens and the stars, inter- 18
mingles the elements and transforms them by their interchange; it
also renews all things which come into existence and die, by the
generation of like offspring and seeds. Further, it constrains the 19
actions and fortunes of men by an unbreakable interlinking of
causes, and since this interlinking takes its origin from unchanging
Providence, the causes themselves must likewise be unchangeable.
For the best possible ordering of the world exists only if the 20
undivided nature which abides in the divine Mind inaugurates an
unvarying sequence of causes, and this sequence with its own
immutability constrains the world of change which would otherwise float away at random.

So although the general picture may seem to you mortals one of 21
confusion and turmoil because you are totally unable to visualize
this order of things, all of them none the less have their own
pattern, which orders them and directs them towards the good.
There is indeed nothing which is done with evil intent, even by 22
those wicked men themselves; as we have shown in considerable
detail,* they seek the good but are deflected by debased error. It is
certainly not the case that the sequence which issues from the axis
of the highest good is diverted from its initial course in any
direction.

But, you will remark, what possible confusion can be more 23
unjust than that good men should experience reverses at one
moment and successes at another, and that evil men too should be
confronted with both what they desire and what they detest? Can 24
it be, then, that human beings are endowed with such clear
intellects that those whom they regard as honourable and dishonourable must inevitably conform to such assessments? And 25
this in spite of the fact that men's judgements differ, so that those
regarded by some as worthy of regard deserve punishment in the
view of others?

'Let us grant, however, that one can in fact distinguish between 26

good and evil men. But to exploit a term from physics, can one
27 possibly probe the inner *temperament* of their minds?* The
situation is rather like that of men unaware of the curious
reason why sweet foods agree with some healthy bodies, and
bitter ones with others; or again, why some invalids are helped by
28 mild potions, and others by sharp ones. Yet this does not surprise
the physician in the least, for he can distinguish between the levels
and the balance of health and sickness as they really are.

29 'But so far as health is concerned, what else in all likelihood is it
if not goodness, and what else is mental sickness if not vices? And
who else preserves the good and eradicates the bad but God, the
30 ruler and physician of men's minds? As he gazes out from his high
vantage-point of Providence,* he recognizes what is appropriate
for each human being, and invests each of them with what is
31 appropriate. It is here that the remarkable phenomenon of the
pattern imposed by Fate is now put in train, carried through by
God who knows, and viewed with astonishment by men, who do
not know.

32 'Let me touch upon a few examples such as human reason can
grasp of God's profundity. Take a man whom you regard as
supremely just, totally upholding the right;* he appears to all-
33 knowing Providence in a different light. Lucan, a poet of our
persuasion, has reminded us that the cause of the victor was
34 pleasing to the gods, but that of the vanquished to Cato.* So all
that in this case falls short of your expectation in fact occurs in due
order, whereas to your thinking it appears a topsy-turvy shambles.

35 'But let us imagine a person whose behaviour is so ideal as to
win the unanimous respect of God and men, but who is wanting
in strength of mind, so that if he meets with some reverse he will
perhaps cease to uphold the integrity which could not guarantee
36 him his good fortune. Accordingly, if adversity can affect him for
the worse, a wise dispensation spares that person, to ensure that
he does not suffer an ordeal which would be unsuitable in his
case.

37 'Another person is perfect in all the virtues, a holy and godlike
individual. Providence decrees that it would be sacrilegious for
him to suffer any reverses whatever, so she does not allow him to
38 be afflicted even by physical illnesses. In the words of one more
outstanding than myself,

'The body of the holy man was formed in heaven.*

'It often happens that good men are entrusted with the supreme 39
government of affairs, to ensure that unscrupulous behaviour
overstepping all bounds can be beaten back. To some men 40
Providence assigns varied fortunes appropriate to the nature of
their minds. Others she stings from time to time, to ensure that
they do not degenerate through continuing prosperity.* To others
she gives a hard time to allow them to strengthen their qualities of
mind by the application and exercise of patience. Some men's fears 41
about their powers of endurance are greater than they should be,
while others show too much contempt in the face of what they
prove unable to bear. Providence imposes harsh experience on
them, to allow them to put themselves to the test. There are some 42
who at the cost of a glorious death have purchased fame and
reverence from posterity; others, by their refusal to cave in before
tortures, have proved to the world that virtue is unconquered by
evils. Of the justice and apt order of such treatment, and of the
benefit it confers on those seen to experience it, there can be no
doubt.

'These same causes likewise ensure that wicked men sometimes 43
encounter hardships, and at other times obtain the blessings they
desire. Of course, no one is surprised at the hardships, because 44
everyone believes that the wicked have deserved to suffer; and
indeed their punishments both deter others from criminal activities, and correct the persons on whom they are imposed. As for
the blessings, they speak volumes to good men on how they are to
assess this kind of happiness which they see often attending on the
wicked.* I think that it is part of this dispensation that a man 45
should perhaps be so headstrong and impulsive by nature that lack
of family possessions can incite him more readily to commit
crimes; Providence heals this sickness by granting him money as
remedy. Another man examines his conscience, and finds it 46
blackened by evil deeds. In comparing his character with his
fortune, he perhaps fears that he may suffer the grievous loss of
what he so pleasantly enjoys; as a result he will change his ways,
and abandon his wickedness for fear of losing his fortune. Others 47
have been plunged into deserved disaster by exploiting their
prosperity for unworthy ends.

'Some men have been given the right to administer punishment.
48 The purpose of this is to test the good and to chastise the bad, for
just as no compact is made between good and wicked people, so
49 wicked people cannot agree between themselves. How could they,
when one and all are at odds with themselves because their vices
lacerate their consciences, and they often do things which when
perpetrated they regret having done?

50 'So it is that the highest Providence often achieves the striking
51 miracle of causing evil men to make other evil men good; for
when some of them are seen to suffer injustice at the hands of
out and out scoundrels, they grow hot with hatred of the
wrongdoers, and they return to the honest path of virtue in
52 their eagerness to be unlike those whom they hate. The only
force which transforms evil things into good is that of God,
when he aptly exploits them to draw out of them an element of
53 good; for some sort of order pervades all things. If something
forsakes the planned order assigned to it, it slips back into some
alternative pattern, admittedly different but none the less a due
order, so that nothing in the realm of Providence may be left to
chance. But

how hard it is to say all this as though I were a god!*

54 for it is not right for a man either mentally to grasp or to explain in
55 words all the workings of God's creation. It must be enough
merely to realize that God, the author of all things in nature,
orders all of them and guides them to the good. He hastens to
maintain in his own image* the things which he has brought to
birth, and through the chain of necessity imposed by Fate, he
56 excludes all the evil from the boundaries of his commonwealth. So
if you were to observe Providence dispensing all the plenty which
men believe exists on earth, you would not imagine that there was
any evil present at all there!

57 'But I see that for some time you have been weighed down by
the burden of this enquiry, and exhausted by this elaborate
reasoning you are pining for some honeyed song. So drink deep;
then, once you are refreshed, you can battle on further with
enhanced strength.

'If with wisdom and clear mind*
The lofty Thunderer's laws you would discern,
   Upward gaze at heaven's heights,
There constellations keep their ancient peace,
   The world's just compact they preserve.   5

The sun, when summoned with his ruddy fire,
   Phoebe's cold car does not halt.
Nor does the Bear, which bends its speeding course
   At the high peak of the world,
Submerge itself within the western deep.   10
   Other stars it sees sink down,
But it has no desire to quench its flames.*

   In balanced periods of time
The evening star proclaims the shades of night;
   Then as bearer of the light,   15
The morning star brings back the fostering day.
   Thus their alternating love
Renews the immortal motions of the world;*
   Thus all conflict stirred by war
Is banished from the region of the stars.   20

   Harmony thus regulates
The elements in equal measure poised;
   Warring moisture therefore yields
By turns before the onset of the dry.
   Cold makes compact with the flames,   25
And thus while fire suspended soars aloft,
   Earth with heavy weight sinks low.*

These are the causes which in balmy spring
   Prompt the blossom-bearing year
To issue its sweet scents upon the air.   30
   Summer's heat dries out the corn;
Next, autumn laden with its fruits, returns;
   Rain then pours on winter's face.*

This due proportion nurtures and gives birth
   To all that breathes life in the world;   35
Then seizes, buries, shifts what was brought forth,
   All plunged in final death.

Meanwhile the high Creator rules aloft;
   Tight rein he wields over the world,
Source and beginning, king and lord and law,   40
   Wise arbiter of just and right,
He first impels all things in motion; then

The errant parts he halts, pulls back,
To regulate their wandering course. Unless
   He then recalled them to their paths,   45
And forced them to resume their circling course,
   All that fixed order now contains,
Detached from its true source, would fall apart.

Love is that common fount of all;
All seek adhesion to that end, the good.   50
   Things cannot otherwise survive
Unless, in Love's renewed embrace, they flow
   Back to that source, their fount of life.'

Chapter 7

1 'So do you now see what follows from all that we have said?'
'What is that?' I asked.

2 'That every fortune is indeed good,' she said.
'But how can that be?' I asked.

3 'Listen,' she said. 'Since every fortune, pleasant or harsh, is bestowed on the one hand to reward or to exercise the good, and on the other to punish or correct the wicked, they are all of them good, for it is clear that they are either just or useful.'*

4 'Your reasoning', I observed, 'has the hallmark of truth, and if I reflect on what you have just taught me about Providence and

5 Fate, your judgement rests on firm foundations. Still, if you agree, I think we should count it as one of the doctrines which you described a moment ago as unthinkable.'*
'How so?' she asked.

6 'Because it is the general view, repeatedly expressed, that some people do meet with a fortune which is bad.'

7 'So would you like us', she asked, 'to air for a while the views of common folk, so that we don't appear to have distanced ourselves too far from human experience?'
'If you like,' I replied.

8 'Well then, I take it that you agree that the advantageous is good?'
'Quite right,' I said.

9 'And the Fortune which tries or corrects people is advantageous?'

'I agree,' I said.

'And is therefore good?'

'Yes, of course.'

'Now this Fortune is experienced either by those who live 10 virtuous lives and battle against hardships, or by those who abandon vices and embark upon the path of virtue. Is that not so?'

'I cannot deny it,' I said.

'So far as the enjoyable fortune bestowed as reward on good 11 men is concerned, common folk do not regard that as bad, do they?'

'Certainly not. They think it the best possible outcome, as indeed it is.'

'What about the other—the admittedly harsh fortune which 12 constrains the wicked with just punishment? Folk can hardly regard that as good, can they?'

'Indeed not', I said. 'They think it the most wretched outcome 13 possible.'

'Just be careful, then, that by aping the attitudes of the common 14 folk we don't end up with something quite unthinkable.'

'What do you mean?' I asked.

'Well, what follows from the arguments already agreed is that 15 every fortune of those who possess virtue, or who advance towards it, or who acquire it, is good, whatever it is, but for those who continue to be wicked every fortune is wholly bad.'*

'That is true,' I said, 'though no one would presume to admit 16 it.'

'This is why', she went on, 'the wise man ought not to chafe 17 whenever he is locked in conflict with Fortune, just as it is unfitting for the courageous man to be resentful when the din of war resounds. For each of them the difficulty offers the opportu- 18 nity; for the courageous man it is the chance of extending his fame, and for the wise man the chance of lending substance to his wisdom. Moreover, virtue (*virtus*) is so-called because it relies on 19 its strength (*vires*)* not to be overcome by adversity. Those of you who are in the course of attaining virtue have not travelled this road merely to wallow in luxury or to languish in pleasure. You 20 join battle keenly in mind with every kind of fortune, to ensure that when it is harsh it does not overthrow you, or when it is pleasant it does not corrupt you. Maintain the middle ground* 21

with steadfast strength. Whatever falls short of it or goes beyond it
22 holds happiness in contempt, and gains no reward for its toil. It
lies in your own hands to fashion for yourselves the kind of fortune
which you prefer; all fortune which seems harsh is punishment,
unless it either tries or corrects you.

'For twice five years the avenging son of Atreus*
Waged fierce warfare, and plotting Troy's destruction
Redeemed the loss of his brother's marriage-partner.
His was the choice that the Greek fleet should set sail,
Buying off the winds at the cost of human bloodshed.   5
He cast off his fatherhood; in the role of grim priest
He ratified the murder of his hapless daughter.*

Ithacan Odysseus mourned the loss of comrades;
Fierce Polyphemus, stretched out in his huge cave,
Devoured and engulfed them in his monstrous belly.   10
But then, to his fury, deprived of his eyesight,
He paid for his joy with melancholy weeping.*

Hercules gained fame by his taxing labours.*
Arrogant Centaurs he overcame in battle.
From the savage lion he bore away the plunder.   15
Birds he impaled too with unerring arrows.
He looted the apples from the sleepless dragon,
His left hand laden with the golden metal.
Cerberus by a triple chain was dragged up.
As victor, they say, he set the cruel master   20
Before his fierce carriage-team to serve as their fodder.
The Hydra perished, and its venom was ignited.
The river-god Achelous, his brow sore disfigured,
Plunged his dishonoured face below the river-margins.
On Libyan sandbanks he laid low Antaeus.   25
Cacus sated the anger of Evander.
Shoulders, soon to bear the weight of the heavens,
Were earlier fouled with the bristly boar's saliva.
On neck unbent he endured as his last labour
The weight of heaven; as reward for that last labour,   30
Heaven was the prize he attained through his great merit.

Go now, intrepid ones, along the lofty highway,
Following Hercules' conspicuous example.
Why so sluggishly expose your backs unguarded?*
Once earth is overcome, the stars are yours for taking.'   35

Book 5

Chapter 1

Following upon these verses, she was diverting the course of her 1
words to discuss and explain certain other matters, when I
remarked: 'Your exhortation is doubtless all it should be, and is 2
wholly worthy of the authority which you lend it. But that
statement which you made a moment ago,* that Providence is
an issue which interlocks with a number of others, I find true from
my own experience. So the question that I pose is whether you 3
think that there is such a thing as chance, and what you think it is.'

To this she responded: 'I am in a hurry to fulfil the promise 4
which I owe you, and to reveal to you the route by which you are
to be restored to your homeland. These matters which you raise 5
are admittedly useful to grasp, but they do divert us for a little
while from the path which we have set ourselves. My fear is that
these digressions will weary you, and that you will not be equal to
completing the road lying straight ahead.'

'You must not have the slightest fear of that,' I said. 'It will be 6
as good as a rest for me to identify the problems closest to my
heart. At the same time, once every facet of your thesis incon- 7
testably holds good, there can be no uncertainty about what
follows.'

Then she said: 'I shall indulge your wish.' At once she began 8
like this: 'If one were to define chance as the outcome of a random
movement which interlocks with no causes, I should maintain that
it does not exist at all, that it is a wholly empty term denoting
nothing substantial; for since God confines all things within due
order, what place can be left for random processes? It is a true 9
saying, never challenged by any of the ancients, that nothing
comes forth from nothing—though this foundation, so to speak,
which they laid for all explanations of nature, they applied not to
the creative originator, but to the matter subject to it.* Now if 10

something should emerge uncaused, it will be seen to have arisen from nothing; and if this cannot happen, chance in the sense in which we defined it cannot exist either.'

11   'So is there nothing', I asked, 'which can rightly be called chance or accident? Or is there something hidden from the public gaze for which these terms are appropriate?'

12   'My Aristotle', she replied, 'in his *Physics* has offered a succinct account of it* which approximates to the truth.'

'How does he put it?' I asked.

13   'Whenever something is done with a particular purpose in mind', she said, 'and as a result of certain causes something other than was intended occurs, it is called chance. For example, when a man is digging the ground to cultivate his field, and he
14   finds a quantity of gold buried there,* people believe that this has happened by accident, but it does not come to pass out of nothing, for it has its own causes, and the conjunction of these unforeseen and unexpected causes seems to have produced a chance happen-
15   ing. But in fact if the cultivator of the field had not dug the ground, and if someone had not lodged and buried his money
16   there, the gold would not have been found. So this is the explanation of that casual acquisition of his. It resulted not from any intention of the man who was digging, but from causes which
17   met and fused with each other. Neither the person who buried the gold, nor the one who dug the field, intended the money to be found, but as I have explained, the place where the one buried it
18   happened to coincide with where the other dug. Thus we can define chance as the unexpected outcome of a conjunction of
19   causes in actions carried out for some purpose.* What causes the conjunction and the coincidence of these causes is that order* which unfolds in an irresistible chain, descending from its source in Providence, and allocating all things to their due place and time.

'Midst Persian cliffs* (where Parthians launch their darts,
As they retreat, in their pursuers' hearts),
Tigris, Euphrates rise from single source.
They then diverge; each takes its separate course.

Should they then merge again, united flow,   5
Should what their waters bear, together go,
Then ships would meet, uprooted trunks combine,
Their mingled streams on random routes entwine.

Yet such chance wanderings both sloping land
And downward course of gliding stream command;   10
So chance, which seems to float on slackened reins,
Endures the bridle; law its course constrains.'*

Chapter 2

'I take heed of your words,' I said, 'and I agree that it is as you say.   1
But in this sequence of interlocking causes, do we have any free   2
will, or does the chain of fate constrain the movements of men's
minds as well?'

'There is free will,' she replied, 'for no rational nature could   3
exist if it did not possess freedom of will. What can by its nature   4
deploy reason, possesses the judgement by which to discern each
and every thing, and thus unaided it distinguishes what must be
avoided from what is desirable. So the individual seeks what he   5
judges to be desirable, and shuns what he reckons must be
avoided. Hence creatures which themselves possess reason also   6
possess the freedom to will or not to will, but my view is that this
freedom does not exist equally in all. Heavenly and divine   7
creatures* command perceptive judgement, uncorrupted will,
and the power to achieve what they desire; human souls, however,   8
though necessarily free when they devote themselves to the vision
of the divine mind, are less free when they slip down to the
physical world,* and less free still when they are bound fast in
earthly limbs. The furthest degree of slavery is reached when they   9
devote themselves to vices, and abrogate the possession of reason
which is theirs; for once they lower their eyes from the light of the   10
highest truth down to the world of darkness below, they are then
shrouded in a cloud of ignorance, and become confused by
destructive emotions. By yielding and lending consent to them,
they intensify the slavery which they have brought upon themselves, and in a sense they become prisoners through the exercise
of their freedom. However, the eye of Providence, which gazes on   11
all things from eternity, observes these developments, and
arranges predestined things according to the merits of each.

'Thus the sweet-voiced Homer sings:
"Phoebus", clear with limpid light,

"Sees all things and hears all things."*
Yet his rays are not so bright
To pierce the depths of earth and sea.   5

Not so enfeebled are the eyes
Of him who made this world so grand.
He sees all, seated in the skies;
Earth's bulk cannot his gaze withstand,
Nor clouds of night a hindrance be.   10

What is, what has been, what will be*
A single glance of mind discerns.
Since he alone all things can see,
The title of "true sun" he earns.'*

Chapter 3

1 At this I said: 'I fear that I am further disconcerted by a still more
difficult doubt.'

2   'What is it?' she asked. 'Mind you, I can guess what is worrying
you.'

3   'There seems to be a considerable contradiction and inconsistency', I said, 'between God's foreknowing all things and the

4 existence of any free will. If God foresees all things and cannot be
in any way mistaken, then what Providence has foreseen will

5 happen must inevitably come to pass. So if God has prior
knowledge from eternity not only of men's actions but also of
their plans and wishes, there will be no freedom of will; for the
only action and any sort of intention which can possibly exist in
the future will be foreknown by divine Providence, which cannot

6 be misled. If such actions and aspirations can be forcibly diverted
in some direction other than was foreseen, certain foreknowledge
of the future will no longer exist, but instead there will be
vacillating opinion; and I regard it as sacrilege to believe this of
God.*

7   'I do not subscribe to the argument by which some believe that
8 they can disentangle this knotty problem.* What they suggest is
that Providence's foreknowledge of a future event is not the cause
of its happening, but that it is the other way round. Since
something is about to happen, this cannot be hidden from

divine Providence, and in this sense, they claim, the element of
necessity is reversed. Their argument is that things foreseen do   9
not therefore happen by necessity, but that things which will
happen are necessarily foreseen. The assumption here is that we
are toiling over the problem of which is the cause of which: is
foreknowledge the cause of the necessity of future events, or is the
necessity of future events the cause of Providence? In fact,
however, we are struggling to show that whatever the sequence
of causes, the outcome of things foreknown is necessary, even if
such foreknowledge does not appear to impose an inevitable
outcome upon future events.

'Take the case of a person who is seated.* The belief which   10
hazards that he is seated must necessarily be true; and conversely,
if the belief that a certain person is seated is true, then he must be
seated. In each of the two formulations some necessity is present: 11
in the one that it is true, and in the other that he is seated. But the   12
individual is not seated because the belief that he is seated is true;
rather, the belief is true because the person was already seated.
Thus, though the reason for its being true emerges from the fact   13
that he was seated, there is a necessity which both statements
share. Clearly the argument about Providence and the future is   14
similar; for even if things are foreseen because they are about to
happen, and they do not in fact happen because they are foreseen,
nevertheless necessity lies either in that future events are foreseen
by God, or that things foreseen happen because they are foreseen.
This alone is sufficient to eliminate the freedom of the will.*

'And besides, how topsy-turvy is the suggestion that the out-   15
come of events in time is the cause of eternal foreknowledge! What   16
distinction is there between thinking that God has foresight of
future events because they are about to happen, and believing that
things which have occurred at some earlier time are the cause of
that highest Providence?* A further point: when I know that   17
something exists, it is necessary that it exists, and likewise when I
know that something will happen, it is necessary that it will
happen. The conclusion therefore is that the outcome of something foreknown cannot be avoided. Finally, if a person believes   18
that something is other than it is, not only is that not knowledge,
but it is a mistaken assumption far removed from the truth of
knowledge. So if something is about to happen in such a way that   19

its outcome is not certain and necessary, how can it possibly be
20 foreknown that it will occur?* True knowledge is not compounded
with untruth, and likewise what is grasped by knowledge cannot
21 be other than what is grasped; for the reason why knowledge
embraces no falsehood is because everything must be as knowledge
understands it to be.

22 'So what is the solution? How, I wonder, can God know
23 beforehand that these uncertainties will come to pass? If he
thinks that things which possibly may not happen will necessarily
occur, he is mistaken—and this is sacrilegious both to contemplate
24 and to utter. But if he decrees that the future is as it really is, in
other words realizes that future events equally may or may not
happen, what sort of foreknowledge is that, since it constitutes
25 nothing definite or unchanging? How does this differ from that
absurd prophecy of Tiresias

                Each utterance of mine will come to pass—or not!*

26 Again, how does divine Providence rise above mere human
opinion, if like human beings she assesses as uncertain those
27 things whose outcome *is* uncertain? But if no such uncertainty
can reside in that most unerring source of all things, then what
God assuredly knows will happen is guaranteed to come about.
28 What follows from this is that there is no freedom for human plans
and actions, since the divine mind foresees all of them without
straying into error; he confines and restricts them to a single
outcome.

29 'Once this is admitted, the extent of the decline in human
30 fortunes becomes evident. Rewards or punishments offered to
good or wicked men are pointless, for they have not been won
31 by any free and voluntary impulse of their minds.* What is now
considered utterly just—punishments for the wicked and
rewards for the good—will be seen to be the greatest injustice
imaginable, because they have been impelled to commit good or
evil not by their own will, but by the unchanging necessity of
32 what will be. So neither vices nor virtues will exist at all; instead
all the deserts of people are mingled and undifferentiated in the
melting-pot. Moreover—and nothing more heinous than this can
be imagined—since the entire ordering of human affairs derives
from Providence, and no discretion is granted to our human

intentions, our vices as well are to be ascribed to the author of all things good.

'So there is no point in hoping to obtain, or in praying to avert, 33 anything, for what is the individual to pray to obtain or to avoid when all that we long for is set fast in an interlinked chain that cannot be set aside? Thus the one and only transaction made 34 between men and God, namely our hopes and prayers for deliverance, will be abolished, if indeed by payment of a proper humility we deserve the priceless recompense of divine grace.* This is the only way in which men are seen to be able to converse with God, and to be united by this means of supplication to that unapproachable Light,* even before obtaining what they ask for. But if we accept that the course of the future is fixed by necessity, 35 and such approaches to God are considered ineffectual, what means will remain by which we can join and attach ourselves to that highest source of all that is? The human race, as your poem 36 proclaimed a little while ago,* will inevitably be walled off and separated from its fount, and will disintegrate.

'What dissonant cause breaks up the compact of the world?*
What god established such great wars between two truths,*
That though when kept apart each in itself holds good,
When brought together they disdain to share the yoke?
Or is there no disharmony between these truths,   5
And to each other do they ever firmly cleave?

Perhaps the mind, when sunk within unseeing limbs,
Because its flaming light is dimmed and almost doused,
Fails to discern the slender links that bind the world?
If that is so, why does it burn with such great love   10
To investigate truth's evidences lying hid?
Does it now know what eagerly it longs to know?
If so, who toils to grasp those things already known?
If ignorant, why does it in its blindness seek?
For who would long for something that he did not know,   15
Or persevere pursuing things beyond his ken?
Where would he find them? Even if such things were found,
Who in his ignorance would recognize their shape?*

The mind, enveloped in the cloud of mortal limbs,
Does not, however, lose all memory of itself;   20
It grasps the whole while failing to retain the parts.*
Therefore the man whose mission is to find the truth

Belongs to neither of two camps; he neither knows,
Yet is not wholly ignorant of all that is.
He keeps in mind, remembers the totality,   25
And ponders it, recalling what he saw on high,
His purpose is to add to all he recollects
The parts forgotten.'

Chapter 4

1 Then Philosophy said: 'This is a long-standing argument about Providence. Marcus Tullius, when he put paid to divination,* had a lively discussion of it, and you yourself have investigated it for quite a time,* but up to now not one of you philosophers has 2 explained it with the necessary care or incisiveness. The reason for the cloud that envelops you is that the process of human reasoning cannot attain to the simplicity of divine foreknowledge. If that simplicity could somehow be grasped, it is certain that no 3 ambiguity would remain. I shall later try to clarify and explain it, once I have dealt with the problems that trouble you.

4   'I wish to know why you regard as ineffectual the argument of those who try to solve the problem: they think that foreknowledge is not by necessity the cause of future events, and so they believe 5 that freedom of the will is not hindered by such foreknowledge. It is surely not the case that the sole basis on which you argue for the necessity of future events is that things foreseen cannot fail to 6 happen? If previous knowledge in fact implants no necessity on future events—and you yourself also conceded this a moment ago*—why should results of acts of the will be restricted to one 7 particular outcome? Let us assume for the sake of argument that foreknowledge does not exist, for this will allow you to see what 8 follows. If this were the case, no outcome of willed events would be inevitable, would it?'

'Certainly not,' I replied.

9   'Let us now in turn assume that foreknowledge does exist, but that it imposes no necessity on events. The same freedom of will 10 is, I imagine going to remain unaffected and entire. But you will retort that foreknowledge, even if it does not impose necessity on future events, is a sign that those future events will necessarily

occur. Thus, even without the existence of foreknowledge, there 11
would be the certainty of a necessary outcome of future events, for
every sign merely indicates what a thing is, and does not bring
about what it signals. Hence what we must first establish is that 12
there is nothing which does not occur out of necessity, so that it
becomes clear that foreknowledge is a sign of this necessity;
otherwise, if the necessity does not exist, foreknowledge cannot
be a sign of it, since it does not exist. Now it is generally agreed 13
that proof which rests on secure reasoning is to be derived not
from signs or from externally adduced arguments, but from causes
appropriate and necessary.

'But how can it possibly be the case that events foreseen as 14
about to happen do not actually come about? Such an assumption
would have us believe that what Providence foreknows will happen
will not come to pass, rather than have us think that though such
things do come to pass, by their nature they have not imposed any
necessity that they should so happen. You will be able to make 15
such a judgement from this: we see a number of things developing
before our eyes, for example, charioteers observed in the act of
controlling and steering their four-horse teams, and other such
scenes. It is not suggested, is it, that any necessity compels any 16
such development to occur?'

'Certainly not, for the exercise of skill would be pointless if all
such activities were not spontaneous.'

'So if such actions when they take place do not owe their 17
existence to necessity, they will likewise involve no necessity in the
future before they take place; and therefore there are certain things 18
which are about to happen whose outcome is free of all necessity. I 19
do not think that anyone will claim that events now occurring were
not on the point of occurring before they came to pass. Thus these
events, even if foreknown, have an outcome free of necessity, for 20
just as knowledge of present events imposes no necessity on them
as they occur, so foreknowledge of future events imposes no
necessity on things still to come.

'But, you will say, this is precisely the point at issue, whether 21
there can be any foreknowledge of things which have no necessary
outcome.* The two concepts, foreknowledge and necessity, seem 22
to be at odds with each other. You believe that if things are
foreseen, then necessity follows, and that if necessity is absent,

there is certainly no foreknowledge; and that only established facts
23 are grasped by knowledge. But if things of uncertain outcome are
foreseen as being certain, this, you maintain, represents not the
truth of knowledge but the haziness of opinion; for you regard it as
a departure from sound knowledge to hold a view contrary to
reality.

24   'The reason for this error is that all men believe that the totality
of their knowledge is obtained solely from the impact and nature
25 of things known. But the reality is wholly different: all that
becomes known is apprehended not by this impact, but rather
26 by the capability of those who grasp it.* Let me make this clear
with a brief example. The roundness of the same physical object is
identified in one way by the eyes, but in another by the touch, for
the eyes remain at a distance, and at one and the same moment
they observe the whole by means of light-rays which they project,*
while the touch clings closely to the sphere, and as it circles round
its perimeter, it apprehends its roundness bit by bit.

27   'In the case of man, the senses, the imagination, the reason and
28 the understanding all regard him in different ways.* The organs of
sense examine his shape in the matter that lies before them. The
29 imagination visualizes his shape independently of the matter. The
reason too rises higher, and surveys the appearance of each
30 individual in the light of the universal to which all belong.* The
eye of the understanding rises still higher, and transcending the
boundaries of the created world, it gazes on the simple Form with
31 the unsullied sight of the mind.* Your most concentrated thought
should be directed on this, for the higher power of the understanding embraces the lower, but the lower in no way rises to the
32 higher. For the senses cannot be exercised at all outside matter;
the imagination does not behold universals; the reason cannot
grasp the simple Form. But the understanding looks down, so to
say, from above. It visualizes the Form, and distinguishes all that
lies beneath it, but in such a way that it apprehends the Form
33 itself, which could not be known to any of the other faculties; for it
recognizes the universal as the reason does, and the shape which
the imagination sees, and the matter which the senses grasp, but
without deploying the reason or imagination or senses. Rather, by
that single appraisal of the mind it regards all these things, so to
34 say, as Form. Likewise the reason, when it observes some

universal, does not deploy the imagination or the senses, but grasps what is apparent to the imagination and the senses; for the 35 reason defines the universal which it has conceived like this: "Man is a two-footed rational animal."* Though this is a universal 36 concept, everyone knows that the object is open to the imagination and the senses, but the reason ponders it not by the imagination or the senses, but by visualizing it rationally. The imagination too, 37 though it takes its starting-point of sighting and fashioning shapes from the senses, even in the absence of the senses surveys all that is accessible to them by the criterion not of sensation but by that of the imagination. So do you see how in the acquisition of know- 38 ledge all these elements deploy their own powers rather than those of the objects perceived? And this is how it should be, for since 39 every judgement emerges as the act of one who judges, it is inevitable that each performs its work by its own power rather than by that of another.

'Elders with doctrine dark and dense*
   The Porch did once provide,
To hold that images of sense
   Issue from things outside,
Then are implanted in the mind;   5
   As with swift strokes of pen
Are letters to smooth page consigned,
   Which bears no marks till then.*

But if the mind which ever thrives
   With movements of its own   10
No explanation thereby gives,
   But passively, alone
Bears marks which every body brings,
   Performs a mirror's role,*
Reflects vain images of things—   15
   Large questions then befall.

How does the knowledge that sees all
   Flourish in human hearts?
What force perceives things great and small,
   Distinguishing their parts?   20
What power those parts again unites?
   On double journey wends,
Lifting its head into the heights,
   Then to the depths descends?

   Into itself mind then withdraws,   25
    Falsehood by truth to bar;
   At work is an efficient cause,
    More powerful by far
   Than one which passively accedes
    To marks which matter takes;   30
   In living bodies there precedes
    An impulse which awakes

   And stirs resources in the mind
    When light assaults the eyes,
   Or ears to voices are inclined.   35
    Then powers of mind arise,
   To summon forms within possessed
    To movements of like kind;
   They join external marks impressed
    With images combined.'*   40

Chapter 5

1 'It is possible that when men perceive material objects, those external properties strike the organs of sense, and the effect on the body precedes the exertion of the active mind; and that effect stirs the mind to activity within itself, arousing the forms previously quiescent within. On the other hand, I suggest, if in the perception of material objects the mind is not stamped by that experience, but assesses by its own power the effect sustained by the body, how much more do those things which are freed from all bodily sensations promote the activity of their minds,* refraining in 2 their discernment from paying heed to external objects! By this process many modes of cognition accrue to various beings of 3 different types. Sensation alone, unaccompanied by all other modes of knowledge, is possessed by creatures without movement, like molluscs and others which are nurtured while clinging to rocks.* Imagination is the property of mobile animals, which at that level already appear to have some instinct of what to avoid and 4 what to seek.* But reason is unique to the human race, just as understanding belongs solely to the divine. Hence this last means of apprehending is superior to the rest, for by its own nature it

recognizes not only the object proper to it, but also all that is accessible to other means of knowledge.

'Suppose, then, that sensation and imagination were at odds 5 with reasoning, claiming that the universal, which reason claims to perceive, is non-existent, on the grounds that what can be grasped 6 by the senses or by the imagination cannot be universal. On this view either the judgement of the reason is valid, and nothing can be grasped by the senses; or alternatively, since the senses and the imagination are well aware that numerous things are perceptible to them, the notion held by the reason, that the individual object which can be grasped by the senses is a sort of universal, is without foundation. Reason might rejoin that in fact she beholds things 7 perceptible to the senses and imagination by virtue of their universality, whereas they cannot aspire to knowledge of universality because their awareness cannot pass beyond bodily shapes; and moreover, that where knowledge of objects is concerned, assent should be lent to the judgement that is more consistent and perfect. Surely in a dispute of this kind we who have the faculty of reasoning as well as those of imagination and sensation should prefer to approve reason's cause?

'Similarly the human reason believes that the divine under- 8 standing observes the future only in the way she herself knows it. What you claim is this:* if certain things do not seem to have an 9 outcome fixed and necessary, it cannot be known beforehand that they will certainly occur. Therefore there is no foreknowledge of 10 these things; and even if we were to believe that there *is* foreknowledge of them, there will be nothing which does not happen of necessity. Well then, if we could possess the judge- 11 ment exercised by the divine mind in the same way as we partake of reason, just as we have decreed that the imagination and the senses ought to yield to the reason, so we would regard it as most just that the human reason should defer to the divine mind. So if 12 we can, let us raise ourselves to the peak of that highest understanding, for there the reason will look upon what she cannot of herself observe: that is, how even things which have no certain outcome are witnessed by an unerring and precise foreknowledge, a foreknowledge which is not mere opinion, but rather the simplicity of highest knowledge confined by no bounds.

'How diverse are the shapes of beasts that roam the earth!*
For some with elongated bodies sweep earth's dust,
And plough unbroken furrows with their bellies' thrust.
Others on wings roam high aloft, assail the winds,
In fluid flight swim through vast tracts of heaven's expanse;   5
While others still prefer to tread the solid ground,
With measured step to cross green plains, to course through woods.

But though all beasts that meet your gaze boast varied shapes,
Their heads hang low, depress their senses dulled.
The human race alone lifts high its lofty head,   10
And poised with upright stance looks down on earth below.*
Unless earthbound you lose your wits, this image warns:
As with head high and brow thrust forth you search the sky,
So you must bear aloft your thoughts.* Let not your mind
Sink downward, lower than your body poised above.'   15

Chapter 6

1 'So since, as we made clear a moment ago, all that is known is
known not through its own nature but through the nature of those
who apprehend it, let us now, in so far as divine law allows,
examine what is the nature of the divine being, so that we may
likewise come to know what his knowledge is.

2 'It is the common view of all who live by reason that God is
3 eternal.* So we must ponder what eternity is, for this will clarify
4 for us his divine nature and his knowledge alike. Eternity, then, is
the total and perfect possession of life without end, a state which
5 becomes clearer if compared with the world of time;* for whatever
lives in time lives in the here and now, and advances from past to
future. Nothing situated in time can at the one moment grasp the
entire duration of its life. It does not as yet apprehend the morrow,
and it has already relinquished its yesterday; and even in your life
of today, you humans live for no more than that fleeting and
transient moment. So anything subject to a status within time,
6 even if it has had no beginning and never ceases to exist, and even
if its life extends without limit in time, as Aristotle argued is the
case with the world,* is not yet such as can be rightly accounted
7 eternal; for it does not grasp and embrace at the one moment the
whole extent of its life, even if that life is without end. It does not

yet possess the future, and it no longer owns time past. So what 8 does rightly claim the title of eternal is that which grasps and possesses simultaneously the entire fullness of life without end; no part of the future is lacking to it, and no part of the past has escaped it. It must always appear to itself as in the present, and as governing itself; the unending course of fleeting time it must possess as the here and now.

'So those people are mistaken who on hearing that Plato 9 thought that this world had no beginning in time and will have no end,* believe that this created world is become coeternal with its creator; for it is one thing to be directed through a life without 10 end, the process which Plato assigned to the world, but quite another to hold in one's embrace, as being in the present, the whole of life without end, a power clearly unique to the divine mind.* God must not be visualized as prior to the created world 11 merely in length of time; rather, it is by virtue of possession of his simple nature. This condition of his, unchanging life in the 12 present, is imitated by the perpetual movement of temporal things.* Since that movement is unable to achieve and to match that unchanging life, it degenerates from changelessness into change. From the simplicity of the present it subsides into the boundless extent of future and past. Since it cannot at the one moment possess the total fullness of its life, because in a certain sense it never ceases to exist, it appears partially to emulate what it cannot totally fulfil and express.

'So it binds itself to the present, such as it is, of this short-lived, fleeting moment. Since this moment bears some resemblance to that enduring present, it bestows the appearance of such enduring existence on whatever it touches. But since it cannot continue at 13 rest, it embarks on a boundless journey through time; thus by its course it extends the life whose fullness it could not attain by abiding at rest. So should we wish to designate things appro- 14 priately, we should follow Plato, and call God eternal, but the world enduring.*

'Therefore, since every judgement which is made comprehends 15 the things lying before it according to its own nature,* and since God's status is abidingly eternal and in the present, his knowledge too transcends all movement in time. It abides in the simplicity of its present, embraces the boundless extent of past and future, and

by virtue of its simple comprehension, it ponders all things as if
16 they were being enacted in the present. Hence your judgement
will be more correct should you seek to envisage the foresight by
which God discerns all things not as a sort of foreknowledge of the
17 future, but as knowledge of the unceasingly present moment. For
this reason it is better to term it *providentia* ("looking forward
spatially") rather than *praevidentia* ("looking forward in time"),
for it is not set far apart from the lowliest things, and it gazes out
on everything as from one of the world's lofty peaks.*

18   'Why, then, do you demand that things surveyed by the divine
light be necessary, when even men do not pronounce as necessary
19 the things they see? Surely, when you observe things before you,
your seeing them does not impose any necessity on them?'
'Of course not.'

20   'But if it is appropriate to compare the divine present with the
human, then just as you men see certain things in this temporal
present of yours, so God sees all things in his eternal present.
21 Hence this divine foreknowledge does not change the nature and
character of things; God sees them as present before his eyes as
22 they will emerge at some time in the future. Nor does he make
confused judgements about things; with a single mental glance he
distinguishes those future events which will occur by necessity
from those which will not. Consider this parallel.* When you
observe at the one time a man walking on the earth and the sun
rising in the sky, even though you see them simultaneously, you
distinguish them, and you judge the first movement to be
23 voluntary, and the second to be necessary. So it is the same
with the divine vision, as it looks out on the whole world; it
certainly does not dislocate the nature of those things which for
God are in the present, but which in their temporal aspect are in
24 the future. So when God knows that something is about to take
place, something which he is well aware need not come to pass,
this is not an opinion but knowledge which rests on truth.

25   'At this point you may say that what God sees will happen must
inevitably happen, and that what must inevitably happen, happens
of necessity. If you tie me down on this term necessity, I shall
concede that this is a concept most substantially true, but one
which scarcely anyone other than the student of theology has
26 grasped. For my response will be that a future happening which is

necessary when viewed by divine knowledge seems to be wholly free and unqualified when considered in its own nature.* In fact 27 there are two kinds of necessity. One is simple; for example, it is necessary that all men are mortal. The other is conditional; for example, a man must be walking if you are aware that he is walking. What a person knows cannot be other than as it is known; 28 but this conditional necessity is far from involving with it that other simple kind. For conditional necessity is shaped not by a 29 thing's particular nature, but by the condition appended to it. When a person voluntarily takes a walk, no necessity impels him to move forward, though it is necessary for him to move forward the moment he walks. Likewise, then, if Providence sees something in 30 the present, that thing necessarily exists, even though of its nature it incorporates no such necessity. But God sees in the present the 31 future events which proceed from free choice. So these things become necessary as related to God's observation of them, through the condition of his divine knowledge; but considered in themselves they do not forfeit the total freedom of their nature.* So the 32 future events which God foreknows will all undoubtedly come to pass, but some of them proceed from free choice. Though these do take place, their occurrence does not mean that they surrender their own true nature, which would have allowed the possibility of their not happening before they took place.

'What difference, then, does it make that those things are not 33 necessary, when the condition of God's knowledge will in all ways result in the equivalent of necessity? Observe the difference in the 34 instances which I adduced a moment ago, the sun rising and the man walking; while these actions take place, they cannot not take place, but in the first example, before it actually happened, it was necessary for it to do so, whereas in the second it was certainly not. Likewise those events which God sees in the present will 35 undoubtedly come to be, but some will result from their innate necessity, and others at the discretion of those who perform them. So we were by no means wrong in stating that these things are 36 necessary from the aspect of divine knowledge, but considered in themselves they are free from the bonds of necessity, just as all things accessible to the senses are universals from the aspect of the reason, but particulars considered in themselves.

'You will respond that if it lies in my power to change my 37

course of action, I will deprive Providence of her role when I
38 happen to change an act which she foreknows. My response will be
that you can indeed divert your course of action, but the truth of
Providence observes in the present your ability to do this, and
whether you are doing it, or in what direction you are changing it.
So you cannot evade the divine foreknowledge, just as you cannot
escape the gaze of a person's eye which observes you at this
moment, even though you vary your actions by use of your free
will.

39   'So your question then will be: will the arrangements which I
make cause a change in God's knowledge, so that when my
intention switches from one thing to another, his knowledge too
40 seems to vacillate? By no means, for God's gaze anticipates
everything that is to happen, and draws it back and recalls it to
his own knowing in the present. There is no vacillation such as
you imagine, with his foreknowledge changing this way and that;
rather, with a single glance it anticipates and embraces the changes
41 which you make, while itself remaining unchanged. God derives
this understanding and vision in the present not from the outcome
42 of future events, but from his own simplicity. This also offers the
solution to your earlier objection, that it is unworthy to suggest
43 that our future actions are the cause of God's knowledge; for it is
the force of that knowledge, embracing all things in its awareness
in the present, which itself imposes a limit on all things, and owes
nothing to events which occur later.*

44   'Since this is the case, man's freedom of will remains intact, and
the laws which prescribe rewards and punishments for acts of will
45 which are free of all necessity are not unjust. Moreover, God
continually observes with foreknowledge all things from on high,
and his eternal vision, which is ever in the present, accords with
the future nature of our actions, and dispenses rewards to the good
46 and punishments to the wicked. The hopes which we rest in God,
and the prayers addressed to him, are not in vain; when they are
47 righteous, they cannot be ineffectual. So avoid vices, cultivate the
virtues, raise your minds to righteous hopes, pour out your
48 humble prayers to heaven.* As long as you refuse to play the
hypocrite, a great necessity to behave honourably is imposed on
you, for your deeds are observed by the judge who sees all things.*

EXPLANATORY NOTES

(Note—m. stands for metrum and so distinguishes the verse notes from the prose.)

Book 1

Chapter 1. As Boethius laments in verse the misery of his arrest and confinement, he is visited by an apparition. He fails to recognize Lady Philosophy in spite of the indications offered by her robe, her appurtenances, and her comments. She peremptorily dismisses the Muses of poetry who are present to inspire the prisoner's lamentation.

m.1–22 *I who with zest*: in Book 1 the poems precede the prose-narratives, because Boethius initially seeks his consolation from literature. In the later books the poems are appendages to the philosophical exhortations. In these first verses (the Latin is in elegiacs, the metre of lament), Boethius suggests that the poetic Muses can see him through his impending ordeal. He draws by reminiscence on the Roman poets who were his companions in happier days. The first line adapts the epilogue to Virgil's *Georgics* (4. 563 ff., *studiis florentem*), and perhaps also the prooemium to the Aeneid (*ille ego . . .*) which is excised from modern editions. Virgil is again evoked in the images of flourishing youth and declining age (*Aen.* 5. 295, 395). The lament that Death refuses to visit the poet recalls Hecuba's forlorn cry in the *Troades* (1170 ff.) of Seneca, a favourite poet. The most pervasive influence is that of Ovid, notably *Tristia*, 5. 1, the lament that recalls Ovid's happy youth and sudden fall. The tissue of commonplaces from these and other poets (Horace and Propertius) is to be swept away by Philosophy, who in the spirit of Plato's condemnations (*Rep.* 548 B, 607 A, etc.) sends the poetic Muses packing.

1 *a lady*: see Chadwick, 225 ff. Various models in earlier literature have been suggested: Sapientia ('Wisdom') in the Old Testament, Ecclesia ('the Church') in *The Shepherd* of Hermas, Parthenia in Methodius, and in the prosimetric tradition of Menippean satire, Philosophy in Lucian's *Fugitivi*. Perhaps most prominent in Boethius' mind is the similar epiphany of Continence in Augustine's *Confessions*, 8. 11, likewise urging a change of heart;

Philosophy personified appears also in Augustine's *Soliloquies* 1. 1. Her varying stature as described here symbolizes the different aspects of philosophy. Her feet are on the ground in the disciplines of logic and ethics, but her head is in and above the heavens when she turns to physics and natural theology.

3 *Her robe*: this is dust-covered because of her venerable age and recent neglect. The Greek letters *Π* and *Θ* stand for Practical and Theoretical Philosophy respectively. The suggestion that *Θ* hints also at Boethius' imminent death (*thanatos* in Greek), seems less likely, but see Chadwick, 225 f. and *Medium Aevum* (1980), 175 ff. In his *Commentary on Porphyry's* Isagoge (*Dial.* 1. 1), Boethius links ethics with the first and physics (including natural theology) with the second. For the notion that philosophy was originally a seamless robe, God's highest gift to mankind, which was later torn by hostile sects, see e.g. Justin Martyr, *Dialogue with Trypho*. The books which Philosophy carries are the works of the major philosophers, and her sceptre indicates her role as queen of the sciences.

10 *the Eleatics and . . . the Academy*: the Eleatic school was founded at Elea in southern Italy in the early fifth century BC by Zeno and Parmenides, whose obscure poem argues that being is one, eternal, motionless, and perfect. See Kirk-Raven-Schofield, chs. 10–11. The Academy, the school founded by Plato, survived into Boethius' day, but was dissolved by the emperor Justinian in 529.

Chapter 2. Philosophy rebukes in verses Boethius' abandonment of his spirit of philosophical enquiry, and his descent into self-absorbed misery. She follows her poetic lines by upbraiding him for his failure to recognize her, but she promises that once he rectifies his ignorance he will then recall his own true identity.

m.1–36 *Dull-witted*: the poetic rebuke contrasts Boethius' earlier sense of intellectual adventure, evocative of Lucretius' eulogy of Epicurus (1. 62 ff.), with his present descent into the concerns of the material world, which is depicted with echoes of Plato, Cicero's *De senectute*, 77, and Neoplatonism, especially in the image of the sea as the material world; see the references in O'Daly, 42 and 108 f. There may also be hints of biblical influence from Ps. 129 (*De profundis*) and Matt. 22: 13 (the outer darkness).

m.15–16 *The planets . . . Charting with mastery*: Boethius' earlier studies had included mathematical astronomy; for the likelihood that a lost work of his was based on Proclus' summary of the *Almagest* of Ptolemy, see Chadwick, 108 ff.

5 *He is suffering from loss of energy*: This medical condition was discussed by Celsus and the elder Pliny, as well as in the poetry of Lucretius and of Horace. There is a powerful description of its effects at Lucretius 3. 463ff., though there it is associated with bodily disease.

Chapter 3. Boethius at last recognizes Philosophy, and is exhilarated. She promises to stand by him, as she has supported other representatives of hers in the past.

m.1–10 *Then darkness left me*: in this poetic excursus in which Boethius describes the dawn of recognition, he evokes the image of Turnus in Virgil (*Aen.* 12. 665ff.), when after being initially dumbstruck by the siege of Laurentum and the death of Amata, the hero's mind clears. The Virgilian phraseology is evoked in the first two lines here, and the metaphors of storm and cloud that follow are anticipated in the language of the Virgilian passage. See O'Daly, 120ff.

6 *he triumphed over an unjust death*: this refers to Socrates' refusal to retire into exile in 399 BC; instead, he resolved to stand trial on the charge of having introduced strange gods into the state and having corrupted the youth. Thirty days after defending himself, as Plato's *Apology* and *Crito* describe, he willingly drank the hemlock.

9 *the flight of Anaxagoras . . . the torturing of Zeno*: Anaxagoras, who posited the existence of Mind (*Nous*) as initiator of cosmic motion and animator of plants and animals, and who argued that initially the world developed from 'seeds' of every natural substance, was condemned at Athens (*c.*450 BC? The date is disputed; see Kirk-Raven-Schofield, ch. 15) on a charge of impiety. Pericles aided him to retire to Lampsacus and further fame. For Socrates' condemnation, see the previous note. The Zeno mentioned here is the Eleatic philosopher cited in 1. 1. 10n. ('the Eleatics', etc.); the sources agree that he was tortured to death, but detail of the identity of the tyrant who punished him and the locale varies so widely that the truth cannot be established.

Canius, and Seneca, and Soranus: as recounted in the following chapter, Canius was accused of being implicated in a plot to assassinate Caligula in the months before that emperor's violent death in AD 41. See 4. 27n. (*Canius*). Seneca was forced to commit suicide by the emperor Nero in AD 65, and the same emperor made Soranus Barea a victim in the following year (see Tacitus, *Ann.* 15.64, 16. 23). All three are associated with the Stoic opposition to

imperial tyranny, and are thus presented as Boethius' spiritual
predecessors.

13 *our leader*: this cannot be Philosophy herself, for she is speaking; it
must be Sapientia ('Wisdom').

Chapter 4. Philosophy in her preliminary verses emphasizes that the man
of wisdom and courage fears neither physical nor moral hazards. When
she subsequently asks the prisoner if he has absorbed the lesson, he
responds with an outburst against the iniquity of Fortune: in spite of his
having embraced the Platonic principle of seeking public office for the
furtherance of justice, and in spite of his noble record as administrator,
he has suffered the injustice and deceit which led to his condemnation.

m.1–18 *He who keeps composure*: in her reflections on the need to face
tyranny with equanimity, Philosophy expresses the lesson in
hendecasyllables. In view of her earlier condemnation of the
Muses of poetry, it seems ironical that she repeatedly echoes the
Odes of Horace (for the opening line, cf. *Odes* 3. 3. 1; for the tumbling
tower, 2. 10. 10 f.; for jettisoning the shield, 2. 7. 10). But these
evocations and the echo of Virgil's description of Etna (*Aen.* 8. 418)
are to bolster the prisoner's courage instead of inciting him to self-
pity. The exhortation to renounce the vicious emotions of fear and
desire, and the condemnation of intemperate anger, are features of
Stoic ethical tenets; see Cicero, *Tusc.* 3. 24 ff.; Seneca, *De beata vita*,
5. 1.

1 *the donkey listening to the lyre*: the proverbial phrase goes back to
Menander (fr. 640 and *Mis.* 295), but Boethius may have been
reminded of it by Martianus Capella (804 ff.), one of his predecessors in the use of the prosimetric form.

Out with it . . . your breast: Homer, *Il.* 1. 363.

2 *Then I pulled myself together*: Boethius now marshals his rebuttal of
the charges laid against him by a sort of forensic speech, with
exordium (cf. Cicero, *Cat.* 1. 1), narration of the case, proof,
refutation of the charge, and peroration. See K. Reichenberger,
Untersuchungen zur literarischen Stellung des Consolatio Philosophiae (Cologne, 1954), 35 ff.

3 *the room in my house*: if we accept the *Consolation* as a historical
document, it seems clear that Boethius is confined under conditions more Spartan than house-arrest, but which permit him access
to books. See the Introduction, p. xix.

5 *this principle*: enunciated at Plato, *Rep.* 473 D, 487 E.

10 *Conigastus... Trigguilla*: little is known of these agents of Theoderic. Conigastus is the recipient of a letter from Cassiodorus, successor to Boethius as Master of Offices (*Var.* 8. 28); Trigguilla (cf. *Var.* 3. 10) may be the Triggua mentioned by Ennodius, bishop of Pavia (9. 21. 2), who had died in 521. Trigguilla's title was *Praepositus Sacri Cubiculi* (court chamberlain; cf. Jones, *LRE* 567 ff.).

12 *public purchase of grain*: this compulsory purchase (*coemptio*) was for feeding the troops (Jones, *LRE* 254, 1117). The Praetorian Prefect in Italy (Flavius Anicius Probus Faustus Niger, consul 490) was responsible for army rations and for the corn supply of Rome. The dispute dated back to 510–11, or less probably to 522. See Gruber, ad loc.: Jones, *LRE* 448 ff.

13–14 *Paulinus . . . Albinus*: Flavius Paulinus was consul in 498; for Boethius' defence of Albinus (consul 493), see the Introduction, p. xvii.

14 *Cyprian*: this courtier, brother of the Opilio mentioned a few lines below, was subsequently promoted to the office of *comes sacrarum largitionum*, a position in which he supervised the mines and the mints, and was responsible for the pay and donatives of the army and civil service; see Matthews, 30.

16–17 *Basilius . . . Opilio and Gaudentius*: for the background to their accusations, see the Introduction, p. xvii f.

24 *the injunction of Socrates*: cf. Plato, *Theaet.* 151 D, *Rep.* 485 C.

27 *Canius*: the anecdote recounted here is the sole evidence for the historical episode; see Matthews, 37.

30 *one of your devotees*: he is usually identified as Epicurus (cf. fr. 374 = Lactantius, *De ira Dei*, 13. 21): 'If he has both will and power, as is appropriate for God alone, what then is the source of evils? Or why does God not dispel them?'

36 *five hundred miles away*: Boethius was indicted and condemned by the senate at Rome.

37 *to stain my conscience with sacrilege*: the imputation is probably that Boethius exploited magic arts to win the support of evil spirits. We recall a similar charge made against an earlier philosopher, Apuleius; accusations of magic were a recurring feature in the years between. See Matthews, 36 f.; Chadwick, 49 f.

38 *'Follow the god'*: a commonplace of ancient philosophy; cf. Cicero, *Fin.* 3. 73; Seneca, *De beata vita*, 15. 5, and *Ep.* 2. 4. 5.

40 *my august father-in-law*: for Symmachus, Roman consular and father of Rusticiana, wife of Boethius, see the Introduction, p. xiv.

Chapter 5. As spokesman of the preliminary verses, Boethius complains to God that the order imposed on the world of nature does not extend to the realm of human conduct. Philosophy counters with the criticism that he has exiled himself from his true home, by surrendering to base emotions. She promises an initial cure of a gentle kind.

m.1–50 *Creator of the starry sphere*: the poem is neatly structured in two parts. The first describes the regularity of the cosmic order; and the second contrasts with it the anarchy of human life, in which the wicked prosper and the good suffer. As Klingner, 4, comments, this poem is the hinge on which the whole of Book 1 turns. The literary inspiration is above all the *Phaedra* of Seneca, 959 ff. The structure in both (invocation, the order of the heavenly bodies, the sequence of the seasons, the divine indifference to human affairs) is identical. See O'Daly, 129.

m.22–3 *Arcturus . . . Sirius*: for Arcturus as symbol of the barren season, see Virgil, *Georgics* 1. 68 ff. (it rises in September). Sirius, the dog-star, rises in late July, when the crops are roasted.

m.29 *slippery Fortune*: the theme is prominent in Seneca's *Phaedra*, 977 ff.

3 *your native land*: the true *patria* of the Platonist philosopher is the heavenly home of the soul. Cf. Cicero, *Tusc.* 1. 24: 'Once souls have left their bodies, they can rise to heaven as to their own abode.'

4 '. . . *one lord and one king*': the citation is from Homer, *Il.* 2. 204.

5 *cannot lawfully be banished from it*: cf. Cicero, *Caec.* 100.

11 *grief, anger, and melancholy*: for harmful emotions condemned by the Stoics, see the note at Book 4 ch. 2 ('lust . . . anger . . . grief . . . hope') and Cicero, *Tusc.* 3. 23 ff. The image of the emotions forming a *tumor* or swelling goes back to the Stoic Chrysippus (see Cicero, *Tusc.* 4. 63). The notion of the application of 'gentler remedies' echoes Seneca's consolation to his mother Helvia in *Dialogi*, 12. 1. 2.

Chapter 6. From this chapter on, Philosophy declaims an extended sequence of poems, so that they become part of the coherent pattern of her teaching. This poem both reinforces the message of that in chapter 5, that nature follows laws divinely imposed, and further suggests that man's behaviour must conform to that pattern. In the prose-sequence that follows, Philosophy elicits the precise nature of Boethius' sickness: he has forgotten how and to what end the world is guided, and his own identity within it.

m.1–24 *When Apollo*: in this poem, Philosophy reviews successively nature's ordinances for summer, winter, spring, and autumn, and the final section underlines the lesson that men must not seek to reverse the order in nature. The advice against sowing seed in high summer is clearly influenced by the teaching in Virgil's *Georgics* (1. 204 ff.), and the warning against harvesting the grape in spring echoes Horace, *Odes*, 2. 5. 9 ff.; see O'Daly, 132 ff. Thus this first plank in Philosophy's demonstration that the world is God's rational creation is underpinned by the authority of antiquity.

m.2 *the Crab's oppressive days*: the sun enters the zone of Cancer (the Crab) between 20 June and 20 July.

m.4 *In the furrows will not grow*: a reminiscence of Virgil, *Georgics*, 1. 223 f.

m.6 *Acorns from the oaks obtain*: cf. Virgil, *Georgics*, 1. 159.

1 *to probe and investigate*: Philosophy plays the role of physician; diagnosis of Boethius' mental state must precede the prescription of salutary medicine.

10 *distress has clouded my recollection*: at the close of 3. 11 Boethius is reminded of what he earlier knew.

15 *a mortal creature endowed with reason*: Boethius offers a similar definition, in response to this frequent philosophical enquiry, What is man?, at his commentary on the *Isagoge* of Porphyry, 3. 4 (CSEL 48, 208).

17 *the further cause of your sickness*: Philosophy is suggesting that Boethius' failure to follow the Delphic injunction, 'Know thyself,' is impeding his awareness of God, the final End. In the Neoplatonists' view, that awareness is gained through knowledge of one's own soul; Boethius' sickness lies in his forgetting that he has an immortal soul.

Chapter 7. With Philosophy's diagnosis of the nature of Boethius' sickness, the subject-matter of Book 1 has been completed in ch. 6. These verses round off the book with a series of images which illustrate the prisoner's malaise. His mind is blinded and impeded by vicious emotions, like the stars when hidden by clouds, the sea-waters when muddied, and the waterfalls when blocked by rocks.

m.1–16 *When black clouds envelop*: the series of images evokes familiar passages of earlier poetry. For the encompassing clouds, see Horace, *Odes*, 2. 16. 2 ff. The sea-storm is a commonplace in Greek and Latin literature from Homer onwards; here Virgilian touches are especially prominent (cf. *Aen.* 3. 196; 7. 759), though the detail of the dredged-up sand may be original. The third image, that of boulders impeding a waterfall, recalls Homer, *Il.* 13. 137 ff., and Virgil, *Aen.* 12. 523 ff. See O'Daly, 126 ff.

m.21–4 *Forgo empty joys . . . come not near*: this emphasis on harmful emotions goes back to Plato (*Laches*, 191 D), but is particularly prominent in Stoic thought; see the note on 4. 2. m.6–8 ('lust . . . anger . . . grief . . . hope'). There are echoes here of Horace, *Epp.* 1. 4. 12; 1. 6. 12.

Book 2

Chapter 1. Philosophy's diagnosis of Boethius' ailment is that he pines for the wealth and position earlier bestowed on him by Fortune, and is bitter because she has deserted him. But he should have remembered that her consistency lies precisely in her inconsistency. Philosophy seeks the eloquence of her ally Rhetoric to underline that the prisoner has no justifiable complaint against the fickle goddess. The verses that follow underline Fortune's capricious treatment of the human race.

1 *She fell silent*: the rhetorical device of the silence serves to separate the topic of Boethius' lament, the theme of Book 1, from Philosophy's consolation proper, which now begins in Book 2.

3 *that monstrous lady, Fortune*: it is impossible to overemphasize the prominence which the figure of Tyche/Fortuna plays in the minds of historians and philosophers of Greece and Rome. For a brief survey of her role in Greek literature, see *OCD*, s.v. Tyche. At Rome the theme was taken up by moralizing historians and especially by Stoic philosophers, who urge suspicion of her favours and defiance of her desertion. Boethius plays a key role in the transmission of the concept of Fortuna into Western medieval thought; for a useful survey, see H. R. Patch, *The Goddess Fortuna in Medieval Literature* (Cambridge, Mass., 1977).

8 *the persuasion of sweet-sounding rhetoric*: rhetoric, as the orderly and persuasive art of presenting a thesis, was earlier regarded by Aristotle and by Cicero as a close ally of philosophy. Boethius, in his *De topicis differentiis*, 4, 'subordinates the whole study of rhetoric to dialectic' (so G. Kennedy, *Classical Rhetoric* (Chapel Hill, NC, 1980), 179). Here Philosophy embarks upon a *suasoria* or speech of persuasion (a traditional exercise in schools of rhetoric) on the theme of the right attitude to Fortune, a topic which repeatedly recurs in earlier literature, most prominently in Seneca (e.g. in his *Epp.* 18. 6, 78. 29).

11 *the blind goddess*: in *The Golden Ass* of Apuleius, 11. 15, the priest of Isis contrasts 'Fortune in her blind course' with his divine patroness, whom he describes as 'Fortune with eyes'.

19 *her whirling wheel*: in Hellenistic and Roman art and literature, Tyche/Fortuna is frequently depicted with her whirling wheel. For a detailed survey of these representations and texts, see Courcelle, 127 ff.

m.2 *Euripus' tidal currents*: the Euripus, the strait lying between Euboea and the mainland of Attica, was notorious in antiquity for the irregularity of its currents, see Plato, *Phaedo*, 90 C; Livy, 28. 6. 10. For the use of the image in earlier literature to describe the instability of human affairs, see O'Daly, 139.

Chapter 2. Philosophy now allows Fortune herself to remonstrate with Boethius for complaining at the withdrawal of her favours. In this rhetorical exercise, the goddess exploits traditional images of the perversity of nature, and exempla from history to justify her treatment of the prisoner. The ensuing verses castigate the human race for making importunate demands.

1 *in Fortune's own words*: prosopopoeia or impersonation is a frequent rhetorical technique in philosophical contexts; see Plato, *Phaedo*, 87 A; Cicero, *Tusc.* 2. 45; Plotinus, 3. 2. 3.

4 *When nature brought you forth*: Fortune underlines the fact that the newborn child has no resources or possessions; for the motif in Classical literature, see Lucretius, 5. 222 ff., Pliny, *NH* 7. 1; it also emerges in Christian writings, following Job 1: 21.

8 *The heavens are allowed . . . dark nights*: in this sequence of changes in nature, Boethius has probably drawn on Seneca, *Ep.* 107. 7 f., a passage which exhorts Lucilius to adapt to such shifts.

11 *Croesus*: the king was taken prisoner after the fall of Sardis, set upon a pyre by Cyrus, but saved by a cloudburst; see Herodotus, 1. 86 f. At Herodotus 1. 207, Croesus warns Cyrus that man's affairs are on a wheel, 'which as it whirls round does not permit the same man to prosper for ever'.

12 *Paulus . . . Perseus*: in the Third Macedonian War, the Roman L. Aemilius Paulus defeated Perseus of Macedon at Pydna in 168 BC. Livy (45. 8. 6) makes Paulus moralize on the uncertainty of Fortune, but without weeping; the tears are supplied by the author of *De viris illustribus*, 56. 3, and Plutarch, *Aemilius Paulus*, 26. 4 f.

13 *the two jars*: at *Il.* 24. 527 ff., Achilles consoles Priam for the loss of his sons: 'Two urns stand on the threshold of Zeus's palace,

containing his gifts, the one of evils, the other of blessings.' Plato, *Rep.* 379 D may have reminded Boethius of the saying, though it is widespread in antiquity.

14 *just cause to anticipate a better future*: the comment suggests that though Boethius has been condemned to death, there is prospect of a reprieve. For the possibility that he (and Symmachus) were hostages to ensure the success of the legation sent to Constantinople to remonstrate with Justin about his persecution of the Goths, see Chadwick, 62; earlier, W. Bark, *American Historical Review* (1943–4), 11–32 (= *Wege der Forschung*, 483 (1984), 11–32).

m1–20 *If from her bounteous horn*: the poem underlines the claim made in the previous passage that Boethius has had more than his share of blessings. Cornucopia ('Plenty') appears frequently in Latin poetry (cf. Horace, *Odes*, 1. 17. 14 ff., *Carm. Saec.* 59 f.; Ovid, *Met.* 9. 88 ff., etc.), and she is often combined with the goddess Fortune in Roman art (O'Daly, 140).

m.3–6 *grains of shifting sand . . . bright orbs in the sky*: these images of grains of sand and star-clusters to depict numbers beyond counting evoke Catullus, 7, in which the poet yearns for countless kisses from Lesbia.

m.17–18 *Thirst for possessions*: cf. Horace, *Odes*, 3. 16. 17 f.; Prudentius, *Hamartigeneia*, 257.

m.20 *The rich man hates to spend*: cf. Claudian, *In Rufinum*, 1. 199 ff.

Chapter 3. Philosophy reminds Boethius of the successive stages of his hitherto prosperous life, in which Fortune favoured him above any other individual. Moreover, the reverses he now encounters are temporary, for Fortune's power ends with the period of this life. The verses at the close present a series of images which depict inconstancy in nature; it is therefore foolish to expect human lives to follow a constant course.

4 *the number and extent of your blessings*: the catalogue of blessings enumerated by Philosophy is Boethius' method of recalling to the reader his distinguished earlier career; for the details, see the Introduction, pp. xiii ff. The 'people of the greatest distinction' who tended him were Symmachus and his circle. The distinctions which 'even men of mature years fail to attain' refer especially to his tenure of the consulship in 510 at the age of less than 30. 'The crowning moment of happiness' came in 522, when his two sons held the consulship together; two members of the same family had not held the office together since 395. This distinction reflects the

favour in which Boethius was held, both at Constantinople, the source of such appointments, and at Ravenna. See Matthews, 29.

8 *you delivered the encomium*: this speech of praise of Theoderic is cited as 'a splendid speech' (*luculenta oratio*) by Cassiodorus in the *Anecdoton Holderi*; see Matthews, 30.

m.1–18 *When Phoebus*: the brusque message of the poem appears clearly in the final lines. Boethius incorporates motifs of a letter of Seneca (107. 8), but whereas Seneca urges acceptance of the dictates of nature, Philosophy here stresses the negative aspects of an inconstant world. See O'Daly, 141.

m.7 *Auster*: the south wind was the purveyor of stormy weather; see Propertius, 2. 16. 56; Ovid, *Met.* 7. 532, etc.

m.12 *Boreas*: the Greek name for the north wind is frequently exploited by the Roman poets.

Chapter 4. Philosophy now appends to her account of Boethius' past happiness (ch. 3) some consoling features of his present condition, in particular the welfare of his family; she suggests that by comparison with the lot of the less privileged, he still enjoys an enviable life. But true happiness, she adds, is to be sought not in material possessions which Fortune controls, but in mastery of self. Moreover, since the mind survives the body, such happiness as material possessions bring must terminate at death. The poem which closes the chapter uses the image of a house established on firm foundations to indicate that true happiness cannot be built on the shifting sands of material prosperity.

2 *the unhappiest aspect of misfortune is to have known happiness*: Dante, who found consolation in this treatise after the death of Beatrice, echoes this aphorism at *Inferno*, 5. 121 ff., in the mouth of Francesca:

> Nessun maggiore dolore,
> Che ricordari del tempo felice,
> Nella miseria; e ciò sa il tuo dottore.

5 *the indignities which he himself suffers*: it seems clear that Symmachus was at this point already suffering harassment through his support of Albinus and Boethius, but that his life was not yet in danger.

8 *You are truly fortunate . . . your blessings*: a conscious echo of Virgil, *Georgics*, 2. 458.

9 *your anchors still hold fast*: perhaps evoking Ovid, *Tristia*, 5. 2. 42, where Ovid laments that his wife is perhaps ceasing to be his anchor.

12–14 *Does any individual*: this moralizing echoes similar sentiments in Horace (*Odes*, 2. 16. 27 f., 'nihil est ab omni parte beatum'); for similar sentiments in Greek literature see R. G. M. Nisbet and Margaret Hubbard, *Commentary on Horace Odes II* (Oxford, 1978), ad loc. The various categories of distress that follow echo Aristotle's list in *Nic. Eth.* 1099 B.

17 *your place of banishment*: if the evidence of the *Consolation* is historical, Boethius is at Pavia, separated from his wife and presumably under house-arrest in a run-down area; see 1. 4 n. ('the room in my house').

22 *when it lies within*: the sentence echoes words of the Stoic Epictetus, *Diatribes* 3. 22. 26 ff.

28 *the minds of men are in no wise mortal*: in Platonist and Aristotelian thought, the mind is the higher and directing part of the soul, which for Plato is immortal. Though Aristotle visualizes the soul as inseparable from the body, as the power of sight to the eye, he appears to believe that the mind survives bodily death (*Protr.* frag. B 10 8 D), and the idea becomes a commonplace in Cicero (e.g. *Tusc.* 1. 66).

29 *but even in pain and torture*: it is tempting to put a Christian complexion on this, but Boethius visualizes his impending martyrdom within the tradition of the philosophers cited in 1. 3 above; see also ch. 6 below.

m.1–18 *The careful man*: in counselling the prisoner to despise the favours of Fortune, Philosophy incorporates in these lines a series of images of insecure house-foundations which recur in Senecan tragedy; see e.g. *Hercules Furens*, 199 f., *Phaedra* 1128 ff., *Oedipus*, 8 ff. For further examples, see Nisbet-Hubbard on Horace, *Odes*, 2. 10. 9. O'Daly, 144, speculates on the possibility of the influence of the gospel of Matthew (7. 24 ff.), in which the Sermon on the Mount contrasts the wise man who builds his house on a rock with the fool who builds on sand.

Chapter 5. In resuming the argument from the previous chapter that men are not to look to the gifts of Fortune to obtain happiness, Philosophy reviews the worldly possessions commonly sought—money, precious stones, handsome estates, attractive clothes, large retinues of slaves. The verses make the same point, by harking nostalgically back to the simple life enjoyed in days of old, before the evils of extravagant living invaded society.

4 *when . . . doled out rather than gathered in*: cf. Horace, *Odes*, 2. 2. 1 ff. for condemnation of the accumulation of wealth by misers.

18 *a baleful burden . . . fiercely hostile to the master himself*: for examples of the murder of masters by their slaves in the early empire ('sufficiently rare to merit attention', in A. N. Sherwin-White's phrase, *The Letters of Pliny* (Oxford, 1966)), see Pliny, *Ep.* 3. 14; 8. 14. 12 (with Sherwin-White's nn.); Tacitus, *Ann.* 14. 42 ff.

23 *"if you have a lot . . . you haven't got"*: the aphorism appears earlier in Aulus Gellius, 9. 8: 'multis egere qui multa habeat'.

34 *fearful of the club and the sword*: according to the differing traditions, Boethius himself was clubbed to death (so the *Excerpta Valesiana*, 2. 85 ff.) or dispatched with the sword (*Liber Pontificalis*, 1. 276); see Matthews, 38 n. 1. But 'the club and the sword' is a literary reminiscence; see the next note.

34–5 *as a traveller . . . with empty pockets . . . with a song on your lips*: in a memorable passage, Juvenal (10. 19 ff.) writes: 'On starting a journey by night, even though the vessels of plain silver you carry are few, you will fear the sword and the club . . . but the empty-handed traveller will whistle in the brigand's face.'

m.1–32 *Happy indeed, those earlier days*: the motif of the Golden Age was a hackneyed one in both Greek and Latin poetry; see especially Hesiod, *Works and Days*, 109 ff. and Aratus, *Phaenomena*, 105 ff.; Virgil, *Georgics*, 2. 532 ff., Horace, *Epodes*, 2 and 16, Propertius, 4. 1, Tibullus, 1. 3; 2. 5. O'Daly, 179 ff., makes a valiant attempt to redeem what seems 'at first sight . . . a striking lack of originality', stressing the poem's reflection of the philosophical tradition (cf. Seneca, *Ep.* 90. 3 and 38). But the series of familiar images and verbal echoes makes the poem an exercise in pastiche rather than an original reflection on Philosophy's preceding observations. For the exordium ('Happy, indeed . . .'), cf. Virgil, *Georgics*, 2. 458, Tibullus, 1. 3. 35 f.; for 'the sheen of silk (*lucida uellera*) with Tyrian dye', see *Georgics*, 3. 307; for 'Not yet did sailors cleave the wave . . . to gather goods', cf. Tibullus, 1. 3. 39 ff., which also incorporates the motif of the absence of war. As O'Daly, 180, observes, the final lines ('Who first, alas . . .') echo a passage in Boethius' North African contemporary, Dracontius (*De laud. Dei*, 2. 459 f.), who depicts the Golden Age before the Fall in the garden of Eden.

Chapter 6. Having rejected wealth as a means of happiness in Chapter 5, Philosophy now similarly rejects aspirations to political power. This, she claims, enables men to dominate bodies but not minds. Tyrants and victors in war may find their roles reversed, becoming victims and not oppressors. High positions often fall into the hands of the wicked, and therefore cannot be good. In the poem that follows, Boethius exploits the stock figure of oppression, the emperor Nero, to make an oblique attack on Theoderic as a tyrannical ruler; see O'Daly, 85.

2 *to rescind the consular authority . . . to expunge the title of king*: Livy records how the last king of Rome, Tarquinius Superbus, was deposed following the rape of Lucretia by the king's son. Twin consuls were then elected; one of them, L. Tarquinius Collatinus, was later deposed or resigned from office (Livy, 2. 2. 2, wonders if the people 'did not go too far in excessive protection of liberty'). It is not clear whether Boethius refers to the abrogation of the consular power of individuals such as Collatinus (and much later, that of Cinna in 87 BC), or to the alleged limitation of consular power in general by the lex Terentilia of 462 BC. See Livy, 3. 9-14, with the note of R. M. Ogilvie.

8 *bit through his tongue*: the anecdote is told of both the philosopher Zeno of Elea (*c.*460 BC) and Anaxarchus of Abdera, who accompanied Alexander the Great on his eastern expedition. Anaxarchus was pounded to death in a mortar by the Cypriot prince Nicocreon (Diog. Laert., 9. 58): the torture and execution of Zeno is ascribed to various tyrants (see Cicero, *Tusc.* 2. 52 with the n. of T. W. Dougan).

10 *Busiris . . . slaughtered by his guest Hercules*: the story of Busiris (actually the name of a town; see Herodotus, 2. 59. 1; 2. 61. 1) occurs first in Pherecydes of Syros (*c.*550 BC); it is mentioned by Herodotus (2. 45. 1), and became the theme of a satyr-drama by Euripides.

11 *Regulus . . . surrendered his hands to the chains of his victors*: in the First Punic War, Regulus commanded the Roman army in Africa; after defeating the Carthaginian forces and seizing Tunis, he was captured by the mercenary general Xanthippus in 255 BC. For the later legend of his release on parole to Rome, and his heroic return to Carthage to face torture and death, see Horace, *Odes*, 3. 5, and *OCD*, s.v. Regulus.

m.1-17 *We know what destruction*: this is the first of the poems devoted to the theme of Nero's tyranny with its oblique allusion to Theoderic; for the second, see 3. 4. The details here reflect the accounts of Tacitus, Suetonius, and Cassius Dio. For the great fire of AD 64 see Tacitus, *Ann.* 15. 38 ff. The slaughter of senators followed the unmasking of the conspiracy of Piso in 65 (Tacitus, *Ann.* 15. 49 ff.). The poisoning of Nero's stepbrother Britannicus (hence the final line of the poem) is described in lively fashion by Suetonius, *Nero*, 33. 2. The account of the murder of the emperor's mother Agrippina, together with the report that Nero praised the beauty of the corpse, is at Tacitus, *Ann.* 14. 8 ff. See in general Miriam T. Griffin, *Nero, the End of a Dynasty* (London, 1984).

m.9–10 *Those which the sun-god . . . beneath the ocean*: for this literary conceit describing the widespread nations of the empire, Boethius evokes Virgil, *Aen.* 8. 720 ff., Tibullus, 2. 5. 59 f.

Chapter 7. Following the condemnation of wealth and ambition for high position as avenues to happiness, Philosophy now attacks the pursuit of fame. She stresses how narrow are the bounds within which men attain it, and how precarious is posthumous reputation because of the absence or disappearance of written records. More generally, within the concept of eternity, no fame is significant. Persons who seek true glory through virtue have no desire for the bubble reputation in this life. The verses in this chapter are closely aligned to the messages of the prose-section.

2 *outstanding achievements in the service of the state*: Boethius echoes Cicero's celebrated definition of *gloria* (*Sest.* 139: 'Praise given to right actions and the reputation for great merits in the service of the state.') This is a significant departure from the attitude of the Homeric hero, for whom personal glory is the highest aim; Roman virtue seeks the good of the community. See Donald Earl, *The Moral and Political Tradition of Rome* (London, 1967), 30.

3 *As you have learnt from the proofs of the astronomers*: in what follows, Boethius draws freely on two sources, Cicero and Macrobius. At *Rep.* 1. 26, Cicero makes precisely the point that nothing is notable in human affairs by comparison with the majesty of the heavens, nothing lasting by comparison with their eternity, and nothing glorious in our tiny earth, especially as we dwell in so small a part of it, 'utterly unknown to most nations'. Macrobius, *Comm. on the Dream of Scipio*, 2. 5–9, discusses the astronomical and geographical lore in greater detail, and concludes: 'The small dimensions of the earth are emphasized so carefully that the brave man may realize that ambition for fame must be accorded little weight, for in such small compass it cannot be great.'

4 *Ptolemy's demonstrations*: the astronomer and geographer, writing in Alexandria in the second century AD, wrote treatises on astronomy (the *Almagest*, which Boethius may have drawn upon,

directly or indirectly, in a work now lost; see Chadwick, 102) and geography.

8   *in some passage*: cf. Cicero, *Rep.* 6. 22: 'Could your name or that of any of our contemporaries have made its way across the Caucasus . . .?' The observation is echoed by Macrobius, *Comm. on the Dream of Scipio*, 2. 9. 3, probably Boethius' immediate source.

20 *". . . if you had kept your mouth shut"*: the anecdote (source unknown) may have arisen from the aphorism that the orator proves himself by speaking, the philosopher 'by silence at the right time as much as by talk' (Macrobius, *Saturae*, 7. 1. 11).

m.15–16 *Fabricius . . . Brutus . . . Cato*: C. Fabricius Luscinus is cited as an outstanding historical figure not only for his military exploits (especially in the war with Pyrrhus) and his civil career as consul (twice) and censor (275 BC), but also for his reputation for probity. The adjective *rigidus* here applied to Cato indicates that the Censor (234–149 BC), likewise celebrated not only for military and civil achievements but also for his defence of public morality, rather than his great-grandson is meant. The identity of this Brutus, whether the traditional founder of the Roman republic or leader in the assassination of Julius Caesar, is not made clear.

Chapter 8. In this closing section of Book 2, Philosophy rounds off her condemnation of Fortune's gifts by claiming that she is more beneficial when hostile than when favourable. Adverse Fortune allows us to identify true friends. This theme of *amicitia* is taken up in the concluding poem, which emphasizes that the harmonious love which governs the world of nature also cements relations between nations, married partners, and true friends.

7   *the most precious of all riches*: friendship occupies a dominant place in the ethical doctrines of antiquity. Plato devotes his *Lysis* to the virtue, teaching that true friendship is based on the common acceptance of good and evil. In his systematic discussion at the close of the *Nicomachean Ethics*, Aristotle distinguishes between the utilitarian, the pleasurable, and that between good men alike in virtue, the third being the highest and rarest mode of friendship. Boethius is driven to contemplate the nature of true friendship following the betrayal of those former colleagues in the Roman senate who condemned him, and the steadfast support shown by Symmachus and presumably others of his circle.

m.1–32 *Why does the world with steadfast faith . . .?*: in this important concluding message to Book 2, Philosophy echoes the theme of order and stability which the prisoner had stressed (in 1. 5) dominates the world of nature. But whereas the earlier poem bewails the absence of such order in human affairs, here the message is that human relationships are likewise governed by love. The exordium of the poem evokes the invocation to Hymenaeus, god of marriage, at the beginning of Martianus Capella's *Marriage of Philology and Mercury*.

m.8 *Hesperus*: the evening star.

m.15–16 *Love governs . . . the heavens above*: the notion of Love as harmonious force goes back to Empedocles. In his poem *On Nature* (*c.*450 BC), Love joins the elements in nature, while Strife separates them; see the testimonies in Kirk-Raven-Schofield, ch. 14. The notion of such harmony in nature is a staple of Stoic physics, and Lucan, reflecting such Stoic influence, can speak in the same breath of Concord, as salvation of the universe, and *sacer orbis amor* (4. 190 f.).

Book 3

Chapter 1. This section serves as introduction to the theme of Book 3, which is the nature of true happiness. Philosophy proposes to outline first the routes to false happiness (thereby resuming in part the topics of Book 2) in order to establish what true happiness is. The poem in this chapter uses images from nature to show that what is desirable emerges more clearly when it supplants the opposite. So the final lines draw the moral; men must abandon false goods to make way for the true good. See O'Daly, 154 ff.

2 *I am eager to hear them*: Philosophy appropriately directs the dialogue on the lines of Plato's *Protagoras*, 328 D (so Gruber).

5 *shadowy figures obtruding on your sight*: perhaps a reminiscence of Plato's myth of the cave in *Rep.* 514Aff., in which the cave-dwellers see only the shadows cast on the wall before them.

m.1–4 *He who intends to sow*: There is clear evocation of Virgil, *Georgics*, 1. 150 ff., in these first lines.

m.8 *Notus' rainy tempests*: like Auster in 2. 3, Notus is the rain-bearing south wind; see Horace, *Odes*, 1. 2. 15.

m.10 *Once Lucifer dispels the gloom of night*: The depiction of the bright dawn at the emergence of the morning star is close to Tibullus, 1. 3. 93 ff.

Chapter 2. Philosophy now defines the happiness to which all men aspire; it is the perfection which encapsulates all goods within itself. When men seek their good in riches, or high position, or political power, or fame, or physical pleasure, the quest for the good is in harmony with the laws of nature, which are celebrated in the verses that follow. Fundamental to those laws is the tendency for things to revert to their beginnings: tamed lions resort to savagery, caged birds aspire to freedom, trees when bent revert to upright growth, and the setting sun returns to its rising, so that nature's course is cyclical. See S. Lerer, *Boethius and Dialogue* (Princeton, 1985), 141 f.; O'Daly, 159 ff., citing Seneca, *Ep.* 36. 11.

2 *the one goal of happiness*: this generalization echoes the ethical doctrine accepted by virtually all ancient philosophers from Plato (*Euthyd.* 278 E f.) onwards, though they differ on the means of attaining that happiness. As Cicero's *Hortensius* (cited by Augustine, *De Trin.* 13. 4) puts it: 'All of us certainly wish to be happy.'

9 *the most sacred category of good, that of friendship*: see the note ('the most precious of all riches') at 2. 7. 7.

12 *Epicurus concluded*: Epicurus (341–270 BC), founder of the school at Athens popularly known as The Garden, taught that pleasure was the highest good; by pleasure he basically meant freedom from bodily pain and mental affliction, but his views were selectively quoted by Cicero (*Fin.* 1. 29, etc.) and later commentators. For a careful analysis of the doctrine, see J. M. Rist, *Epicurus, an Introduction* (Cambridge, 1972), ch. 6.

13 *to rediscover their proper good . . . the path which would bring them back home*: the language recalls the Platonist doctrine of the pre-existence of the soul in the world of the Forms; thus the process of recognizing the good is one of recollection (*anamnesis*). For the image of the drunkard losing his way, see Plato, *Phaedo*, 79 C.

m.1–8 *It is my whim on pliant strings*: the exordium to the poem underlines the fact that man's search for the good is aligned with nature's grand design; 'nature' here is identical with Love in the poem in 2. 8. The theme of reversion to origins is picked up in the next chapter, in which Philosophy stresses that mankind likewise searches for its origin.

m.9–20 *Though Punic lions proudly wear*: African ('Punic') lions were hunted and brought to Rome for both public entertainments and private ownership; for the latter, see Juvenal 7. 75 ff. The image of the caged beast resorting to savagery at the taste of blood seems clearly derived from Lucan 4. 237 ff. Martial, 2. 75. 1 ('the lion, accustomed to endure lashes from an untroubled master') may also have been exploited here.

m.21–32 *The bird who whistled without end*: the motif of the caged bird pining for its freedom is equally familiar. Ovid, *Ex Ponto*, 1. 3. 39 ff., laments his exile by comparing himself to a caged nightingale; and Epictetus, 4. 1. 24 ff. combines the caged bird and the tamed lion as examples of loss of freedom.

m.33–6 *A sapling bends its topknot low*: Boethius may have derived this example from Ovid, *Ars amatoria*, 2. 179 f.

m.46 *And make the world a stable zone*: in this final section of the poem, Philosophy by ring-composition reverts to 'the laws of nature' motif with which she began; the reversion to origins is nature's way of preserving order in the world.

Chapter 3. Having posited that the true way to happiness is by reversion to one's origins, Philosophy now substantiates her claim that the gifts of Fortune cannot win happiness by challenging Boethius about his former possession of wealth, and establishing that it did not fulfil his needs in entirety, that it required additional protection, and that greed for possessions is insatiable. The verses concentrate on this final argument: the greedy miser who accumulates great wealth is wretched in life, and must leave it all behind at death.

1 *a dreamlike notion . . . of your beginning*: but Boethius, in 1. 6, has already acknowledged that his origin is from God, Creator of all.

m.1–4 *The miser may wax rich with streams of gold*: Boethius may be evoking lines of Prudentius (*Ham.* 254 f.; so Scheible, 85) in this imagery of the boundless stream of the miser's wealth.

m.3 *bent low with pearls from India's shore*: for *bacis . . . rubri litoris* as pearls from the Indian Ocean, see Trimalchio's laboured verses in Petronius, *Sat.* 55 l. 9.

Chapter 4. Philosophy next dismisses public offices as an avenue to true happiness. She argues that they are frequently held by depraved individuals who incur increased notoriety thereby; the esteem in which they are held does not extend to foreign parts; and magistracies formerly eminent have sunk in public estimation. The verses, in which Nero for a second time is a thinly veiled representation of Theoderic, underline the first and third of these judgements.

2 *Catullus calls Nonius an excrescence*: cf. Catullus, 52. 2, 'sella in curuli struma Nonius sedet'. The identity of this Nonius is uncertain; neither Nonius known to us, Nonius Sufenus, plebeian tribune in 51 BC, nor Nonius Asprenas, Caesar's legate in Africa in

46 and later in Spain, is known to have held curule office, though both could well have done. See C. J. Fordyce, *Catullus* (Oxford, 1961), 222, on Catullus 52.

4 *Decoratus*: he held a minor magistracy *c.*508 (see Cassiodorus, *Var.* 5. 3 f.).

15 *the praetorship*: during the Republican period, praetors were the chief judicial officials at Rome, or they served as governors of provinces overseas. But the office subsequently declined in importance until it eventually became a purely honorary position. It 'weighed heavily on the resources of senators' because the city-praetor on taking up office was expected to mount games for the diversion of the populace.

held to be magnus . . . *what meaner position is there?*: the use of the adjective *magnus* encourages the supposition that Boethius refers to the investiture of Pompey the Great, by the *lex Gabinia* of 67 BC, with *imperium infinitum* throughout the Mediterranean to safeguard the Roman corn supply. By contrast, in the late empire the *praefectus annonae* had become a minor official. See Jones, *LRE*, 697 ff.

m.1–8 *Nero lived*: Gruber and O'Daly suggest that the poem turns on the contrast (*quamvis . . . tamen*) between the emperor's outward appearance and the hatred his tyranny awoke in his subjects. But there is a good case for arguing that the contrast is between his regal splendour and the tawdry offices which he imposed on distinguished senators. Such a decline in the praetorship and the corn-prefecture has less relevance to the age of Nero than to the regime of Theoderic.

m.4 *In . . . crimson cloak*: with *Tyrio superbus ostro*, cf. Virgil, *Georgics*, 3. 17; *Aen.* 12. 126.

Chapter 5. After dismissing riches and high offices as means to true happiness, Philosophy now turns to the exercise of power, with particular reference to the kingship under which Boethius himself had suffered. The lives of kings are dominated by fear; their satellites often fall victims to the royal power. The verses emphasize that the only power worth seeking is that over one's own vicious emotions.

2 *antiquity . . . exchanged for disaster*: for the exemplars from antiquity, cf. e.g. 2. 2. 11. So far as contemporaries are concerned, Boethius doubtless has in mind Odoacer, the first barbarian king of Italy, who after deposing Romulus Augustulus, the last Western

emperor, was himself overthrown by Theoderic, and after surrendering Ravenna to him was treacherously murdered.

6 *a sword poised overhead*: Cicero, *Tusc.* 5. 61 f. (cf. also Macrobius, *Comm. on Dream of Scipio* 1. 10. 16) records how Dionysius I of Syracuse (430–367 BC) reacted when assured by his courtier Damocles that 'no man had ever been more blest'. The tyrant surrounded him with the trappings of luxury, but then ordered a sword to be suspended from the ceiling by a horse's hair over his head.

7 *Kings . . . would prefer to live untroubled lives*: cf. Euripides, *Iphigenia in Aulis*, 16 ff., where Agamemnon makes a similar confession to the elder.

10 *Nero forced . . . Seneca to choose his own form of death*: Tacitus, *Ann.* 14. 53 f., 15. 60 ff., records how Seneca, who had earlier sought to retire from the court, was charged with complicity in the conspiracy of Piso, and was ordered by Nero to end his life (AD 65). He chose hemlock in conscious imitation of Socrates.

on the swords of his own soldiers: Aemilius Papinianus, the celebrated jurist and praetorian prefect from AD 203 under Septimius Severus, was executed in 212 on the orders of the new emperor Antoninus Caracalla for having criticized the murder of the emperor's brother Geta; the version of the execution recounted here is found in the *Historia Augusta* (Spartianus, *Antoninus Caracallus*, 8).

13 *a foe in the time of misfortune*: Boethius appears to allude to his own condemnation by the fair-weather friends in the Roman senate.

m.1–11 *If power is what you seek*: whereas in 1. 7 Philosophy had donned the Stoic mantle in urging excision of the emotions, here the emphasis is on control over them, a doctrine familiar from Plato and Aristotle. See O'Daly, 97 f.

m.7 *furthest Thule*: this remotest western land, counterpoint to India in the east, is usually regarded as Iceland or Norway, but at Virgil, *Georgics*, 1. 30, a passage evoked here, Britain appears to be meant.

m.9 *If black cares are not routed*: cf. Horace, *Odes*, 3. 1. 40.

Chapter 6. The opening salvo of Philosophy's attack on the fourth aspiration to false happiness, the desire for fame, inevitably recalls Juvenal's satire on the vanity of human wishes (10. 158, *O gloria!*). Such glory as is won is often unmerited, or is merely locally based. Associated with it is the lustre of noble birth, which descendants do not deserve through their own merits. The verses are concentrated solely on this last observation; all men, whether nobles or commoners, boast an equally distinguished progeny from God.

1 *O bubble reputation . . . you have raised on high*: the citation is from Euripides, *Andromache*, 319 f.

5 *as I maintained a moment ago*: see 2. 7; 3. 3.

7 *how empty and worthless that title is*: the contrast between noble birth and personal merit is a commonplace in ancient literature (cf. Aristotle, *Rhet.* 1390 B; Seneca, *Ben.* 3. 28. 1; *Ep.* 44, 'True nobility lies in philosophy'; Juvenal, 8. 30, 'Merit is the one and only true nobility'), but the most striking discussion of it is in the speech attributed to Marius by Sallust, *Jug.* 85. 17 ff.

m.1–10 *All men on earth from one source take their rise*: as O'Daly, 162, observes, this poem on the one hand reasserts the claim that fame dependent on noble birth is hollow, and on the other points forward to the more developed discussion of God as the source of all at ch. 9 and following.

Chapter 7. Philosophy's final assault on the false claim to realization of happiness is directed at bodily pleasure, which results in melancholy or anxiety. The verses underline the lesson with the traditional motif of the bitter-sweet legacy of the bees.

4 *devote themselves to . . . bodily needs*: this comparison of those who devote themselves to the pleasures of gormandizing and sex goes back to Plato, *Rep.* 586 A.

5 *his children turned the screw on him*: perhaps an allusion to Creon's remark in Sophocles, *Antigone*, 645 f.: 'He who begets unprofitable children—what would you say he has sown for himself but troubles?'

6 *the misfortune of the childless man is a happy one*: so Euripides, *Andromache*, 420.

m.1–2 *All pleasures . . . they goad*: for the thought, cf. Horace, *Epist.* 1. 2. 55: 'Spurn base pleasures; pleasure purchased by pain brings harm.'

m.3 *like the bees that swarm*: the comparison of pleasures resulting in pain with the bees' legacy of sweet honey with bitter sting goes back to both Greek (Scheible, 95, well cites Meleager in *Anth. Pal.* 5. 163) and Latin contexts (e.g. Trimalchio's airing of the hackneyed theme at *Sat.* 56. 6).

Chapter 8. Philosophy now draws together her criticisms of the five false goods which she discussed separately in chs. 3–7; Plutarch, in his treatise

The Education of Children (Moralia, 5 C), summarizes them similarly. The fifth false good, physical pleasure, leads on to a short disquisition on the fatuity of reliance on bodily strength and beauty. The concluding verses summarize the lesson, that men should not seek happiness by embracing false goods, by exploiting the rhetorical figure of *adynata* ('impossibilities'), a motif much favoured by Augustan poets.

7 *elephants . . . bulls . . . tigers*: this topic of the superiority of brute animals to men in physical stature, strength, and speed goes back to Aristotle (*Protr.* fr. 29 D), and later becomes a commonplace. Boethius may have recalled it from Seneca, *Ben.* 2. 29. 1; *Ep.* 124. 22.

9 *How short-lived is . . . the body's beauty*: echoing Ovid, *Ars amatoria*, 2. 113, 'Beauty is a frail good'; cf. Sallust, *Cat.* 1. 2; *Jug.* 2. 4.

10 *to quote Aristotle*: the aphorism about the keen sight of the Argonaut Lynceus, who had 'the keenest sight of all who dwell on earth' (Pindar, *Nem.* 10. 62), is in Aristotle, *Protr.* fr. 105 D, and is widespread in later literature.

    the celebrated physique of Alcibiades: for his male beauty, cf. Plato, *Symp.* 217 A; *Protagoras*, 309 A, and often thereafter.

11 *tertian fever*: the ancients categorized fevers recurring every third or fourth day as 'tertian' or 'quartan'; see Pliny, *NH* 8. 50; Cicero, *ND* 3. 24.

m.1–8 *What ignorance, alas*: the theme of the preceding prose-discussion, the misdirected vision which diverts men to false goods, is elaborated by a sequence of *adynata* in these first lines; such proverbial 'impossibilities' are found as early as Archilochus (see Nisbet and Hubbard, *Commentary on Horace, Odes*, 1. 2. 9). For seeking gold on trees, see Virgil, *Eclogues*, 8. 52 ff.; netting fish on land, Horace, *Odes*, 1. 2. 9 (on elm-tops); hunting goats in sea-waters, Horace, *Epodes*, 16. 34.

m.11–12 *snowy pearls . . . purple murex-dye*: for the pearls, see above, 3. 3. m.3 n. ('bent low with pearls . . .') for the purple dye, Apuleius, *Apol.* 39, citing Ennius' lost poem *Hedyphagetica*.

m.14 *prickly urchins*: see Horace, *Sat.* 2. 4. 31 ff.: 'Not every sea abounds in choice crustaceans . . . sea-urchins come from Misenum.'

Chapter 9. At this mid-point in the treatise, Philosophy turns from the negative aspect of her teaching, the rejection of false goods, to engage with the prisoner on the nature of the true good. Her thesis is that it is an indivisible whole, subsuming the positive aspects of all the false goods. Whereas in the previous chapters she has lectured the prisoner, briefly rejecting the five common pursuits of men as separate avenues to happiness, she now adopts the Socratic technique of dialectic, encouraging her pupil to co-operate with her in the search for the true good. The conscious imitation of Plato's dialogues can be observed in the phraseology of the conversation, as when Boethius says 'I would rather hear you state them [sc. the reasons] more clearly' (cf. *Phaedrus*, 263 A); 'It seems so' (*Euthyphro*, 10 D, etc.); 'But even a blind man can see it clearly' (*Soph.* 241 D). Similarly Philosophy's words, 'My pupil, how blessed you are . . . if you add just one thing', recalls the Socratic technique in such passages as *Rep.* 440 D; see Klingner, 76–9. The turning-point from the negative condemnation of false goods to positive enquiry into the true good is further marked by the verses, a solemn aretalogy of the Father, whose aid is now sought in the search for the true good.

32 *in his* Timaeus: at *Tim.* 27 C, Socrates invites Timaeus to speak, 'after you have duly invoked the gods'; Timaeus responds that since they are about to discuss the creation of the universe, they should indeed invoke the deities' approval of their words.

m.1–40 *Father of earth and sky*: this is the central poem of the treatise, in which Philosophy, in her own words, seeks to discover 'the abode of that supreme good'. It is noteworthy that the Latin employs the dactylic hexameter, the traditional metre of the Classical hymn, and not the four-line iambic stanzas (the Ambrosian hymn) now established as the conventional Christian medium; notice too the traditional feature of the Graeco-Roman hymn, the triple invocation (in the Latin, *tu . . . tu . . . tu*; *da . . . da . . . da*). Thus Boethius 'places the Creator and his works in a specifically Platonic context' (O'Daly, 163). The content derives largely from Plato's *Tim.* 27 C–42 E, supplemented by the *Commentary* of Proclus (ed. E. Diehl, Leipzig, 1903–6), the fifth-century Neoplatonist who was head of the Athenian Academy. The poem also introduces echoes of Plotinus, Marius Victorinus, and Martianus Capella; see Gruber's *Commentary*. The poem is structured in three parts, invocation, aretalogy, and prayer:

(*a*) Invocation (1–3): The address to the Creator is on the lines of the traditional Graeco-Latin address as in Cleanthes (see A. A. Long and D. N. Sedley, *The Hellenistic Philosophers* (2 vols.; Cambridge, 1987), 326 f.), Proclus, and Lucretius, 1. 21.

(*b*) Aretalogy (4–30):

m.3 *Yourself unshifting*: the notion of God as unmoved mover is at *Tim.* 42 E, but more famously and in more extended description in Aristotle, *Met.* 1072 A.

m.7 *the ungrudging highest good*: see *Tim.* 29E.

m.8 *From heavenly patterns . . . all things*: this is an affirmation of Plato's Theory of Forms; in Neoplatonism the Forms are regarded as thoughts in the mind of God.

m.10–12 *a world of beauty . . . a perfect world*: see *Tim.* 30Bff.

m.13 *Its elements you bind in harmony*: the harmony in the world is achieved by the balance between the elements; so *Tim.* 32B–C, and Martianus Capella, 1. 1. 9.

m.17–18 *The soul . . . as its middle part*: this is a notoriously obscure aspect of the mystical doctrine of the *Timaeus*; at 35A we read that God forged the eternal Same with the changing Other, and placed between them the form of Essence; and then divided the whole 'into as many parts as was fitting'. We are to visualize this as the combination of mind and matter, with the soul (*anima*) as the middle part.

m.21 *Within two orbits*: presumably the celestial equator and the orbit of the sun.

m.22–4 *encircling the mind . . . its very self*: the World-Soul's movement round the mind (here visualized as the supreme Godhead) at the very centre of being induces the heavens to initiate their circular motion in the material world. Aristotle, (*Met.* 1072E) prefers to speak of the outer heaven being stirred into circular motion by aspiration to imitate the unmoved mover, and Plotinus, 2. 1. 1, states: 'Why does the world move in a circle? Because it imitates the mind.'

m.26 *Both human souls and those with lesser lives*: at *Tim.* 41E–42D, we read that souls are first established in stars 'as though in a chariot', in order to survey the nature of the universe. Those souls which after dwelling in human bodies are deemed to have lived degenerate lives are then translated into beasts. Such a distinction between human and bestial souls is the obvious sense implied here; Tester's translation of *animas . . . vitasque minores* as a hendiadys, 'lesser living souls', strains the Latin.

(*c*) Prayer (31–40):

m.31 *Let my mind rise to your august abode*: there is an echo of Martianus Capella 2. 193 here.

m.38–40 *calm brightness and the rest of peace . . . way, and final end*: it is tempting to regard these lines as evocations of the Christian liturgy ('Grant us a place of refreshment, light, and peace') and of the New Testament (John 14: 6: 'I am the Way, the Truth, and the

Life'), but similar imagery is found in Classical hymns, especially in Neoplatonism.

Chapter 10. The existence of imperfect goods making for imperfect happiness implies the existence of the perfect good which brings perfect happiness. That perfect good resides in God, and is identical with him, and since happiness is the highest good, God and happiness are one and the same; they cannot exist separately as two highest goods. Thus when men attain perfect happiness they share in God's divinity. When men seek sufficiency, power, respect, fame, and pleasure, they are aspiring to the highest good where God resides. The verses invite men to abandon blind concern with earthly things, and to direct their eyes to the dazzling light of the perfect good.

5 *it issues . . . into this parlous and sterile world of ours*: that is, it started from the One, the highest category of being. Cf. Proclus, *Elements of Theology*, 12: 'Of all that exists, the beginning and first cause is the Good . . . all emerges from the one Cause.'

7 *nothing better than God can be imagined*: this formulation, which goes back to Aristotle, *De philosophia*, fr. 16 ('In things in which there is a better, there is also a best; since therefore in things that exist one thing is better than another, there is a best, and this would be divine.'), attains fame as Anselm's ontological argument for the existence of God in his *Proslogion*, and thereafter in Aquinas, *Summa Theologiae*, I q.2. a.3.

15 *all agree that nothing is more outstanding than he is*: the appeal to the universal belief of mankind for the validity of a thesis goes back to Aristotle (*Nic. Eth.* 1172 B), and becomes a main plank in Stoic arguments for the existence of God (Cicero, *ND* 2. 12 ff.).

22 *porismata*: the Greek word *porisma*, originally 'a bonus', is used by Euclid, 3. 1 and other mathematicians to denote a deduction from a previous demonstration.

25 *every happy person is God . . . sharing in that divinity*: this notion is particularly strong in Stoic thought. At Cicero, *ND* 2. 153, the spokesman claims that the gods are superior only in their immortality, and Seneca (*Ep.* 53. 11) goes so far as to say that the wise man in a sense rises higher, for 'God is wise by benefit of nature, not by his own'. The belief that Christians 'become partakers of the divine nature' is expressed at 2 Peter 1: 4.

m.3–5 *Come, journey here . . . Sole refuge which for wretched souls remains*: Boethius may have in mind Christ's words at Matt. 11: 28 ff., 'Come to me, all you who labour, and I will give you rest'; but similar sentiments are found in the Neoplatonist tradition at Plotinus, 6. 9. 62 (so Scheible, 113).

m.6–11 *Green emeralds . . . blind in mind, men stand*: the combination of pearls and emeralds evokes Petronius, *Sat.* 55. As O'Daly, 166, remarks, the brightness of the gems paradoxically symbolizes the darkness overshadowing men's sight. The deposits in the Tagus (modern Tajo in the Iberian peninsula) were a main source of gold for the Romans (cf. Catullus, 29. 19; Ovid, *Am.* 1. 15. 34, etc.); the Hermus in Lydia too was 'thick with gold' (Virgil, *Georgics*, 2. 137). The Indus is appended to extend the geographical range from which the Romans sought such profit.

Chapter 11. The defective goods sought by men must be gathered into a unity, for the one and the good are identical. If things lose their unity, they lose their identity. All things, animate and inanimate alike, are induced by the thrust of nature to survive, and they achieve this only if they remain a unity. Thus all men seek the one and the good. The verses urge us to seek this truth not by external scrutiny but by introspection, for the truth is lodged within us, and we can recall it from our earlier existence.

8 *by sharing in the good*: the Latin has *boni participatione*. In the *Phaedo*, Plato's earliest exposition of his Theory of Forms, he argues that all things on earth 'participate' in the Forms, and at *Rep.* 476A, the first of the three classes 'participates' in the good and the virtues approximating to it.

9 *the one and the good are the same*: in the Neoplatonist philosophy, the One and the Good are alternative titles for the highest category of being; see the Introduction, p. xxv.

11 *no longer a living being*: the point is earlier made by Cicero, *Tusc.* 1. 90; cf. Plato, *Phaedo*, 88A–B.

16 *to avoid death and destruction*: Boethius here recalls Cicero, *De finibus* 5. 24, where in discussion of the chief good it is argued that such self-preservation is a law of nature.

18 *plants and trees grow in places that suit them*: the argument continues to draw on *De finibus* (5. 33) in this claim that the law of self-preservation extends to trees and plants. The observation that different types of terrain suit different species is found in Virgil, *Georgics*, 2. 109 ff.; cf. Ovid, *Ars amatoria*, 1. 757 f.

21 *imbibe nourishment through their roots . . . their pith and bark*: the whole of this section is modelled on Cicero, *ND* 2. 120; cf. Aristotle, *De anima*, 416A.

23 *the proliferation of seed*: this too forms part of the Stoic argument for the providential ordering of the world at Cicero, *ND* 2. 127.

26 *fire . . . upwards . . . earth . . . downwards*: at *ND* 2. 44, Cicero ascribes to Aristotle the doctrine that 'things moved by nature are borne either downwards by their weight, or upwards by their lightness'. The citation is probably from Aristotle's lost *De philosophia*.

38 *you can define the good . . . all things*: Philosophy echoes the exordium to the *Nicomachean Ethics* (1094 A) of Aristotle.

40 *you said you did not know*: see 1. 6.

m.1–16 *He who with deep reflection tracks the truth*: following the conclusion in the preceding dialogue that the end of all things is the good, the verses add the rider that this truth lies within us already; the soul, though oppressed by the body, can dimly recall from its previous existence among the Forms the Good to which it longs to return.

m.9 *The body's weight imparts forgetfulness*: Cicero's introductory comment to the third book of *Tusculans* is closely relevant here. Reflecting Stoic teaching, he argues that nature has given us tiny sparks (*parvulos igniculos*) by which to behold her, and innate seeds (*semina innata*) of the virtues, but we extinguish these when depraved by evil manners and beliefs. Seneca likewise combines the images of spark and embers (*scintilla . . . semina*) at *Ep.*, 94. 29.

m.15–16 *Plato's Muse . . . forgetful he recalls*: at *Phaedo*, 72 E, Cebes interjects to remind Socrates of his frequent claim 'that our learning happens to be nothing other than recollection (*anamnesis*)'; what we now 'recall' we must have learnt at an earlier time. This doctrine of the soul's earlier knowledge when reposing among the Forms is also found at *Meno*, 81 ff.

Chapter 12. When Philosophy raises the issue of government of the universe, the prisoner vehemently argues that its orderly progression must be guided by a single intelligence. In applauding this response, Philosophy adds that all things willingly submit to that highest good, and if they did not, they would be constrained to do so. Boethius confesses his bewilderment at the 'labyrinthine' argumentation of Philosophy, a device which allows the author to summarize the progress of the discussion for the benefit of the reader. The extended verses exploit the celebrated myth of Orpheus and Eurydice to underline the lesson that our eyes must be fixed on the true goal above, and must not look back into earth's abyss below.

5 *such varied and opposing parts*: Lucretius 2. 686 f., may have inspired this description, though Boethius does not of course accept the Epicurean explanation of the evolution of the universe.

12 *through himself alone*: see Seneca, *Ep.* 16. 5.

22 *God . . . orders them sweetly*: this echo of the book of Wisdom (8: 1) is the most specific biblical evocation in the whole treatise. Boethius may be citing the Old Testament directly, or Augustine's frequent exploitation of it (so A. Souter, *CR* (1935), 210), or most probably the Advent Antiphon, 'O Sapientia . . . fortiter sua- viterque disponens omnia' (so J. A. Cabaniss, *Speculum* (1947), 441 ff.). The prisoner's praise of the expression in his response may be an acknowledgement of the scriptural source.

24 *the Giants who laid siege to heaven*: the point of the reference is contained in Philosophy's observation that nothing impedes the divine will. The myth of the Gigantomachia (in which the Giants piled Pelion on Ossa to lay siege to heaven) is recounted in several authors; see Cicero, *ND* 2. 70, Ovid, *Metamorphoses*, 1. 152 ff., Horace, *Odes*, 2. 19. 21 ff. (with nn. in Nisbet and Hubbard, *Commentary*, on Greek predecessors in literature and art).

25 *a splendid spark of truth to fly out*: the metaphor is perhaps borrowed from Plato, *Rep.* 435 A; the 'spark of truth' may be the Neoplatonist doctrine that evil is the privation or absence of good. See the next note.

29 *and so evil is a nothing . . . he cannot commit evil*: this central thesis of Neoplatonism on the problem of evil is introduced somewhat inconsequentially here. The germ of the doctrine is found in Plato, *Rep.* 379 B–C. Augustine (*Conf.* 7. 12. 18) adopted it from the Neoplatonists to solve the problem of evil which obsessed him, and from Augustine it became a plank in scholastic teaching from John Scotus Eriugena onwards.

35 *the internal proofs proper to our discipline . . . from its predecessor*: Boethius makes the point that Philosophy is adopting the dialec- tical method of Socrates; it is tempting to suggest that 'any external authority' here refers to Christian revelation.

37 *'Tis like the substance of a perfect rounded sphere*: in Plato's *Sophist*, 244 E, the Eleatic stranger cites this and two further lines from Parmenides' poem, *The Way of Truth*. A longer extract, including the three lines, is found in Simplicius, the sixth-century Aristo- telian commentator (see Kirk-Raven-Schofield, ch. 10). The passage expounds Parmenides' view that reality is spherical;

Boethius adapts the lines to the Aristotelian doctrine that the outer heaven is set in motion by the unmoved Mover.

38 *from Plato's prescription . . . the topics under discussion*: at *Tim.* 29 B, Timaeus insists that in all description of the universe as the creation of the Demiurge, 'the words must be akin to the subjects which they interpret', that is, incontrovertible and immovable.

m.1–2 *How blest is he . . . of the good*: the exordium, which proclaims the blessedness of those who can escape the slavery of earthly concerns to gain a vision of the true good, echoes Virgil, *Georgics*, 2. 490.

m.5–62 *Of old, the Thracian poet . . . his wife's unhappy death*: Boethius recounts the myth of Orpheus and Eurydice by drawing extensively on the poetic versions of Virgil, *Georgics*, 4. 453 ff., Horace, *Odes*, 1. 12 and 24, Ovid, *Met.* 10. 1 ff., and above all Seneca, *Hercules Furens*, 569 ff. For a detailed account of the adaptation of these treatments by Boethius, see O'Daly, 192 ff.

m.23 *His goddess-mother's noble springs*: Orpheus' mother was the chief of the Muses, Calliope; her 'noble springs' were those of Hippocrene on Mt. Helicon in Boeotia.

m.27 *the cave of Taenarus*: in his descent to hell to rescue his wife Eurydice, Orpheus proceeded by this promontory in the Peloponnese, now Cape Matapan; this mention of Taenarus is one of several echoes of Seneca's *Hercules Furens* (587).

m.31 *The three-formed guardian*: for the three-headed dog Cerberus' role in the myth, see Virgil, *Georgics*, 4. 483, etc.

m.36 *Bedewed their cheeks in grief*: so Ovid, *Met.* 10. 45 f.: 'Then for the first time so the story goes, the cheeks of the Eumenides, overcome by the song, were wet with tears.'

m.38–42 *Ixion . . . Tantalus . . . Tityus' liver forsook*: the three celebrated victims of infernal punishment are earlier assembled in Ovid, *Met.* 10. 41 ff., and also in Seneca (?), *Hercules Oetaeus*, 1068 ff. (less likely as a source, since the ascription of the play to Seneca is doubtful).

m.44 *"He wins"*: this and what follows is a close evocation of *Hercules Furens*, 582 ff.

m.51 *Yet who for lovers can prescribe?*: Seneca, *Hercules Furens*, 588, is again the inspiration: 'True love loathes and cannot brook delay.' Boethius here succumbs to the pathos of the story, and undercuts the philosophical message with which the poem ends.

Book 4

Chapter 1. Philosophy has now completed her exposition of the true good and where it is to be found, and she now embarks on the second main topic of the treatise: does God, the true good, justly apportion justice in the world? In this preliminary chapter, the prisoner, reflecting on his own situation, complains that virtue suffers while vice flourishes. Philosophy promises to provide him with answers to his quandary. (Plato's *Gorgias* is to be an important quarry for the arguments.) The appended verses form a general exhortation to abandon the corrupt world of tyranny, and to ascend to the true good.

5 *boundless surprise and complaint from all*: the fact that innocent persons suffer and guilty men prosper had also preoccupied Augustine in *The City of God* (20. 2). He was concerned to demonstrate the apparent irrationality of the situation: good men sometimes suffer, but they may also prosper, and contrariwise evil men often prosper, but usually come to a bad end. God's judgements are perfectly just, but his justice will become clear to us only at the Last Judgement.

6 *in the carefully ordered house . . . lay neglected*: it is tempting to believe that the image is inspired by Paul's second letter to Timothy (2: 20): 'In a great house there are not only vessels of gold and silver, but also of wood and earthenware, and some for noble use, some for ignoble. If anyone purifies himself from what is ignoble, then he will be a vessel for noble use . . .'.

7 *powerful men . . . always the good . . . the wicked suffer misfortune*: the notion that the virtuous life is the happy one is a familiar theme in Plato; cf. *Rep.* 354 A, *Charm.* 172 A, 173 D, and pervasively in *Gorgias*.

m.1–30 *For I have wings . . . the high vault of the sky*: the inspiration for the entire composition is clearly Plato's *Phaedrus*, 246 B–247 C. In that dialogue, the human souls wing upwards, and after standing 'on the back of the world' (cf. 'Swift Aether's frame below depress' here) they 'look upon the regions beyond'.

m.7 *Up through the sphere of fire can go*: the journey upwards takes in the lower air of clouds (*aer*) and then the 'sphere of fire' (the upper air or *aether*).

m.11–12 *the frozen Ancient's car . . . the fiery star*: these are the planets Saturn (traditionally cold; cf. Cicero, *ND* 2. 119) and Mars ('fiery', ibid. 2. 53).

m.13 *or stellar orbit*: the sphere of the fixed stars.

m.16 *the topmost seat*: the account in the *Phaedrus*, 247B, is close.

m.22 *Himself unmoved, guides that swift car*: Boethius amalgamates Plato's Zeus (*Phaedrus*, 246E) with Aristotle's unmoved Mover.

m.23–4 *you can return . . . forgetfully you yearn*: the language evokes the doctrine of the soul's earlier existence in the world of the Forms, to which it longs to return, though the constricting body dims its recollection.

m.29 *in exile there*: exiled, that is, from the realm of the true good.

Chapter 2. Philosophy responds to Boethius' lament that a good God allows vice to flourish and virtue to flounder; she argues that true power lies with the virtuous, while the wicked are enfeebled. Since all men seek to attain the good, and evil men fail in this aim through attempting to acquire it by gratifying their desires, natural instinct is thereby abandoned, and by thus abandoning their nature they cease to be human. The evil which they seek is a nothing; hence in performing it they have no power. The verses (again composed with Theoderic in mind) demonstrate that evil men have the trappings of power, but in reality are slaves to their own vicious emotions.

2 *power always lies with the good . . . strength forsakes the wicked*: the argument is developed from Plato, *Gorgias*, 466Bff.

5 *will and capability*: this section too is inspired by the *Gorgias* (509D), and echoed in Seneca, *Ep.* 71. 36 ('an important element in success is the will to succeed').

10 *to hasten towards happiness*: see 3. 2.

21 *by resting on his hands*: see the amusing anecdote in Valerius Maximus 7.5.2. When P. Scipio Nasica was canvassing for the aedileship, he grasped a rustic's horny hands of toil, and jocularly enquired if he walked on them. As a result he failed in his candidature, since none of the country tribes voted for him.

28 *"no paltry and playground prizes"*: the citation is from Virgil, *Aen.* 12. 764f.

32 *Or do they abandon the good, and turn to vice . . . in full knowledge?*: the series of questions probing the reasons why men abandon virtue is largely adapted from Aristotle, *Nic. Eth.* 1146B (cf. also 1151A).

45 *that saying of Plato's*: there is no exact counterpart in Plato's *Gorgias*, but the whole section 466B–481B revolves round the content of the aphorism, especially 466D–E.

m.1–5 *You see kings seated high on lofty thrones*: in summary of the lesson of the chapter, the poem contrasts the appearance of power with the reality: tyrants are evil men whose oppression is 'empty show'; so far from possessing the virtue which has true power, they are slaves to their vices.

m.6–8 *lust . . . anger . . . Grief . . . hope torments*: the earlier Stoics classified the four main vicious emotions as appetite (*epithumia*), fear, grief, and pleasure (see Long and Sedley, *Hellenistic Philosophers*, i. 410 ff.). Cicero renders *epithumia* as *libido* or lust; anger, originally a subdivision of appetite, emerges later as a main target for Stoics (see Cicero, *Tusc.* 4. 78; *Off.* 1. 69; Seneca, *De ira*). Hope, or anxious concern for the future, likewise meets with greater condemnation at Rome; see Horace, *Epist.* 1. 4. 12; Seneca, *Ep.* 5. 7 ff.; and O'Daly, 99 ff.

m.8 *captives*: reading *captos* with some MSS against *capti* in Bieler and Tester.

Chapter 3. Since all men seek the good, and good men attain it while wicked men do not, good men win the reward which makes them divine; evil men by contrast incur the punishment of being wicked. This punishment relegates them to subhuman status; they become animals. The verses fittingly append the myth of Odysseus' followers transformed by Circe into beasts; the final stanza clarifies the allegory: Odysseus' men represent the wicked of the world.

2 *the crown of the victory . . . the reward*: for the application of this illustration to the moral life, see Aristotle, *Nic. Eth.* 1099 A, which is evoked here.

6 *since it is bestowed . . . by his own worth*: in the *De republica* of Cicero (6. 8), Scipio Africanus appears in a dream to his adoptive grandson to explain that 'for the wise, knowledge of their outstanding deeds is the most honourable reward of virtue'.

8 *a short while ago*: 3. 10.

10 *to become gods*: 3. 10. 24.

12 *goodness . . . the reward . . . wickedness . . . the punishment for bad men*: this explanation derives from Neoplatonism; see Proclus, *In Timaeum*, 1. 378.

14 *A little while ago*: 3. 10.

16 *dislodged from the human condition*: so Cicero, *Off.* 3. 82: 'What difference is there between a man's physical transformation into a beast and one who has the appearance of a man but the monstrous nature of a beast?' This argument, the germ of which appears in

Plato's *Timaeus*, 42 C–D, becomes prominent in Augustine; see G. O'Daly, *Augustine's Philosophy of Mind* (London, 1987), 72 ff.

17 *comparable to a wolf*: cf. Plato, *Phaedo*, 82 A.

considered a dog: cf. Cicero, *Pro Roscio Amerino*, 57: 'Some of you are geese who merely cackle and cannot do harm; others are dogs who can both bark and bite.'

18 *likened to young foxes*: cf. Persius, 5. 117; Plutarch, *Solon*, 30. 2.

a lion's disposition: so Plato, *Rep.* 588 D–E, 620 B.

19 *compared with hinds*: the traditional analogues for cowards from Homer, *Il.* 1. 225 onwards.

a donkey's life: cf. Plato, *Phaedo*, 81 E.

20 *no different from the birds*: so Aristophanes, *Birds*, 169 f.: 'The man's a bird, flighty, feckless, inconsistent, never remaining in the one place.'

like a filthy sow: so Horace, *Ep.* 1. 2. 26: 'like a sow that loves the muck'.

m.1–44 *the Ithacan leader's billowing sails*: the encounter of Odysseus with the divine magician Circe in Homer, *Od.* 10, became a popular text for moralizing allegory. The moly (mystical herb) which Hermes gave to Odysseus to counteract the magic of Circe becomes for the Stoics the symbol of Logos or Reason, enabling man to resist the vicious passions of the flesh; for Neoplatonists it represents Paideia or spiritual education. See H. Rahner, *Greek Myths and Christian Mystery* (London, 1963), ch. 5. Boethius here concentrates on the negative aspects of the myth, the transformation of Odysseus' followers into beasts, as an allegory of men whose decline into wickedness has rendered them bestial.

The first section of the poem follows closely the Homeric account (*Od.* 10. 135 ff.): 'We came to the isle of Aeaea where dwelt Circe . . . begotten of Helios.' The 'magic charms' are an addition from Virgil, *Eclogues*, 8. 70 and from Ovid, *Met.* 14. 301.

m.9–20 *So masterful with herbs . . . she ranged* the emphasis on herbs echoes Virgil, *Aen.* 7. 19 (*potentibus herbis*) as well as *Od.* 10. 236. The transformations into boar, lion, wolf, and tigress are artistic elaboration from the *Odyssey*, in which 'wolves and lions which Circe had bewitched' roamed round the palace (10. 212 f.). The 'meek and gentle tigress' evokes the civilized behaviour of the wolves, bears, and lionesses in Ovid (*Met.* 14. 258 ff.).

m.21–32 *the winged Arcadian god*: the god is Hermes, whose gift of moly to Odysseus counteracts the drug of Circe (*Od.* 10. 277 ff.) which transformed the oarsmen into swine, though their minds remained human (ibid. 10. 240).

33–44 *That hand of Circe was too weak*: it is notable that Boethius does not recount the retransformation of the swine into men (Homer, *Od.* 10. 393 ff.; Ovid, *Met.* 14. 297 ff.). His treatment demands concentration on the correspondence between the metamorphosis into beasts and the moral degeneration of the wicked in the preceding prose-section.

Chapter 4. The wicked are wretched in their desire and ability to perform evil deeds; moreover, since life is short, the scope for such wickedness is limited. They are happier when they undergo punishment for their crimes, for such punishment, being just, grants them a measure of good. The prisoner, while assenting to the chain of arguments, observes that the generality of men do not subscribe to them. Philosophy laments that the common herd fails to appreciate that the perpetrator of crime rather than the victim is the sufferer, and suggests that it would be more appropriate if such criminals were sympathetically enabled to see that their punishment is remedial. This final plea for compassion towards the wicked is echoed in the verses.

3 *evil men must be unhappier . . . if they cannot achieve them*: this paradox is taken over from *Gorgias*, 509 A; cf. also Seneca, *Ep.* 97. 14.

7 *that the mind finds waiting for it tedious*: Cicero makes a similar observation in the *De senectute*, 69.

8 *extended depravity must make people unhappier still*: so the *Gorgias*, 480 E–F.

13 *happier if they suffer . . . constrains them*: likewise inspired by the *Gorgias*, 472 E.

17 *than the one whose misfortune . . . share in the good*: cf. *Gorgias*, 476 A–478 E.

20 *an evil by virtue of its being unjust*: so *Gorgias*, 480 E–F.

23 *with a kindly process of cleansing*: in view of the close connection with the *Gorgias* throughout this chapter, and the close parallel there with this observation (525 B ff.), it is unlikely that the phrase *purgatoria clementia* makes specific reference to the Christian doctrine of Purgatory, though that doctrine is pervasive in the Fathers from Clement of Alexandria onwards and especially in Augustine, *City of God*, 21. 13 and 21; see *ODCC* s.v. Purgatory.

24 *my aim*: like the good pedagogue he is, Boethius has Philosophy present to the reader a summary of her earlier findings on the impotence and wretchedness of the wicked.

26 *the judgement of men . . . not worth listening to*: In the *Gorgias* (474 B), it is Polus the interlocutor who waxes sceptical about Philosophy's thesis.

27 *those birds . . . blinded by daylight*: the analogy is taken over from Aristotle, *Nic. Eth.* 993 B, who however, cites bats rather than owls.

38 *nowadays advocates claim the opposite*: it is of some interest that whereas in the parallel passage of the *Gorgias* (480 A) Socrates condemns rhetoric as a technique defending injustice, Boethius does not make this criticism, doubtless mindful of Cicero's judgement that rhetoric is the ally of philosophical discourse. See P. MacKendrick, *The Philosophical Books of Cicero* (London, 1989), 13 ff., and the note on 2. 1. 8 above.

  as . . . sick men brought to a doctor: cf. *Gorgias*, 469 A, 480 A–C.

40 *they would not regard them as pains . . . by attainment of goodness*: so also *Gorgias*, 480 C–D.

42 *pitied rather than hounded*: a judgement shared by the later Stoics; see Epictetus, 1. 18. 9; Marcus Aurelius, 7. 26. 1.

m.1–12 *Why take delight in rousing mass disorder?*: at first sight, the theme of the poem bears little resemblance to the preceding prose-passage, but there is a subtle connection. The condemnation of civil war (evocative of Lucan's epic and of Petronius, *Sat.* 119 ff.) illustrates the degradation of human behaviour into which wicked men fall; they sink lower than the beasts catalogued in the previous chapter. But such delinquency, as Philosophy has argued, should command our pity since it is a sickness of the mind. For the images in the poem and their possible sources, see O'Daly, 170.

m.2 *to tempt the hand of Fate*: The line may have been inspired by Seneca, *Hercules Furens*, 867.

Chapter 5. The prisoner now switches the focus of enquiry from human wickedness to the apparent injustice and irrationality which prevails in the world of spite of the governance of a good ruler. Philosophy begins her response in the verses by contrasting men's ignorance of the laws governing heaven with their sang-froid when contemplating the forces of nature on earth. This is to serve as prelude to discussion of the role of Providence in the next chapter.

  2 *an element of good and evil in . . . Fortune*: the prisoner turns from the previous discussion of wrongs committed by men to consider

the role of Fortune. In their analyses of the causes of events, Roman writers allot the major responsibility to men's virtues and vices, but beyond these lies the element of the unforeseen, popularly ascribed to Fortune. Boethius now seeks instruction on how such apparent workings of chance can be reconciled with God's wise government.

3 *the happy existence of rulers . . . transmitted to the folks dependent on them*: one wonders if this notion bequeathed by Homer (*Od.* 19. 109 ff.) and taken up by some Stoics (see Sharples' n. on this passage) is adduced as an implicit defence of the comfortable lifestyle of philosophers such as Seneca and Boethius himself.

6 *kindnesses to good men . . . their dearest wishes*: as noted at 4. 1, Boethius may have drawn this observation from Augustine, *City of God*, 20. 2; Philosophy's response here echoes Augustine's view.

7 *the final end*: translating *causam*. Aristotle in his discussion of causes in the *Physics* (2. 3) distinguishes four categories: the formal (the law or pattern determining the shape of a thing), the material (the matter from which a thing derives), the efficient (the agent originating the existence or movement of a thing), and (as here) the final (the end or purpose towards which a thing is directed). See D. Ross, *Aristotle*[5] (London, 1949), ch. 3.

m.1–22 *He who does not know . . . Arcturus*: the verses, as often earlier, stress that the entire universe is governed by law; the irrationality in human fortunes of which Boethius complains is apparent rather than real. The contrast drawn between men's fearful ignorance of the laws of heaven and their ready acceptance of nature's workings here below underlines their unwillingness to train their eyes upwards, and their imprisonment in things of earth.

m.1–5 *Arcturus . . . Boötes . . . rising very swiftly*: strictly speaking, Arcturus is the brightest star in the constellation Boötes, which is also known as Arctophylax or Bear-keeper, because the 'Wagon' it drives is the constellation of the Great Bear; hence the stars of Arcturus here refer to those in Ursa Maior. Since both constellations (Boötes and Great Bear) hug the celestial North Pole, they are 'close to the hinge of heaven'; they rise earlier and set later than stars further south. The description of Boötes guiding his Wagon echoes Ps-Seneca, *Octavia*, 233 f.

m.7–12 *the horns of Phoebe . . . perpetual beating*: the cause of eclipses of the moon (= Phoebe) was well-known to the Presocratics; Thales is said to have predicted them (see the texts in Kirk-Raven-Schofield, ch. 2). But the average Roman's notorious ignorance of natural science is reflected in the numerous references to the superstitious practice of the clashing of cymbals to restore the vanished moon. These are documented not only in the time of the Second Punic War (Livy, 26. 5. 9), but also in the Augustan age (Tibullus, 1. 8. 21; Ovid, *Met.* 4. 333) and later (Tacitus, *Ann.* 1. 28. 2; Juvenal, 6. 442 f.).

m.13 *the blasts of Corus*: Corus (or Caurus) is the north-west wind; for its wintry violence, cf. Caesar, *Bell. Gall.* 5. 7; Virgil, *Georgics*, 3. 356.

Chapter 6. In this, the longest chapter of the entire work, Philosophy offers her rationale of the relationship between Providence, the divine reason which directs the course of the world, and Fate, the realization of that direction in the world of change; the second emerges from, and is subject to, the first. An immutable chain of causation proceeds from Providence through Fate in order to control the destinies of men. Mortals are not equipped with sufficiently clear intellects to comprehend the divine order as it relates to human beings. Though they can observe some of the evidences of rational processes, men must be content to acknowledge the beneficent ordering of the world by God without a full understanding of it. The culminating verses resume the pervasive lesson taught throughout the poems in the treatise: the order in the natural world reflects the wise and rational rule of the divine Creator who is cosmic Amor.

1 *which I mentioned*: the prisoner refers to the apparently anarchic world in which Fortune rules capriciously; see the previous chapter.

3 *the Hydra's heads*: one of Hercules' labours was to slay the nine-headed snake of Lerna near Argos. For every head severed, two others sprouted until the wounds were seared with burning brands by Hercules' charioteer Iolaus. Hence here the application of 'the fire of the mind'.

4 *the single nature of Providence . . . the freedom of the will*: these topics are to form the third and final part of the *Consolation*. A lost work of the Neoplatonist Proclus was entitled *Providence, Fate, and What lies within our Power*.

8 *Providence . . . Fate*: as Courcelle, 203 f., indicates, Stoics did not make this distinction between the two concepts, so that it does not appear in either Cicero's *De fato* or Seneca's *De providentia*. It is in Neoplatonism that this relationship between the two is prominent; as Plotinus, *Enneads*, 3. 3. 5, has it, 'There is only one Providence;

beginning with lower things, it is initially Fate; above, it is only Providence.' Cf. also Calcidius, *Comm. in Timaeum*, 151, 177.

11 *the order of Fate emerges from the indivisibility of Providence*: so Calcidius, ibid. 203: 'According to Plato, Providence precedes, and Fate follows.'

12 *the craftsman . . . a single moment*: Aristotle, developing the image of the craftsman in Plato's *Timaeus*, states: 'From art proceed the things of which the form is in the soul of the Artist.' (*Met.* 1032 A).

13 *by divine spirits . . . the chain of Fate . . . the whole of nature . . . the power of angels . . . demons . . . all of these*: In this mélange of Platonic and Stoic views of the governance of the world, some have suggested that the reference to *virtus angelica, daemonum sollertia* introduces a Christian element into the philosophical framework, but as Courcelle, 205, notes, Proclus not only combines the terms 'angels' and 'demons' in his own writings (*De decem dub.* 62. 2), but also cites Plato's use of 'angels' in *Cratylus*, 457 E, 408 B. Demons as intermediaries between heaven and earth feature prominently in the Middle Platonists Plutarch (*De gen. Socr.*) and Apuleius (*De deo Socr.*).

14 *Fate itself is subject*: so Proclus, *De Providentia*, 14. 9 ff.

    some things . . . transcend the chain of Fate: presumably the Forms, envisaged by Neoplatonists as thoughts in the mind of God.

15 *a series of concentric circles . . . a sort of axis . . . can turn*: for the various theories prompted by this geometric image of the relationship between Providence and Fate, see Sharples, ad loc.

22 *in considerable detail*: see 4. 2.

26 *a term from physics . . . temperament of their minds*: *temperies* (or *temperamentum*) is a technical medical term for 'mixture'. Galen, the medical writer of the second century AD, wrote a work *De temperamentis*. On the concept, see now P. N. Singer's World's Classics edition of Galen's *Selected Works* (Oxford, 1997), 202 ff.

30 *his high vantage-point of Providence*: for the image, see Plato, *Statesman*, 272 E.

32 *supremely just, totally upholding the right*: the phrase echoes the description of the Trojan hero Rhipeus in Virgil, *Aen.* 2. 426 f.

33 *Lucan . . . of our persuasion . . . Cato*: Lucan is described as 'of our persuasion' because he writes as a committed Stoic. The celebrated citation from *Pharsalia*, 1. 128, is a commentary on the victory of Julius Caesar over the senatorial party in the Great Civil War; the

Younger Cato, senatorial and Stoic, committed suicide after the Caesarean victory at Thapsus in Africa in 46 BC.

38 *The body of the holy man was formed in heaven*: Since the citation is from one 'more outstanding' than Philosophy herself, it has been ascribed to the *Chaldaean Oracles*, which Neoplatonists regarded as a sacred text (see Chadwick, 243), or alternatively as a Gnostic utterance (see Bieler, ad loc.).

40 *to ensure . . . through continuing prosperity*: so Seneca, *De providentia*, 4. 5 ff.

44 *happiness . . . often attending on the wicked*: Augustine's advice (*City of God* 20. 2) is that we should not set much store by such things.

53 *How hard it is . . . god!*: a citation from Homer, *Il.* 12. 176.

55 *in his own image*: see *Tim.* 29 E: 'Let us state, then, why nature and all creation was fashioned by him who fashioned them. He was good . . . he desired that all things should be as like himself as possible.'

m.1–53 *If with wisdom and clear mind*: this is 'the last great celebration of divine order and cohesion in the universe . . . the counterpart of I m.5 . . .' answering 'the questions in that poem about the apparent discrepancy between order in nature and order in human affairs'. The poem is 'a *summa* of the cosmic themes of the work' (O'Daly, 171). The verses attest the cosmic order among the heavenly bodies, the elements, and the seasons.

m.6–12 *The sun . . . the Bear . . . to quench its flames*: the order in the heavens is demonstrated by the simultaneous presence in the sky of sun and moon (= Phoebe), and (echoing the verses in the previous chapter) by the Great Bear's lingering presence high in the sky. Echoes of Virgil, *Georgics*, 1. 246 and 2. 481 are perceptible here.

m.14–18 *The evening star . . . The morning star . . . their alternating love . . . the world*: the regular appearance of Venus, alternating as evening and morning star, has already been cited in the verses in 1. 5 as evidence of order in nature. The power of Love, identified with God at the close of the poem, is celebrated earlier in the verses at 2. 8.

m.23–7 *moisture . . . the dry . . . Cold . . . with the flames . . . fire . . . Earth*: Boethius here too, in the celebration of the harmony between elements, returns to a theme earlier aired; see 3. 9.

m.28–33 *spring . . . Summer's heat . . . autumn . . . winter's face*: for the regularity of the seasons as reflecting order in nature, see the verses at 1. 2. The Augustan poets repeatedly advert to this theme: so

Horace, *Odes*, 1. 4, 4. 7; Virgil, *Georgics*, 2. 319 ff.; Ovid, *Met.* 2. 27 ff.; *Tristia*, 4. 1. 57 ff. See O'Daly, 112 ff.

Chapter 7. Philosophy's assertion that every fortune is good is challenged by the prisoner, who appeals to the general belief that some men meet with an evil fortune. Philosophy suggests that together they analyse this general attitude, which rightly supposes that good fortune attends the virtuous, but erroneously maintains that evil fortune attends the wicked. She does not, however, condemn this misapprehension; instead, she counsels the virtuous to adopt the doctrine of the mean towards Fortune, enduring her blows and remaining on guard against her favours. The verses focus on three mythological figures as exemplars of attitudes towards Fortune; for the problem of their relevance, see below.

3 *Since every fortune . . . it is clear that they are either just or useful*: Simplicius, the Aristotelian commentator contemporary with Boethius, closely echoes this paragraph; see the citation in Courcelle, 219, who suggests that both are indebted to a common Alexandrian source.

5 *a moment ago as unthinkable*: see ch. 4 above.

15 *every fortune is wholly bad*: Philosophy is reporting, not espousing, this common view.

19 *virtue* (virtus) *. . . strength* (vires): *virtue* is the quality of a *vir* (cf. Cicero, *Tusc.* 2. 43), but strictly speaking *vis* is cognate with the Greek *is*, which likewise means strength.

21 *Maintain the middle ground*: this is the Aristotelian concept of virtue as the mean between extremes; see *Nic. Eth.* 1115ʌ ff., and D. Ross, *Aristotle*[5] ch. 7.

m.1–35 *For twice five years the avenging son of Atreus*: this poem, a triptych of mythological figures hounded by Fortune, has been condemned on the grounds that only the third exemplar, that of Hercules, is apposite to the previous discussion; the experiences of Agamemnon and Odysseus are less relevant (see Gruber, 372). O'Daly, 221 ff., mounts a spirited defence, arguing that Agamemnon is not being condemned here, but is depicted as grappling with a testing fortune; Odysseus for his part represents the struggle to overcome vice and acquire virtue. It is worth noting that Philosophy's previous discussion has been concerned with the contrast between her own view (that every fortune is good) and the general perception that for the wicked every fortune is bad. The poem may be exploiting this ambivalence. Agamemnon's behaviour (*pace* O'Daly) is stigmatized as wicked; we are left to infer that his fate (assassination by his wife and her lover), unmentioned here but known to every reader, is evil in the eyes of the world, but good because just in the view of Philosophy. In the Odysseus–Polyphemus episode, it is Polyphemus who takes centre stage; he too in the eyes of the world meets a hostile fortune, which again in Philosophy's view is good because just.

m.7 *He ratified the murder of his hapless daughter*: Agamemnon, son of Atreus, led the Greek expedition against Troy after the Trojan Paris had carried off Helen, wife of Agamemnon's brother Menelaus. The Greek fleet was delayed at Aulis by unfavourable winds, and he was persuaded to sacrifice his own daughter Iphigenia to Artemis to ensure good sailing-weather. Roman poets (Lucretius, 1. 82 ff.; Seneca, *Agamemnon*, 160 ff.; cf. Cicero, *Off.* 3. 95) are unanimous in condemnation of this barbarous act. Seneca's recasting of the theme from Greek tragedy conspicuously influences Boethius' account, as verbal reminiscences indicate.

m.12 *He paid for his joy with melancholy weeping*: when Odysseus reached the land of the Cyclopes (Homer, *Od.* 9. 106 ff.), the giant Polyphemus devoured six of his comrades. Odysseus and the rest took revenge before their escape by plunging a red-hot stake into the giant's single eye.

m.13 *Hercules gained fame by his taxing labours*: different versions of the twelve labours of Hercules appear in different authorities. Boethius' list is derived mainly from Seneca, *Agamemnon*, 829 ff., and Ovid, *Met.* 9. 182 ff., supplemented by reminiscences from other Senecan plays, *Phaedra*, 317 ff., and *Medea*, 634 ff., and other poets. The twelve labours included here are as follows:

1. Taming of the centaurs: cf. Ovid, *Met.* 9. 191; Ps-Seneca, *HO* 1195, 1925.
2. Plundering of the Nemean lion's skin: *Ag.* 829 f.; Seneca, *HF* 1150 f.; *Met.* 9. 197.
3. Slaughter of the Stymphalian birds: *Ag.* 849 ff.; *Met.* 9. 187.
4. Seizure of apples of the Hesperides: *Ag.* 852 ff.; *Met.* 9. 190.
5. Cerberus dragged up from Hades: *Ag.* 859 f.; *Met.* 9. 185.
6. Capture of horses of Diomedes who was then devoured by them: *Ag.* 824 ff.; *Met.* 9. 194.
7. Slaughter of the Hydra: *Ag.* 835 f.; *Met.* 9. 192 f.
8. Wrestling with river-god Achelous: *Met.* 9. 85 f.; Ps-Seneca, *HO*, 495 ff.

9. Strangling of giant Antaeus: Seneca, *HF* 482 (cf. *Medea*, 643, 653); *Met.* 9. 183 f.

10. Slaughter of Cacus at behest of King Evander: Virgil, *Aen.* 8. 190 ff.; Propertius, 4. 9.

11. Subjugation of Erymanthian boar: *Ag.* 832; *Met.* 9. 192.

12. Bears heavens on his shoulders: *Met.* 9. 198; Seneca, *HF* 70 ff.; Ps-Seneca, *HO* 1905 f.

m.32–3 *Go now, intrepid ones . . . your backs unguarded*: Philosophy here exploits Seneca, *Hercules Furens*, 89 ff. (where Juno taunts Hercules at the close of his labours: 'Go now, make for the abode of the heavenly dwellers, and spurn the affairs of men') to exhort her followers to emulate Hercules, patron saint of Stoics, in abandoning earthly concerns and making for heaven. The line which follows, 'Why so sluggishly expose your backs unguarded?' reinforces the admonition to abandon with all speed the concerns of earth, and to rise to heaven.

Book 5

Chapter 1. As preliminary to the main theme of the final book, which is Philosophy's explanation of how Providence and free will are to be reconciled, the prisoner asks for guidance on the possible existence and nature of chance. Philosophy replies with the celebrated definition and illustration of Aristotle, that chance is the conjunction of unforeseen causes which are initiated by Providence and carried through by Fate. The verses exemplify this thesis by demonstrating the natural cause of the apparently random course of river waters.

2 *a moment ago*: see 4. 6.

9 *nothing comes forth from nothing . . . subject to it*: this aphorism was a commonplace among Presocratic philosophers as applied to material substances, and it is echoed later by Plato and Epicurus; see the references in Sharples, ad loc. Lucretius (1. 149 f.) in support of the Epicurean thesis states that 'nothing is ever begotten from nothing by divine agency'; this qualification ('by divine agency') may be the reason for Philosophy's 'applied not to the creative originator' here.

12 *a succinct account of it*: the discussion which follows draws upon Aristotle's account in *Physics*, 197 A.

13 *he finds a quantity of gold buried there*: this example appears first in abbreviated form in Aristotle's *Metaphysics*, 1025 A, and thereafter

is widely found in philosophical writers; for the citations, see Sharples, ad loc. The combination of the definition in the *Physics* and the example from the *Metaphysics* is found later in Simplicius and Philoponus, leading Courcelle (218f.) to argue that both draw upon Ammonius' lost commentary on Aristotle's *Physics*, and that Boethius likewise is indebted to Ammonius; but this theory is disputed by other scholars.

18 *Thus we can define chance . . . to some purpose*: the definition is close to the Aristotelian analysis; for discussion in the framework of Aristotle's account of causality, see Ross, *Aristotle⁵*, 75 ff.

19 *that order*: i.e. Fate.

m.1–2 *'Midst Persian cliffs*: the verses exemplify that apparently chance events are governed by the laws of causality. The mistaken assertion that the Tigris and Euphrates arise from the same source is a misinterpretation of Lucan, 3. 256ff.; Lucan (8.224) may also have inspired the epithet *Achaemeniae* ('Persian') in the first line, but cf. also Propertius, 2. 13. 1. The parenthetical description of the fighting technique of Parthian mounted archers is a commonplace in Augustan poetry; see Virgil, *Georgics*, 3. 31, Horace, *Odes*, 1. 19. 11f., 2. 13. 17f., etc.

m.12 *law its course constrains*: The course of waters is dictated by the natural causation of sloping terrain, and not by chance.

Chapter 2. The prisoner now asks if men have free will. Philosophy is emphatic that free will exists, but distinguishes its operation at four levels. The more an individual soul is locked into things of earth, and especially into vices, the less is its capacity to deploy reason in making free choices. The verses develop Philosophy's final comment in her discourse; the poem identifies the eye of Providence with the gaze of God, who is depicted as the true sun.

1 *Heavenly and divine creatures*: these are souls free of bodies, resident in the world of the Forms.

8 *when they slip down to the physical world*: since this second level is distinguished from the occupancy of human bodies which follows, this must reflect the Platonist notion of the ensoulment of the stars; see Plato, *Phaedrus*, 247 D; Plotinus, 3. 8.

m.1–5 *Thus . . . 'Sees all things and hears all things'*: throughout the first section of the poem, Boethius evokes Homeric passages. For the epithet 'sweet-voiced', cf. *Il.* 1. 248f. (used of Nestor). For the description of Phoebus (= the sun) as 'clear with limpid light', see ibid. 1. 605. The formulaic 'sees all things and hears all things' is used of the sun, ibid. 3. 277; *Od.* 11. 109, 12. 323, and is a favourite quotation of Neoplatonist philosophers.

m.11 *What is, what has been, what will be*: an echo of *Il.* 1. 70, imitated by Virgil, *Georgics*, 4. 392 f.

m.14 *the title of "true sun" he earns*: the symbolism of God as sun and source of all light goes back to Plato, notably in the myth of the cave in *Rep.* 7. It becomes a recurrent feature in Neoplatonist texts; see the references in Sharples, ad loc.

Chapter 3. In this chapter, which is the sole occasion on which the prisoner makes an extended contribution to the debate other than the self-pitying recital of his complaints in 1. 4, the fundamental issue of Book 5 is raised: how can God's foreknowing be reconciled with the existence of free will? The solution advanced by earlier thinkers, that foreknowledge does not necessarily imply predetermination, is attacked in a series of counter-arguments. The prisoner concludes that the existence of free will is an illusion, with the depressing consequence that all rewards and punishments are arbitrary, and prayer to God is futile. The verses reflect on the apparent inability of the human mind, trapped in its earthly prison, to recapture the knowledge of the truth in all its parts which it had earlier possessed.

6 *I regard it as sacrilege to believe this of God*: in this first objection to the simultaneous operation of free will and divine foreknowledge, the prisoner argues that the existence of the first would necessarily result in divergence from the second.

7 *some believe that they can disentangle this knotty problem*: Courcelle, 216, suggests that Boethius is citing Ammonius, *De interpretatione*; Klingner, 97 f. points to the Platonist–Christian tradition represented by Origen as the source.

10 *a person who is seated*: this example appears earlier in Ammonius, *De interpretatione*, 153. 24, and in Boethius' own *De interpretatione*, 122. 1 ff.

14 *This alone is sufficient to eliminate the freedom of the will*: thus the first main argument against free will is that things foreseen must necessarily come to pass.

16 *things which have occurred at some earlier time are the cause of that highest Providence?*: criticism here is directed against the notion that God's knowledge is dependent on the development of shifting events in time.

19 *how can it possibly be foreknown that it will occur?*: the third argument recapitulates what is implicit earlier, that if free will makes an outcome uncertain, God cannot possibly foreknow it.

25 *that absurd prophecy of Tiresias . . . or not!*: at *Satires*, 2. 5. 59, in a comic extension of the dialogue between Odysseus and Tiresias at *Od.* 11. 90 ff., Horace makes Odysseus enquire how he may enrich himself before reaching home in Ithaca. This reply of Tiresias is a mocking commentary on the nature of oracular utterances.

30 *by any free and voluntary impulse of their minds*: the argument may be drawn from Cicero, *De fato*, 40.

34 *a proper humility . . . divine grace*: the emphasis on these Christian concepts encourages the speculation that Boethius draws on Christian sources here; see Klingner, 101. The thesis carries more weight because it is the voice of the prisoner, and not of Philosophy, which utters these sentiments.

that unapproachable Light: the similarity of the phrase (*inaccessae luci*) to Paul's *lucem inaccessabilem* at 1 Tim. 6: 16 adds weight to the argument for Christian inspiration here; but see Sharples, ad loc.

36 *a little while ago*: 4. 6m. 44 ff.

m.1–28 *What dissonant cause . . . the world*: this is the sole poem declaimed by the prisoner since that in 1. 5, and the same metre in both (the anapaestic dimeter) underlines the connection. In that earlier composition, a contrast is drawn between the order in the world of nature and the apparent anarchy in human affairs; here the acknowledgement is made that man is unable to discern fully the divine pattern imposed on the world. This limitation is expressed in a series of questions, to which the Platonist solution is tentatively offered: the soul recognizes the outline of the truth by reminiscence from its previous existence, but its vision is only partial because of its imprisonment in the body.

m.2 *between two truths*: the immediate impasse is the difficulty of reconciling divine Providence and free will.

m.18 *Who in his ignorance would recognize their shape?*: this is the culmination of the series of questions in which the prisoner expresses bafflement: on the one hand man unceasingly seeks to know (so the exordium to Aristotle's *Metaphysics*: 'All men by nature desire to know'), but on the other hand he is uncertain of the object of his search. The whole passage reads as an evocation of Plato's *Meno*, 80 D–E, where Socrates acknowledges that he does not know what virtue is, and Meno scathingly asks: 'How will you search for a thing whose nature you do not know at all?' Socrates condemns the argument that a man cannot enquire about what he knows because he knows it, nor about what he does not know since he does not know the object of his search.

m.21 *It grasps the whole . . . the parts*: in this final section of the poem, Boethius argues that in this life the questioning mind seeks to fill out the detail of the picture whose general outline it recalls from its earlier existence in the world of the Forms.

Chapter 4. Philosophy now reverts to the traditional argument rejected by the prisoner that foreknowledge is not by necessity the cause of future events. She develops the case by arguing that such necessity does not exist in all cases. The prisoner's misapprehension that if things are foreseen they must necessarily occur demands an explanation of the nature of cognition, which operates at the four levels of sensation, imagination, reason, and understanding. The verses that follow reject the Stoics' empirical approach to the acquisition of knowledge in favour of the Neoplatonist notion that the mind possesses its own dynamic, with its own access to knowledge through recollection; it can combine such knowledge with that received through the senses.

1 *when he put paid to divination*: reading *destruit* (Theiler) for *distribuit*. Cicero's *De divinatione* offers no indication of either word. Klingner suggests that Boethius has taken the reference to Cicero from Augustine, *City of God*, 5. 9, which states that Cicero sought to dispense with divination. Courcelle defends *distribuit* by citation of *De divinatione*, 1. 125, where Cicero's brother Quintus argues that divination springs from God, Fate, and nature; but the phrase *divinationem distribuere* is an improbable combination in Latin.

you yourself . . . for quite a time: Boethius has discussed the concept earlier in his *De interpretatione*, 225. 9 ff.

6 *a moment ago*: see ch. 3 above.

21 *any foreknowledge of things which have no necessary outcome*: Philosophy has so far argued that foreknowledge of an event does not mean that the event is necessary rather than contingent. She has now to deal with the problem of how a contingent event can be foreknown.

25 *by the capability of those who grasp it*: this distinction goes back via Ammonius to the Neoplatonist Iamblichus (*c.*AD 300); see Gruber, ad loc.

26 *light-rays which they project*: this Stoic concept in epistemology, anticipated by Plato, *Tim.* 45 B, is outlined at Gellius, 5. 16. 2.

27 *in different ways*: this fourfold classification of modes of cognition, which is a necessary preliminary to an explanation of how Providence can be reconciled with free will, is a fusion of Platonist and Aristotelian categories similarly combined in Proclus; see Sharples, ad loc.

29 *the universal to which all belong*: Aristotle in his *Metaphysics* argues that objects confronted in the world have shared characteristics; hence the notion of universals (e.g. tree, horse, man), which he regards not as mere concepts, but as objective realities. They do not, however, exist in a detached world, but as characteristic of individuals. See Ross, *Aristotle*[5], 157 f.

30 *it gazes on the simple Form with the unsullied sight of the mind*: unlike Aristotle, who rejects the notion of the Platonic Forms as a separate world of universals, Boethius explains them as existing as thoughts in the mind of God. The location of the Forms beyond the bounds of the created world is suggested by Plato, *Phaedrus*, 247 C.

35 *"Man is a two-footed rational animal"*: at 1. 6, the prisoner's definition of man is 'a mortal creature endowed with reason'. Philosophy here dispenses with man's mortality.

m.1–40 *Elders with doctrine dark and dense*: in the verses, Philosophy continues to instruct on the theory of knowledge by contrasting the Stoic view with that of Plotinus; see Scheible, 166 ff. The Stoics (commonly called the Porch because the school was situated in the Painted Porch at Athens) followed Aristotle in maintaining that all knowledge comes through the senses; objects imprint themselves on the soul like a seal on wax. The Neoplatonists rebut this notion of the mind/soul as a *tabula rasa*, as a mere recipient of sensations. Such an empirical outlook was opposed to the traditional Platonist view that the mind has its own dynamic, recalling its earlier experience from the world of the Forms.

m.6–8 *swift strokes of pen . . . no marks till then*: this image of characters inscribed on a wax tablet goes back to Plato (*Theaet.* 191 C ff.) and Aristotle (*De anima*, 430 A).

m.14 *Performs a mirror's role*: similarly the image of reflection in water or a mirror is borrowed from Plato, *Rep.* 402 B; *Theaet.* 206 D; *Sophist.* 239 D.

m.40 *With images combined*: Philosophy here suggests that the mind

combines the perceptions obtained via the senses with the knowledge recalled from the world of the Forms.

Chapter 5. Following upon the disquisition on epistemology in the
previous chapter, Philosophy now categorizes modes of knowing at the
four levels of immobile life, the lower animals, man, and divine creatures.
She argues that just as the reason is to be preferred to the senses and the
imagination in the interpretation of reality, so the divine understanding
is to be preferred to the reason. It is that divine understanding, in so far
as man can apprehend it, which will reconcile the apparent contradiction
between God's foreknowledge and free will. The verses underline the
differences between the lower animals, whose eyes are riveted on the
earth, and man, whose thoughts, like his gaze, should be directed
upwards.

1 *those things which are freed . . . their minds*: Philosophy refers to
spiritual creatures. Chaucer's gloss names them as God and his
angels (so O'Donnell); philosophers in the Platonist tradition think
of the demons on which Apuleius in *De deo Socratis* waxes
eloquent.

3 *molluscs . . . clinging to rocks*: cf. Aristotle (?), *On Plants* 816A:
'Sensation is the only faculty which allows them to be termed
living.' Cf. Pliny, *NH* 9. 90.

Imagination . . . what to seek: cf. Aristotle, *De anima*, 433A: 'no
thought nor reasoning, but merely imagination'; avoiding and
seeking, 432B.

9 *What you claim is this*: see ch. 3 above.

m.1–15 *How diverse . . . the earth!*: this is 'the verse prelude to the final
great argument which reconciles the conflict of free will and divine
foreknowledge' (O'Daly, 177). More immediately, it underlines
the difference between the lower animals and man; the animals are
rooted in the earth, but man can and should aspire to the divine
understanding. The first section is a virtual mosaic of Augustan
poetry, especially the *Aeneid*. For the beasts that sweep the earth,
Ovid *Met.* 10. 701; birds that assail the winds, swim through
heaven's expanse, *Aen.* 11. 756, 5. 217; animals which tread solid
ground and course the plains, ibid. 11. 788, 4. 154.

m.9–11 *Their heads hang low . . . on earth below*: the thought is
characteristically Platonist (*Tim.* 91E, etc.), but the expression is
Ovidian (*Met.* 1. 84 ff.): 'Though all other animals face downward
and fix their gaze upon the earth, [the god] gave to man a face

uplifted, and bade him gaze on the sky, and raise his face aloft to the stars.'

m.14 *bear aloft your thoughts*: cf. Cicero, *ND* 2. 140; (Nature) 'made man stand tall and erect, so that by gazing on the sky he could acquire knowledge of the gods'.

Chapter 6. The apparent conflict between divine Providence and free will can be resolved only by an understanding of God's nature and knowledge. By contrast with our world of time, he is eternal; he lives an unchanging life always in the present. His knowledge therefore transcends the world of time; he sees future events, whether occurring by necessity or not, as happening before his eyes. So far as necessity is concerned, from the viewpoint of divine knowledge all future events will be necessary, but of their own nature some will be necessary and some freely chosen. The changes freely adopted in courses of action will be foreseen by Providence. Thus the freedom of the will, the rewards and punishments which free choices merit, and prayers to God for future blessings remain intact and valid.

2 *the common view . . . that God is eternal*: the appeal to the authority of the whole of mankind (*ex consensu gentium*) goes back to Aristotle (*NE* 1172B), who likewise posits God's eternity (*De phil.* fr. 16).

4 *compared with the world of time*: for this definition of eternity by contrast with the temporal order, see Plato, *Tim.* 37D; cf. Plotinus, 3. 7. 3.

6 *as Aristotle argued is the case with the world*: see *De caelo*, 283B.

9 *Plato thought . . . no beginning . . . no end*: this belief occurs in both *Tim.* 28Bff., and repeatedly in *Politicus*, 270A, 273E.

10 *one thing . . . quite another . . . unique to the divine mind*: the distinction is similarly found in Proclus, *Elements of Theology*, 55.

12 *imitated by the perpetual movement of temporal things*: so *Tim.* 37D–38A.

14 *eternal . . . enduring*: this distinction is implicit in *Tim.* 37Dff.

15 *every judgement . . . according to its own nature*: so Ammonius, *De interpretatione*, 9.

17 *as from one of the world's lofty peaks*: this image has given rise to an argument frequently adduced in later times to reconcile all-knowing Providence with free will: if from a height you observe two cars on a collision course at a junction, does your observation render the collision necessary? Aquinas, *Summa Theologiae*, I q.

14 a. 13 ('Has God knowledge of contingent future events?') has detailed discussion of the problem.

22 *Consider this parallel*: the sun's rising as a necessary future event was earlier adduced by Boethius in *De interpretatione*, 241. 4, following Ammonius.

26 *when viewed by divine knowledge . . . when considered in its own nature*: this solution to the problem of necessary future events, briefly raised in chs. 3–4, had been proposed earlier by Aristotle, Ammonius, and Boethius himself in his *De interpretatione*. See the citation in Sharples, ad loc.

31 *they do not forfeit the total freedom of their nature*: this doctrine, inherited from Ammonius, is adopted by Aquinas, *Summa Theologiae* I q. 14 a. 13.

42–3 *your earlier objection . . . owes nothing to events which occur later*: the objection is raised in ch. 3 above. As Sharples observes, the solution thus propounded raises the further question: does God's foreknowledge predestine what is to occur rather than merely foreknow it?

47 *raise your minds . . . pour out your humble prayers to heaven*: this is one of the passages for which Christian liturgical influence is claimed; see C. J. de Vogel, *Vivarium* (1972), 1 ff.; C. Mohrmann in J. J. O'Meara and B. Naumann (eds.), *Latin Script and Letters, AD 400–900* (Leiden, 1978), 60 f.

48 *the judge who sees all things*: this rather abrupt conclusion, without accompanying verses, is one of the features which prompted H. Tränkle (*Vig. Christ.* (1977), 148 ff.) to argue that the *Consolatio* as we have it is incomplete. But the contrary argument, that verses to lighten the reading of non-philosophers are no longer required, makes the suggestion superfluous. D. Shanzer, *Hermes* (1984), 352 ff., suggests that the close of the treatise consciously imitates the end of Plato's *Phaedo*; like Socrates, Philosophy has completed her lesson by leading her auditor to an understanding of the mind of God.

INDEX AND GLOSSARY OF NAMES

(References to the prose-passages are by book, chapter, and section; to the verses by book, chapter (m. stands for *metrum*), and line).

Academy, Academics, school of Hellenistic philosophy, Introd. VI; 1. 1. 10; closed by Justinian, Introd. IV

Achelous, Greek river, 4. 7. m.23

Aemilius Paulus Macedonicus, L., victor over Perseus in Third Macedonian War, 2. 2. 12

Aetna, volcanic mountain in Sicily, 2. 5. m.27, 6. 1

Ager Calventianus, location of B.'s exile at Pavia, Introd. II

Alan of Lille, 12th-c. French poet, Introd. VIII, X

Alaric, Visigothic leader, Introd. I

Albinus (cos 493), Roman senator cause of B.'s condemnation, Introd. II; 1. 4, 14. 32

Alcibiades, (*c*.450–404 BC), Athenian general and statesman celebrated for his beauty, 3. 8. 10

Alcuin of York (*c*.735–804), Introd. X

Alexandria, Neoplatonism at, Introd. IV

Alfred the Great, translator of the *Consolation*, Introd. X

Altar of Victory, Introd. II

Ambrose, bishop of Milan, originator of Ambrosian hymn, Introd. IX

Ammonius, son of Hermias, philosopher at Alexandria, Introd. IV, VII

Ammonius Saccas (3rd c. AD), teacher of Origen, Introd. IV

Anastasius I, eastern emperor 491–518, Introd. I

Anaxagoras (*c*.500–428 BC), first philosopher to practise at Athens, 1. 3. 9

Anicii, Roman aristocratic family, Introd. II

Antaeus, giant strangled by Hercules, 4. 7. m.25

Antoninus Caracalla, M., emperor who ordered Papinian's execution, 3. 5. 10

Apollo (the sun), 1. 6. m.1

Arcadian god (Hermes/Mercury), 4. 3. m.21

Arcturus, brightest star in constellation of Boötes, 1. 5. m.22; 4. 5. m.1

Arians, harassed by emperor Justin, Introd. II; Ambrose opposes them, Introd. IX

Aristotle, B.'s researches on, Introd. III; as a source for the *Consolation*, Introd. VII; popularity in 13th-c., Introd. X

De caelo, 5. 6. 6

Metaphysics, Nic. Eth., Introd. VII

Physics, 5. 1. 12

Asser, biographer of Alfred the Great, Introd. X

Asterius, literary contemporary of B., Introd. III

Athena, possible model for Lady Philosophy, Introd. VI

Atreus' son (= Agamemnon), 4. 7. m.1 ff.

Augustine, admirer of Marius Victorinus, Introd. III–V; his enthusiasm for philosophy, Introd. VIII

De ordine, Introd. VIII

Soliloquies, Introd. VI

Ausonius, 4th-c. Christian poet, Introd. VIII

Auster (south wind), 2. 3. m.7

Bacchus, god of wine, 1. 6. m.16

Basilius, accuser of B., Introd. II; 1. 4. 16; 2. 5. m.7

Bear (constellation), 4. 6. m.8 ff.

Bede's *Ecclesiastical History*, trans. Alfred, Introd. X

Bhagavad Gita

The Bible Authorized King James Version
  With Apocrypha

Dhammapada

Dharmasūtras

The Koran

The Pañcatantra

The Sauptikaparvan (from the
  Mahabharata)

The Tale of Sinuhe and Other Ancient
  Egyptian Poems

Upaniṣads

ANSELM OF CANTERBURY	The Major Works
THOMAS AQUINAS	Selected Philosophical Writings
AUGUSTINE	The Confessions On Christian Teaching
BEDE	The Ecclesiastical History
HEMACANDRA	The Lives of the Jain Elders
KĀLIDĀSA	The Recognition of Śakuntalā
MANJHAN	Madhumalati
ŚĀNTIDEVA	The Bodhicaryàvatàra

Women's Writing 1778–1838

WILLIAM BECKFORD   Vathek

JAMES BOSWELL   Life of Johnson

FRANCES BURNEY   Camilla
Cecilia
Evelina
The Wanderer

LORD CHESTERFIELD   Lord Chesterfield's Letters

JOHN CLELAND   Memoirs of a Woman of Pleasure

DANIEL DEFOE   A Journal of the Plague Year
Moll Flanders
Robinson Crusoe
Roxana

HENRY FIELDING   Joseph Andrews and Shamela
A Journey from This World to the Next and
  The Journal of a Voyage to Lisbon
Tom Jones

WILLIAM GODWIN   Caleb Williams

OLIVER GOLDSMITH   The Vicar of Wakefield

MARY HAYS   Memoirs of Emma Courtney

ELIZABETH HAYWOOD   The History of Miss Betsy Thoughtless

ELIZABETH INCHBALD   A Simple Story

SAMUEL JOHNSON   The History of Rasselas
The Major Works

CHARLOTTE LENNOX   The Female Quixote

MATTHEW LEWIS   Journal of a West India Proprietor
The Monk

HENRY MACKENZIE   The Man of Feeling

ALEXANDER POPE   Selected Poetry

The Oxford World's Classics Website

www.worldsclassics.co.uk

- Information about new titles
- Explore the full range of Oxford World's Classics
- Links to other literary sites and the main OUP webpage
- Imaginative competitions, with bookish prizes
- Peruse the Oxford World's Classics Magazine
- Articles by editors
- Extracts from Introductions
- A forum for discussion and feedback on the series
- Special information for teachers and lecturers

www.worldsclassics.co.uk

American Literature

British and Irish Literature

Children's Literature

Classics and Ancient Literature

Colonial Literature

Eastern Literature

European Literature

History

Medieval Literature

Oxford English Drama

Poetry

Philosophy

Politics

Religion

The Oxford Shakespeare

A complete list of Oxford Paperbacks, including Oxford World's Classics, Oxford Shakespeare, Oxford Drama, and Oxford Paperback Reference, is available in the UK from the Academic Division Publicity Department, Oxford University Press, Great Clarendon Street, Oxford OX2 6DP.

In the USA, complete lists are available from the Paperbacks Marketing Manager, Oxford University Press, 198 Madison Avenue, New York, NY 10016.

Oxford Paperbacks are available from all good bookshops. In case of difficulty, customers in the UK can order direct from Oxford University Press Bookshop, Freepost, 116 High Street, Oxford OX1 4BR, enclosing full payment. Please add 10 per cent of published price for postage and packing.